GEORGIA
ARMENIA
AGU City Campus
VAN
Çukurova Regional Airport Complex
Antakya Museum Hotel
IRAQ
SYRIA

EAA
Emre Arolat
Architects
CONTEXT AND PLURALITY

Philip Jodidio and **Suha Özkan**

New York · Paris · London · Milan

First published in the United States of America in 2013
By Rizzoli International Publications, Inc.
300 Park Avenue South, New York, NY 10010
www.rizzoliusa.com

Designed by HvADesign, NY
Henk van Assen, with Loide Marwanga and Sarah Eidelson
Rizzoli Editor: Ellen Cohen
EAA Editor: Nil Aynalı

ISBN: 978-0-8478-4085-4
Library of Congress Control Number: 2013936513

Printed in China

2013 2014 2015 2016 2017 / 10 9 8 7 6 5 4 3 2 1

Context and Plurality:
The Architecture of Emre Arolat and EAA / 5

Suha Özkan

Drawing What You Think:
The Work of EAA / 13

Philip Jodidio

PROJECTS

Context and Plurality The Architecture of Emre Arolat and EAA

Suha Özkan

BACKGROUND

To understand and appreciate the professional context in which Emre Arolat and EAA practice, a brief overview of Turkish architecture since 1923 is essential.

Contemporary architecture in Turkey and its response to modernity are part of a complex story that can be highlighted through a few key concepts. The proclamation of the Republic of Turkey in 1923 was the most important event in the recent history of the country. This political change had an impact on all modes of expression in both the visual and the performing arts. Architecture was no exception.

When the new republic chose Ankara as its capital, the country's center of gravity was displaced, engendering major investments and the construction of much-needed government buildings. At that time three notable architects were called on: Vedad Tek, who had attended the École des Beaux-Arts in Paris; German-trained Kemalettin Bey; and the self-trained builder Arif Hikmet Koyunoğlu. Giulio Mongeri from the Fine Arts Academy quickly joined their ranks. All four were followers of Ottoman court tradition and built notable buildings in the classical idiom. Their work had developed as cross-fertilization of the French and German neoclassical styles blended with Ottoman influences. Though these men produced masterpieces in Ankara, their careers were short-lived. In Turkish academia this period has been referred to as the First National Movement of the new Republic, but this is a misnomer. Rather than being a new national style, the architecture that emerged during this period must be understood within the history of Ottoman designs, together with a strong European influence.

Those who were committed to Kemalist modernity rightfully informed the leader Atatürk that these post-Ottoman "classical" styles should not be favored when expressing the ideals of the modern republic in public edifices. Architects who were critical of the classical styles asserted that architecture had to correspond to the message of the republic. Bauhaus-inspired modernism was to be the style of the new regime. The modern movement was studied by the succeeding generation of architects, and Turkish modern architecture emerged to replace what was deemed to be inappropriate. Seyfi Arkan, Sedad Eldem, Şevki Balmumcu, and Ahsen Yapaner were the chosen modernists for the new governmental buildings. They produced magnificent modern architecture, especially in Ankara. During the same period, the Austrian architect Clemens Holzmeister designed buildings in heavy stone cladding in line with the architecture of Austria and Germany of the 1930s, and he left his mark as well.

During the Second World War, Turkey did not form any alliances. As a consequence of this political and military decision, Turkey was in a sense locked within its own borders for what amounted to a period of austerity and self-reliance. During this time, Sedad Eldem and Emin Onat, both professors in Istanbul, developed an architectural idiom that would deserve to be called "regional" (national). It was in this context that Paul Bonatz, who was not on good terms with Heinrich Tessenow and Albert Speer, came to Turkey with his exhibition "New German Architecture." He remained in Turkey and was influential as a professor and an architect. He clearly engaged the search for a regional idiom that would be uniquely Turkish.

During the postwar years, multiparty democracy emerged and political elitism faded away, allowing architecture and planning to be "democratized." Post-1950s architecture lent itself to meaningless and massive building wherein quality was not sufficiently taken into account. Simplistic, low-quality building practices took the major cities hostage. A process colloquially called "build and sell" (*yap-sat*) was the architectural currency of the moment.

The de facto development of architecture in Turkey involved a process of building as an extension of rural tradition, accommodating newcomers to the cities. Derived from the process of building "overnight" (*gecekondu*), this type of construction became a way to shelter the neediest urban populations. The process was based on the legal premises of "what is a shelter for a citizen or citizens is untouchable and cannot be demolished against the will of the occupant."

With political expectations and compromises, squatters became landowners first and later speculators as the land they possessed on the periphery of the central business districts from the 1950s to the late 1970s became extremely valuable for development during the twenty-first century. From the 1970s onward, master plans were developed for these squatter neighborhoods, and the speculative initiatives of small contractors caused Turkish cities to become petrified in a seemingly irreversible process, the result of inadequate planning.

During the past decade, the political powers have not been at peace with squatters, nor have they worked well with the petty contractors, intervening in a heavy-handed manner. Vast stretches of public land have been turned over to a new judicially and financially empowered process of massive construction. Consequently, meaningless tower blocks—with no social, environmental, or urban design qualities—have since mushroomed all over the country. This Soviet-style solution for housing yielded a new architectural disaster, engendering serious societal consequences that the country must now cope with. In the meantime, as industry and services have developed, urban life has grown in leaps and bounds. Istanbul has reached a population of more than ten million, and Ankara almost five million.

The unfortunate result of these massive building exercises is that Turkey has produced neither an architect with an international reputation nor buildings that will in any sense mark architectural history. There have been exceptions, however. Sedad Eldem (1908–1988) endeavored to address geography, culture, and heritage in his own work. Even though substantial efforts have been made to promote contemporary architecture in Turkey, publications remain focused on the Turkish intelligentsia and are published almost exclusively in Turkish.

EMRE AROLAT'S MISSION

Emre Arolat was born into the architectural scene where his parents, Şaziment and Neşet Arolat, had been practicing with a tremendous professional commitment. They respected their profession, and those involved in architecture in Turkey regard them highly. Their efforts for "good architecture" and professionalism were engaging, and their involvement has been long-lasting and genuine. However, like many of their contemporaries, their influence was national, and they did not endeavor to gain renown in the wider world. At the time the principles of modernist architectural design were generated by Western, principally German, sources that were willing to adapt themselves to Turkish building technology. Here, the respectable efforts of Doğan Tekeli, Sami Sisa, Vedat Dalokay, and Hayati Tabanlıoğlu, among many others, should be cited.

Emre Arolat began to practice with his parents. His mother, Şaziment, was a strong and determined person, whereas his father, Neşet, played the role of the reserved but assertive talent. Emre Arolat's engagement with his parents represented a commitment to learn and coexist in the most inspiring architectural environment of the moment in Turkey. Step-by-step, his solutions and architecture emerged as being "different." He has been consistently open-minded, creative, and conversant with what was happening in the world beyond Turkey.

Emre Arolat with his parents in the 1980s

At the outset his contributions echoed the global discourse. His architecture dating from his early years has been published in Turkey, and it deserves further research by academics who may be interested in the influences of postmodernism that originated in the West.

The present book considers the postmillennium projects of Emre Arolat, perhaps better known as EAA (Emre Arolat Architects). His work in the twenty-first century has been significant in that the architect never committed himself to a personal design idiom, style, or school.

The route to fame in architecture is frequently the one established by Andrea Palladio, which is to say the development of an attitude or even an ideology that evolves even as it is being propagated. Ludwig Mies van der Rohe is probably the most powerful proponent of this attitude, followed later by Kenzo Tange, Frank Gehry, Tadao Ando, Richard Meier, Norman Foster, and Zaha Hadid—all architects who offer what no one else dared to propose before them, and who generate new solutions within the realm of the personal styles that they originally developed.

The line that Frank Lloyd Wright and Le Corbusier initiated and practiced is different. That is to say that they eschewed the sustenance and development of self-created architectural approaches or idioms, searching instead for originality in each of their major projects. More recently, Toyo Ito and Herzog & de Meuron could be considered the leaders of this approach. Arolat has set out to take each and every project as a new beginning, where the solutions are potentially found within the circumstances or the conditions of the context. This attitude has made him a sought-after design consultant for many major clients.

BEING AT PEACE WITH WHAT EXISTS

Post-1950s architecture in Turkey has been profoundly affected by uncontrolled widespread urban development that has yielded a low-quality urban environment and provided only rudimentary housing conditions. The driving force of "Freedom to Build" has transformed the urban environment into an unrecognizable setting. The former "Freedom to Build" dynamics are an exponential derivative of rural development fueled by technology and an extralegal existence considered as temporary, whereas "Freedom to Develop" resulted in a series of concrete blocks erected with questionable engineering and lacking architectural style or expertise. The "noble" and discerning architectural profession in Turkey has maintained a dismissive and pejorative attitude toward these fast and lucrative "build and sell" practices, which have long been taken for granted and unquestioned within political or larger economic circles. As time has passed, the concrete blocks have acquired a sense of permanence and gained a battered aspect, the result of neglect and lack of maintenance.

In 2005, as a part of the World Architecture Congress, Turkish architects took architect Robert Venturi to the urban areas they considered to be haphazard, low quality, and indicative of an architecturally sick environment. Venturi observed the urban scene with its variety of forms, colors, and masses and stated: "Magnificent! What freedom." Venturi regarded the spontaneous, unself-conscious, modest, and pragmatic building practices in a positive manner. Those in Turkey who had defended a one-dimensional modernist search for the integrity of forms were puzzled. They thought that only solutions envisaged by legitimate architectural practices could be executed. When they heard the appreciative remarks of Venturi on what had been happening in Turkey, they were taken aback or, rather, disappointed. They did not understand at all what Venturi admired. According to them, the "Architect" (with a capital A) was to be likened to an iron fist that would regularize everything.

Emre Arolat does not share the conviction that everything that develops spontaneously is good and must be cherished. However, he is modest and willing to understand varying points of view. He has been at peace with what has happened in Turkey, despite the difficulties outlined here. He does not seek an architectural revolution in every project. Instead, he strives to find the seeds of an evolution in what everyone else considers a form of "sickness." He senses that the seeds of what could be better have always existed within what has taken place in his country.

For the Tekfen Kağıthane Office Park in Istanbul, Arolat developed a novel and healthy analysis of the broader built environment, one that nobody else had dared formulate. The rejection of the "low-quality" practices that formed the major part of the "legal" urban development scheme was a clear part of the thinking of those who consider themselves to be "Architects." Arolat dared to distill the decency that ultimately does exist in the dominant practice.

Often in modern Turkey, the practice of building on identified plots does not take into account the surrounding environment beyond roads and sidewalks. Arolat homogenizes the texture and color of blocks and brings a richness of variety to fenestration, rather than the regimented windows usually seen in new projects, and offers soft, well-landscaped outer spaces that make for a pleasant environment. The usually neglected exterior spaces of office environments come to life in his work. Instead of dismissing what has become common practice, Arolat endeavors to discover the dynamics of existing architecture and uses those as potent elements of his own "new" ("old"?) architecture.

As recently as late 2012 Turkey passed new legislation concerning urban development. This legislation, "among other objectives," aims in particular to improve the de facto haphazard urban environment into what might be a healthy, contemporary, and "civilized" urban environment. Unfortunately, emerging solutions would seem to be standard, aggressive tower blocks. One may see Arolat's office park as a model to guide the aspirations that do exist to transform the problematic Turkish urban environment into something new, with the intrinsic potential inherent in its formation. Here, Arolat is not preoccupied with architectural form. He provides the needed elements for urban structuring as an ensemble of open and closed spaces where buildings become an integral part of the urban fabric.

LAYERING

In the 1960s, Metabolist utopians such as Arata Isozaki and Kiyonori Kikutake proposed novel, but rather simple, layers of urban existence above congested cities to provide a new order. Imagining a new order that covers, protects, and coexists with the existing urban fabric is a daring, and at the same time challenging, responsibility. In his Antakya Museum Hotel, Arolat confronts precisely this challenge. The hotel and museum are being built on a site that unexpectedly yielded historic treasure.

Here, Arolat places strong foundations on pillars that minimally disturb the site. His building does not touch the unearthed heritage of ancient Antioch. This challenge was also one that Bernard Tschumi grappled with in the Acropolis Museum. Unlike the site conditions of Athens, the situation in Antakya is much more complicated. The site does not allow the architect to place a reinforced concrete slab over the archeological area. Instead, the hotel building had to be placed on huge girders with long spans to protect and display what was discovered and allow archeological work to progress. Peter Eisenman's theory of the "palimpsest" calls for expression of the traces of history, and it is definitely a source of inspiration here. However, the transformation of the palimpsest into a living and clearly observable architectural work furthers theory by a large margin. The difficult problems encountered by Arolat in Antakya and the elegance of his technical and artistic solution, which allows the ancient past and near future to coexist, form an architectural story that deserves to be featured in textbooks. The Antakya Museum and Hotel is destined to become a showcase for future generations of architects and decision makers in Turkey and, perhaps, abroad.

The project for the renovation of the Entrepôt Royal in Brussels has similar dynamics, wherein Arolat aims to keep and project memory in the form of traces of a previously undervalued industrial heritage. Along similar lines of thinking, the AGU will leave a lasting mark through the treatment of previously ignored industrial architectural heritage. In Kayseri, a redundant and unused textile factory and its ancillary facilities suddenly benefit from a sophisticated treatment, adding new life to their existence. The Kayseri Sümerbank textile factory was built as a machine shelter in the 1930s by Russians within the parameters of industrial efficiency. The only exception is the coal-operated electrical plant designed by the distinguished architect Ivan Nikolaev. This building complex, designed in the late Constructivist idiom, is the most notable structure of the entire site. Vast spaces that shelter textile manufacturing machinery are also scheduled to be treated at a later date.

To accommodate the pressing need for educational spaces, Arolat chose to alter the most insignificant part of the former storage yards. A road and railway tracks flanked by derelict buildings are to be transformed into studios, class-rooms, and laboratories. With this urban university campus, Arolat has endeav-ored to create a closely knit outdoor social space. This linear area is made up of closed, colonnaded, and open spaces and will add to the urban life in Kayseri. The storage spaces are completely ordinary structures from the point of view of discerning architectural standards. The insignificance of what exists is precisely the energy that Arolat wishes to bring back to life. For him, even though the buildings are aesthetically or architecturally poor, the historical patina that has accumulated in the aura of open and closed spaces can make the whole environment worth experiencing.

The urban pattern proposed by Arolat within the fabric of structures on the verge of collapse is a gesture intended to restore dignity to ignored architec-ture, regardless of its intrinsic quality. Implicitly, Arolat returns a sense of honor to structures that served their industrial purpose for almost eighty years. He does not dismiss them but recognizes the services they rendered and offers them a new life. Because the client is indirectly the current president of the republic, the project will have substantial ripple effects on ignored industrial heritage elsewhere in Turkey.

THE WALL

The wall is an essential and generic element of architecture. In the scale of buildings, walls define and protect spaces. In urban terms, walls either retain, circumscribe, or divide. When used at a large scale in an urban context, "the wall" is by definition a divisive element. Walls separate one from the other. There are many sad examples of walls as divisive features used to separate or contain. In two major projects, Arolat uses the wall as a separator but gives it different interpretations. In his designs, the wall separates at the same time as it belongs functionally to two different sides. The wall thus gains a new momentum and becomes an integrating element rather than a divisive one.

Yalıkavak is a fishing village located near Bodrum that is famous for its single, lonely windmill on the seashore. During the past three decades, the town has grown into a major tourist attraction, with thousands of secondary resi-dences and tourist facilities. Fine hotels and a marina have become important parts of the town. Dozens of bays, islands, and peninsulas dot the seascape of Yalıkavak. Nearly every point on the coast offers spectacular views of the shore-line and the sea. The rapid development of the town, accomplished in part with

foreign capital, necessitated the creation of a new marina for large yachts. The expansion had a strict deadline. Thus the project had to allow for rapid construc-tion without risking the overall quality, a capacity that EAA aims to respect. The Yalıkavak Marina Entertainment Island project needed a windbreak to protect vessels from the damaging storms of the Aegean. In the Arolat proposal, the windbreak became a massive and spectacular wall. This wall shields the yachts from heavy winds and storms but also separates the social, commercial, and en-tertainment functions of the complex from the landing services. Finally, it mani-fests itself as a dominant and expressive landmark. Decades before, the "lonely windmill" on the shore was the town's modest landmark. Today, Yalıkavak has a new landmark for the twenty-first century. The landscape conceived for the area is sensitive and sustainable, composed mostly with indigenous Mediterranean plants. The surface treatment, combining hard and soft materials, brings comfort to the pedestrian who may initially be overwhelmed by the scale of the project.

Minicity Theme Park in Antalya is a project that was recognized by the Eu-ropean Union Prize for Contemporary Architecture / Mies van der Rohe Award. There is an inherent duality in this building complex. On one side are tourist facilities with shops, and on the other is a park with scale models. The investor insisted on separating the two activities. One area is commercial, recreational, and busy, with direct outdoor access; the other is cultural, calm, and exclusively indoors. Arolat creates another wall that separates and, by definition, integrates the two sides. The two sides have different architectural expressions. The com-mercial side is linear, rectangular, and half shaded, whereas the Minicity side is covered by a roof with richly articulated triangular forms that fold in a sheltering continuity, providing light and opening to the less busy edge of the site.

ENVELOPE

Allowing architectural spaces to float freely under a unifying cover is an idea generated by Cedric Price in the 1960s that has resulted in many examples around the world. The idea that brought the Centre Pompidou in Paris into existence was not only Archigram's techno-romantic expression but also Price's dynamic spaces that are formed independent of their exterior envelopes. Arolat has used this solution in two different ways. The Raif Dinçkök Cultural Center is more in line with Price's inspiration, whereas in the SantralIstanbul Contem-porary Arts Museum, the envelope is an intrinsic development of solutions that have been used over scores of years in the same complex.

SantralIstanbul is a power plant that was built early in the twentieth century to generate electricity from coal. Since about 1910, each architect in Turkey who was entrusted to build a shell over a generator has prioritized the valuable machinery and built modest, even flimsy envelopes to protect it. In the end these unassuming structures took the form of simple technological lattices used for protection. Seyfi Arkan, a talented and dedicated modernist of the 1930s, followed this tradition of enveloping instead of building. Bilgi Univer-sity, now one of the leading institutions of private higher education in Turkey, ventured to transform the derelict power plant into its third urban campus. Under the leadership of İhsan Bilgin, leading architects such as Nevzat Sayın and Han Tümertekin, along with Emre Arolat, joined a think tank to develop ideas for regenerating the area to fulfill its new educational function. All the site conditions, ranging from the soil to industrial pollution to the existing buildings, were seriously problematic. Even though a substantial stock of buildings was available to conserve and reuse, new academic buildings and other structures, such as the museum of contemporary art, also needed to be erected. For the museum, Arolat proposed a light, protective steel mesh to envelope a freely formed functional setup with large and small spaces, each of which was designed to embrace different types of artistic production. The steel mesh of the main facade looks out onto a haphazardly developed housing area, an "ordinary" urban setting of Istanbul. Through Arolat's steel mesh, the view is filtered, complicated, and honored to become the celebration of the neighborhood.

The Raif Dinçkök Cultural Center is the result of a dialogue among events, activity, and the envelope. This type of dialogue was intended but never functioned in the Centre Pompidou: the main space was supposed to be formed and reconfigured continuously; it was set in place and remained as it was for decades. The Millennium Dome in London by Richard Rogers was a more efficient expression of this idea. The dome was the envelope, and different functions were placed freely inside. In the Raif Dinçkök Cultural Center, the idea is not to house freely formed activities but freely formed spaces and individual buildings wrapped up by a steel lattice in order to integrate and protect the whole. Here, freedom is the pedestrian movement that flows on decks and terraces from one activity to the other. Time will determine how this idea of integrating a complex group of activities under a vast expressive envelope will function.

MEGA

Arolat has been among the few architects who dare to "think big." In doing so, he has never ignored the reality of the situation. Matching a large-scale building with urban realities initially brought him the commission for the Zorlu Center in Istanbul, which he won with Tabanlioğlu Architects, another Turkish firm. Later in the project development, EAA advanced alone. In this project, Arolat proposed a novel urban structure on an island circumscribed by roads and the heavy traffic of the central business district of Istanbul. Unlike many urban projects that seek to structure existing urban life, the Zorlu Center aims to generate life from within. In fact, this was what the Istanbul Metropolitan Municipality was envisaging at the outset. The land-sale conditions required the coexistence of a clearly defined urban mix consisting of residences, commerce, hospitality, and culture. Arolat's competition-winning idea was an urban continuity that flows from the business district to the terraces overlooking the unique landscape of the Bosporus. The population mix of the complex has been envisaged broadly, so that when people flow down into the central plaza, there is a range of ages, income groups, and genders represented. When realized in early 2013, the central plaza will be the gift of the Zorlu Group and Arolat to the city of Istanbul, which unfortunately has never succeeded in creating designed and finished urban spaces of high quality.

The Mecidiyeköy Towers and Seyrantepe Complex are two other mega projects entrusted to Arolat following his success with the Zorlu Center. The Mecidiyeköy project is in the process of realization, but unfortunately the client vision, determination, and power necessary to realize Arolat's vision Seyrantepe did not coalesce. The Mecidiyeköy Towers are on a vast site where a liquor factory was once situated. The project is next to a major overpass of the E5 highway in Istanbul. Predictably, Arolat is very much at peace with this noisy, polluted environment. It is part of Istanbul's reality, where Arolat believes the "new" complex will generate its own life and induce the urban quality that this particular area deserves. Located next to the site, the old Ali Sami Yen Stadium was also entrusted to Arolat to be integrated as mixed-use development. With large stretches of protected urban green areas, the project represents a symbiotic integration of two vast areas.

The Seyrantepe Complex consisted of three towers rising from a huge urban courtyard defined by a dozen galleries and multiple functions. Had the project been approved by the client, it would have become another novel development for Istanbul. Perhaps it would even have been able to compete with the Sony Center in Berlin in terms of its urban presence. The best aspect of these mixed-use projects is that they include a resident population, thus making the complexes a real part of urban life.

PLURALITY

Plurality is a common thread in Arolat's architecture, with two different aspects within EAA's practice. First, consider the selection of building types the firm has worked on. Arolat has tackled almost every kind, with the exception of a large-span sports complex. The richness of the EAA portfolio might not be considered an expression of plurality but rather a variety of subjects. However, a look at the firm's housing projects indicates the number of approaches that EAA exercises. This book describes many examples of buildings in which different attitudes develop from within the project's scope and environmental conditions.

Arketip Housing involves the integration of rows of houses around a large and very generous courtyard containing a huge swimming pool. Arolat provides private gardens at ground level, and at the upper levels are large terraces, the outdoor spaces. The ingenious form of the courtyard closes the compound onto itself in order to generate a sense of community.

In his Evidea Housing project, Arolat uses a peripheral building that forms a large square, similar to Victorian housing developments but on a bigger scale. Here, the idea is to amalgamate the existing building rights into an architecturally meaningful setting. The planning rights required a certain amount of built-up space and took for granted the presence of freestanding medium-rise blocks. The building rights became a given for Arolat, and he treated them as the energy of the project. By bringing together the bits and pieces of open spaces, EAA configured a huge common yard for all.

The bylaws of Turkish master planning define *planning control* exclusively in terms of streets and plots. In fact, streets circumscribe plots that appear as islands. Oddly enough, the ensemble of building plots is called *ada* in Turkish, meaning "island." In the Evidea Housing project, Arolat challenges those bylaws imposing standard streets and blocks. Instead, by employing the same ratios of land occupation and built-up areas, he composed a new urban structure that includes a vast common space for all. The project deserves the name *Evidea* (i.e., ev = house + idea). The final architectural expression may seem rather standard from the formal, innovative architectural point of view. However, one has only to compare this project with the hundreds of hostile and aggressive housing developments in Turkey to appreciate its merit.

Arolat's often novel approaches to housing have influenced Turkish architectural discourse substantially. Bodrum is a small town of 35,000 whose population increases to almost a million in summer. Town officials have reacted by severely limiting construction, mostly through rules that make innovative or creative solutions extremely difficult to realize. The result is that common practice on the Bodrum Peninsula is in keeping with the rest of the "sugar cubes" of the Aegean. In his Vicem Bodrum Residences, Arolat converses with the landscape. A rocky peninsula has been crowned by buildings that contribute to the topography, thus the whole complex becomes a continuum of the rock formation. The masses are broken into narrow, fragmented fronts, radiating in all directions, allowing the complex to blend into nature and embellish the setting. It is conveivable that the landscaped compound will merge into the rocks as though it had been there forever.

In the Şalvarağa Residences, Arolat used a similar approach but a completely different design concept intended to develop the required mass. The building compound has layered slabs that are reduced in size and treated with softened, angular edges instead of rectangular forms. Landscaping on terraces protrudes to form the soft edges of a well-designed artificial hill. The building itself forms a small, green, artificial hill. Therefore, the context has been accentuated by creating an additional hill on top of an existing one. The existence of ruins under the site is highly likely. If that is the case, the Antakya Museum Hotel experience will provide the guidance and expertise to meet the challenge.

The planned configuration of the Folkart Narlıdere Housing complex in Izmir represents a creative leap from what would otherwise have been an ordinary project. The continuous street-type access to the flats brings different qualities of space into the complex. The circulation gallery is separated from the main building block and covered with a light structure to create a microclimate. On the view side, the undulating balconies provide different possibilities of use for every household. The softness of the curvilinear form challenges prevalent rigid block-type housing solutions.

ABOVE, TOP
Discussion on a project

ABOVE, BOTTOM
Zeynep Uşşakli, Sezer Bahtiyar,
and Gonca Paşolar

OFFICE

EAA has been entrusted with many commissions in every realm of architecture within Turkey. Large or small in scope and size, designed for clients who are public or private, the projects selected by EAA enable the firm to develop novel grounds for the staff's expertise. EAA's portfolio is a subject of nationwide envy in architectural circles. The secret of its success is an impeccably organized office.

The office concentrates on a "design an innovation" process wherein Emre Arolat is involved in every project during the design phase. It is not a corporate organization, where jobs are forwarded to a subteam. On the contrary, significant members of the design team participate in open discussions under the leadership of Arolat and his partners. In addition to three family members, two other staff members hold strong and decisive positions in the practice. Gonca Paşolar and Sezer Bahtiyar belong to the generation after Emre Arolat. In fact, three generations are active in the firm's management, and the office has a fresh group of architects from many different schools.

The six project groups are composed of more than sixty architects on the design team. The partners wish to have a smaller number of architects and a more concentrated focus on portfolio of projects, but the firm and its architects are still young—and demand for their design work is intense. Decreasing the size of the practice will require more than a decade to realize, if it is even possible.

EAA allows members of the design team to cite their names and obtain credit for intellectual and creative work. Team members also participate under their own names in international awards competitions for the projects they design under the auspices of EAA. Arolat is personally very happy when young talents from his firm are recognized in these situations. In the past, Gonca Paşolar and Kerem Piker (2010) and Başak Akkoyunlu (2012) have received European "40 Under 40" awards for projects they produced at EAA.

The bureaucracy and project-fee scale of public institutions do not allow them to benefit from the quality of services offered by EAA. For this reason, the firm offers complete design consultancy as a public service. The Bergama Cultural Center, Eyüp Cultural Center and Marriage Hall, and Istanbul Museum of Contemporary Art can be considered among EAA's public contributions. For public clients with restricted funds, EAA offers nonprofit services. The designs for AGU City Campus and the METU Research Center Ankara can be noted among these. A new initiative of EAA is to host professional conferences and workshops in the office. "What Space Is," by notable planner and urban geographer Dr. Murat Güvenç, was the pioneering event in that series.

PLURALITY AND CONTEXT

In short, the key words for EAA and Emre Arolat would be *context* and *plurality*, the former being where the solution lies. The architect must uncover aspects of the context that will become the basis for EAA projects. He must not be ideologically or stylistically prejudiced. This supple unself-conscious attitude allows him to propose novel solutions for each project. Needless to say, this attitude also calls for bringing plurality to solutions as well as richness to the young architectural portfolio of an up-and-coming master of architecture.

Suha Özkan
FOUNDER OF WORLD ARCHITECTURE COMMUNITY

Ulus Savaş Topografya etüdü
Emre Arolat 2009

Drawing What You Think The Work of EAA

Philip Jodidio

Turkey is slightly larger than Texas and has a population of nearly eighty million people, of whom 99.8 percent are Muslim (mostly Sunni). The real growth rate of the economy (GDP) was 8.5 percent in 2011.[1] The country's largest city, Istanbul, one of the world's historically most significant capitals, has a population of nearly 10.5 million. These facts may suffice, together with the location of the country at the juncture between Asia and Europe, to explain why Turkey has played an increasing role in regional and world politics, and also why construction has become a strong part of the economy. History too is a key to the depth and significance of the culture of Turkey. When the Roman emperor Constantine (272–337) converted to Christianity, he made Byzantium, which had been founded by the Greeks in 657 B.C., his capital in the year 324. Constantinople would later be the center of power of the Ottoman Empire that embraced much of the Mediterranean world, stretching from Baku in the east and beyond Budapest in the west in the late sixteenth century. Thus, as Turkey builds anew and reaches out toward Europe and the Middle East, it is very much within its historic prerogatives, surely a country to observe and learn from in the twenty-first century.

LEARNING FROM ISTANBUL

Born in Turkey's second largest city, Ankara, in 1963, Emre Arolat is one of the first Turkish architects to emerge as a creative force in his country and, to some extent, beyond its borders. He was educated in Turkey, receiving bachelor's and master's degrees in architecture from Mimar Sinan University in Istanbul (1986 and 1992). He spent a year working as an assistant architect at Metcalf and Associates in Washington, D.C. (1986–87), before returning to

Turkey and joining his parents' firm, Arolat Architects, as an associate designer and, later, a senior partner (1987–2004). He founded his present firm, EAA–Emre Arolat Architects, in May 2004 together with Gonca Paşolar in Istanbul. The text that follows is based on a conversation between Emre Arolat, Suha Özkan (former director of the Aga Khan Award for Architecture), and the author (Zurich, November 18, 2012).

Though he might seem to be severe at first glance, Emre Arolat is a gentle man who readily admits his mistakes and explains the development of his talent as being a difficult learning process. He insists often that architecture is a hard profession, requiring long hours in the office. He also deploys a particular energy to convince clients of his reasoning, which often surprises them. He has a clear commitment to respecting context and thus can be said not to have any immediately recognizable style. Rather, the style of Arolat is one of finding solutions to the specific problems posed by any given project. After a time of emulating American postmodernism, which he now regrets, it would seem that Arolat has clearly understood his own calling and capacities, underlining the fact that he believes architecture is and must remain a "local" profession.

As Suha Özkan explains elsewhere in this volume, Arolat's parents formed a successful architectural partnership. "I was always in their office, beginning when I was ten or twelve years old. I can say that I grew up there," says Arolat. "I went to the office to do my homework after school." The architect recalls today that he was not a brilliant student. "After primary school," he says, "I went to the Lycée Galatasaray in Istanbul, and I was what you would call a flâneur in French, enjoying the street life. In terms of education, it was a disaster for me. We had professors who came from France, but I skipped their lectures. After my graduation from the university, I was with a friend in Paris. We saw a line with hundreds of people waiting for an event, and I thought it must be for a new movie,

Study for Ulus Savoy Residences, topography, 2009

but I realized it was for a lecture by my philosophy teacher from the lycée. A sort of illumination came to me precisely because I had skipped his lectures when I had the chance to hear him." As it is, Arolat has the lucidity to admit that he made mistakes, and he explains in a modest way that he had the courage to learn from these errors.

"I worked in my parents' office, and they were quite successful in Turkey, but I was rather lazy," admits the architect. "I thought it was a nice profession, where one could earn a decent amount of money. But I realized that the money my parents used did not come from their work as much as it did from their in-heritance from my grandfather, who had made a fortune in the textile business in the city of Bursa. I realized that it is a hard world. I understood that I had to become serious, to be someone different than I had been, and I believe that I changed a lot. I was about twenty-five years old, and I can say that my education began again at that point." That architecture is a "hard" profession is an idea that recurs frequently in Emre Arolat's discourse. So, too, is a self-deprecating tone that gives way to an assured one when he speaks of his current work.

SEARCHING FOR THE SPIRIT

"After university," explains Arolat, "I went to the United States for a year and worked in the office of architects my parents knew in Washington called Metcalf Associates. It was a good experience—there were fifty architects in the office." At the time Arolat vowed he would never want to have an office with so many staff members, though not long ago, his Istanbul practice employed a hundred architects. Clearly, he is not only able to learn from mistakes but also to allow his own conception of architecture to evolve, a quality that may be too rare in the profession. "Though I studied architecture at the university," he says, "I feel that my real learning began as I followed the work of my parents—for example, when they discussed projects they were undertaking. But at that time, Turkey was in a different world as far as architecture is concerned, as compared to Europe, for example. I spent my first five years in their office without saying anything about the nature of their work. I did what I was told to do."

Perhaps because of his experience in the United States, Arolat was open to current international trends in architecture. "In those days," he says, "post-modernism was a big thing all over the world, and in Turkey as well. I felt that the work my father was doing had no spirit. What he did was very much in a modernist style, and what I had seen in the United States made me feel that an orientation to the past was more appropriate. Traditionalism, vernacular, and the importance of context were the ideas that were in my mind. Simplic-ity and a feeling that place did not matter were more the rule in Turkey then." Though clearly a dedicated participant in the work of Arolat Architects, the younger member of the family began to assert his own ideas. "My father was

not easy about these things, but I started to propose alternatives to his designs. My mother tried more than he did to accept my thoughts, and with her help I became the head designer of the office, about ten years after I had started out."

Arolat looks back on his early years working in his parents' firm with a cer-tain amount of regret. "I was young, and in my opinion I was not well educated. I did a number of things that I should not have done in terms of design in the late 1980s," he admits. "But these projects nonetheless generated a certain amount of interest in my work. I was influenced by postmodernism—Michael Graves and James Stirling were my heroes. Putting American postmodern high-rise buildings in the middle of Istanbul was a mistake. I did not try to use Turkish forms but opted instead for an international vocabulary. I designed a building that was inspired by something I saw in Boston. I still see it every day, and it is a kind of punishment for me."

A MATTER OF THINKING

Just as Arolat's stylistic references have evolved, so too has his way of obtain-ing work and even of conceiving a project. The capacity to evolve and to learn emerges as a central feature of his talent. "My parents obtained work mostly through the competition process," he explains. "My current firm EAA is a kind of continuation of my parents' company, Arolat Architects, and we did continue at the outset to work in the same way. But when an office is well known, clients do come on their own. Today, we are no longer involved in competitions, with a few exceptions. Sometimes we do participate in order to make a comment or a statement, not necessarily to win. In the case of the Zorlu project in Istanbul, where we did participate in the competition, I asked my partner for her agree-ment because I was so sure that we would not win. We proposed a rather radical solution that I believed the jury would not accept, but as I knew beforehand, the jury was very 'architectural' in its composition."

Just as competitions are no longer a central part of the work of Arolat, so too have his work methods changed over time. Nor are the changes involved cosmetic; rather, they are fundamental and explain the present success of the architect more pertinently than any critique of his work. "When I worked with my parents' firm, I used sketchbooks very frequently," he recalls. "Over the years, however, I have come to the conclusion that architecture is not so much physical as it is a matter of thinking. I began to sketch less frequently. Rather than drawing and thinking, I started to think first, to talk to other people, and to do research. After this process, I am often able to draw the final design. For some projects, I do no drawings, and people in our office do that work. I actually like that process better, although I still enjoy drawing very much. We have six work groups in the office, and each day I work with a different group, six days a week. The leaders of the groups have been with me for five to ten years, and they are quite young. When we talk, we do sketches on a large board. Before advancing too far, we talk a good deal, and I think that this is a very productive way of doing architecture. Rather than drawing, thinking is more important. In my opinion, there are two ways to organize work in an architectural office. One is thinking by drawing, which I am no longer comfortable with, and the other method is drawing what you think. Drawing should be the final result of the thought."

Thinking and then drawing are part of the work method of EAA, but so are computers and models. "We have a well-organized scale model shop in the office," says the architect. "We have intelligent and skilled 3-D professionals. The most productive program of the moment is SketchUp, in my opinion. It is easy to use and to manipulate, shall we say. Scale models are made in parallel, in some cases. In about 70 percent of our work, SketchUp is used." The use of these methods is fundamentally related to the people who work in Arolat's office. "I was lucky to be able to hire more people because we had more work to do, and I began to think about the process. I feel that producing architecture with a team is the ideal situation. Another ideal situation might be having a much smaller office—say, a maximum of six or seven, and drawing everything yourself. I like the way Peter Zumthor works. We are Mediterranean, and he is a Protestant from the mountains. His is a different world, a different understanding of architecture. I am sure we don't even eat the same way. I eat a lot, and I am sure that he doesn't. I believe, though, that everyone looks for what they do not have. If somebody had told me a number of years ago that I would have an office with one hundred persons and that I would be building tens of thousands of square meters, I would not have believed it. Sometimes when you obtain what you want, you start to look for something else, a time when things were simpler. About fifteen years ago, I saw a picture of Rem Koolhaas driving to Lille in his Maserati. I thought, This is architecture! But I don't believe that anymore."

SOLVING THE PROBLEM

Though Arolat may have given up the more romantic idea of architecture that he had in his youth, he retains a clear sense that he is the central person in his office. His conception of his own role is another measure of what sets him apart from other architects of his generation, or other architects in Turkey. "Even if we build a lot, I would say that every project our office designs is my project. If I were not there, I do not believe that people would do the same thing. I put them in an architectural jail, in my opinion. I talk a lot, and they can't beat me at that game; I am always the one who directs the situation. Ours is not a corporate office."

Though he has worked in cities such as Brussels or Prague, Arolat today affirms the interest in and importance of a more local and contextual architectural practice. "Fifteen years ago," he says, without the slightest trace of nostalgia, "I dreamed of working in other countries. In those days, I felt that architecture was a global profession. Today, I believe that architecture is a very local profession more than a global one. I believe that context is very important. It must be well understood before doing a project. Our embassy building in Prague required ten trips for me. I read numerous books about the Czech Republic, but I was not very comfortable with the project. This is an embassy building that could reflect the Turkish mentality, but I think it should be a building that is ultimately related to a place. Even if it is the Turkish Embassy, perhaps in twenty years it will no longer serve that function. Because of this, it should not reflect the Turkish mentality or Turkish architecture. It should reflect the aura of the place. This gave rise to a long discussion with the person responsible for this project at the Turkish Ministry of Foreign Affairs, who felt it had to be 'Turkish.' I feel that I have to solve the problem of the client, but that I have to bring the client to my point of view."

The attitude of Arolat might well be called pragmatic. He does not reject programs and clients because of their nature, but rather he tries to form situations according to his own ideas. "I have no problem with producing in a system," he says. "If you do a large project in the middle of Istanbul, you have to obey the program and the site specifications. If you want to place a building on a given location and to create an urban space, you have to convince the client that it is important to leave space for the urban context. I refer to this problem because many new developments in Istanbul are gated communities surrounded by walls. They want to close themselves off from the public, or to the city. Clients in Turkey curiously feel that their success is related to how well they close off their buildings, but this is not true. Shopping malls are the urban centers of this era, as Baudrillard states, and yet in Istanbul you have to pass through a metal detector to get into them. In the case of the Zorlu project, we had problems with the client because we rejected the idea of metal detectors or X-ray machines. The whole city is becoming a sequence of islands with streets that run between them. All the real urban amenities are inside the islands."

Zorlu, which is one of Arolat's largest current projects, raises numerous issues into which the architect readily delves. "We did something very special in Zorlu," he states. "Creating a wall around a complex like that is what I would call an urban sin. Instead, we created a shell, with the urban elements and the private buildings above. There is a gap between the shell and the buildings— this is an idea employed by Le Corbusier in the Ville Radieuse project (1924). We leave the ground to the urban fabric. People can enter and see the Bosporus view and public spaces. We have elevators up to the towers, where you have to check in and the public cannot enter. This is secure enough according to English specialists who reviewed the plans, and this convinced our client."

LIGHT OF ISLAM

Arolat is obviously interested in the influence that Islam can have on his work, but his approach is a subtle, intelligent one, from which many others might readily learn. "In the Western world," he says, "the influence of Islam has been understood as a formal thing. I believe that it is more a question of feeling, the use of indirect light, shadow, and space. Islamic architecture is more social than it is formal. I am always keen to use the spirit of Islam that Le Corbusier understood, for example. Louis Kahn also understood the aura of Islamic architecture, but he did very formal things nonetheless. Understanding a way of using space, the fluidity of the space, is part of what might be called Islamic architecture." Arolat evokes specific elements that he feels are part of the tradition, not so much of a religion as of a region and a culture. "Sometimes invisible barriers can be created by working with the plan or with the section, allowing the creation of invisible barriers between private and public zones. I learned a lot from Islamic architecture, but I don't use formal devices like cupolas and domes. To work with this kind of architecture, you have to understand what I would call its aura. You have to understand the society. I am not only thinking of mosques but also of palaces or houses in Turkey, from which you can learn a lot. In a way, they are very modern."

Arolat is comfortable with references to Islamic architecture, but these are clearly not the surface decoration that characterized the postmodern approach. "The use of space, shadows, and microecology in a building is of interest," he affirms. "We learned from landscaping related to buildings," he says, "as is the case with the *asma* [a grapevine often used in Turkey to cover pergolas] to reduce the effect of the sun. We used this idea for the design of Dalaman Airport, replacing the plants with aluminum sunshades. Our design made the energy consumption 40 percent lower than other similar airport buildings. Islamic architecture has a great deal to do with the hot climate we live in. In my opinion, it is a very pragmatic type of architecture." Though he readily defines Islamic concerns as being social ones, Arolat states, "There is no sense to using aspects of old Islamic architecture that have to do with social structures that no longer exist. What I call the aura of Islamic architecture, its use of light and shadow or space, is still very much something that we can be inspired by."

Today, having reached an obvious level of success, Arolat views the future of his practice with a certain introspection. "My aim," he says, "is to reduce the size of my office. My ideal office will have about twenty architects. At present we have eighty-five. I would like to build fewer buildings but to concentrate on each one very well. I put a great deal of effort into each project, and it is hard to do that when you have a very big office. There is too much to do." Among other elements that put EAA in a category different from other offices in Turkey, the matter of gender can easily be raised. "We have a large number of women in the office, most of whom were originally my students," says Arolat. "I don't know why, but in the architectural schools in Turkey there is a majority of women. Women are hard workers, perhaps more so than men. Of the six group leaders in the office, only one is a man. My two partners are also women, as is our manager."

ON THE PILLARS OF ANTIOCH

The projects of EAA are presented elsewhere in this volume, but the architect evokes four with a particular passion and in the process reveals central aspects of his work and his method. The first of these presents the unusual juxtaposition of a museum and a hotel, perched above a remarkable archaeological site.

Antakya, once known as Antioch, is located in southern Turkey, near the Syrian border. Founded in 300 B.C., it was one of the largest cities of the Roman Empire and of Byzantium. According to church tradition, the patriarchate of Antioch was founded by St. Peter. Antioch was the base for St. Paul's missionary journeys, where Jesus's followers were first called "Christians" (Acts 11:26) and where the Gospel of Matthew was probably written. The city remains a site for Christian pilgrims. Its layers of history are everywhere apparent as soon as construction projects dig into the soil.

EAA is involved in a complex project that concerns a hotel in Antakya. "At the outset," says Arolat, "the client Necmi Asfuroğlu, who is from Antakya, had another architect and wanted to build a Hilton hotel on the site. Hilton's brief required two basement levels. This is unheard of in Antakya because as soon as you dig anywhere, you find the vestiges of old civilizations. Without the basements, Hilton was not interested in the project. But the client had exploratory archaeological work done with machines on the 100-by-200-meter site to see what, in fact, was beneath the earth, in the hope that his hotel idea could be saved. When it became clear that the site was very rich in archaeological remains, the museum and the heritage committee had the work stopped. They told the client that archeological work had to be done by hand and controlled by a scientific committee, headed by a well-known archaeologist. For seven and a half months, Dr. Hatice Pamir, a professor of classical archaeology at Antakya's Mustafa Kemal University, led almost thirty scientists from around the world, aided by about one hundred workers, in a massive dig funded by Asfuroğlu. One member of the committee was an architect and critic. He called me because he felt that the original architect was incapable of dealing with this situation. The committee was not hostile to the idea of a hotel but insisted that the archaeological site had to be protected." The problem became one of building not in the site, but above it. "I immediately noticed that a stream, which had apparently gone through the site, had been diverted," explains Arolat. "I asked the archaeologists to specifically check the area where I imagined the river must have been, and they found retaining walls. Since there was never construction within the walls of the river, we were able to use that area for structural supports. This made it possible to have forty-five- to fifty-meter spans over the known archaeological area, which is affordable."

The architect was thus convinced that, in spite of the particularly dense and rich archaeological elements present, it was possible to insert columns into the earth that would support the new building. "There are sixty-six columns," says Arolat, "each inserted into the earth to a depth of twenty-five meters. They are two meters in diameter. Because of the archaeological site we are working in, they could not use the usual heavy machinery, and I can say that these columns were handmade. Although we worked with the archaeologists for four months before placing the columns, some locations had to be changed when a previously unknown mosaic was found at a depth of six meters, and that required redesigning the building. What they had found in this accidental way was one of the largest intact Roman tile mosaic floors in the world, measuring just over 835 square meters. It was probably part of a sixth-century public building, possibly a house of government or a temple, according to the archaeologists. The design is of a series of nine panels, each decorated with a variety of geometric patterns in different colors. Our plan was to raise the hotel seven meters off the ground level and to place lobby areas or conference spaces well above the archaeological site, which is situated at six or seven meters below grade. The overall clearance is thus about fourteen meters. Prefabricated units form the 220 hotel rooms and other elements of the design, offering views of the rest of the hotel or the site. A public museum is also part of the scheme. I have used the design of the section to create barriers that are not perceived as such between public and private space."

A SIMPLE SPACE THAT IS NOT DESIGNED

Emre Arolat makes clear that his interest in Islamic architecture is important for his work, and yet he has not often worked on religious buildings. The mosque is a very particular aspect of Islamic architecture, sometimes surrounded by a series of "codes" that apparently require architects to imitate older buildings. Arolat has of course not taken this point of view, but rather tried to look back to the very history of Islam to discover the real, significant aspects of mosque design. As he explains, "The Sancaklar Mosque, located near Istanbul, is for five hundred worshippers; it is not huge. Prayer is an important subject of discussion in Islam. We studied prayer spaces carefully over a period of five months. I read the Quran carefully, where it is written that every place that is clean can be used for prayer. The Prophet prayed in a cave that is called Hira. He said that there, nothing could stand between him and God. This is the place where he received the first revelation from the angel Jibril. The cave is a simple space that was not designed. This was one source of our thinking." In itself, this return to the sources of Islamic architecture is of interest, even if it does appear to contradict other currents in contemporary design. On the whole, the mosque is surprising because of its lack of any ostentation or references to the vocabulary that has become popular for mosques in recent times. It is simple to the point of austerity, but this rhymes with the architect's understanding of Islam.

"Culture obviously has oriented us toward certain forms," says Arolat, "particularly for the religious function. The earliest prayer spaces that have come down to us are quite simple. In Islam you have to be very modest; you should not eat too much and you must help people. It is very humanistic. The rise of the power of money and oil somehow made the simplicity disappear in favor of the brilliant and powerful. The most famous mosques of this era are ones like the Sheikh Zayed Grand Mosque in Abu Dhabi, which is huge and was made with very sophisticated materials. We wanted to make a point, a small statement, with our mosque."

Arolat goes on to describe his thinking for this project in more detail. "It is built in a sloped site and is partially built into the hill. When there were no mosques, people prayed in simple open-air prayer areas called Namazgâh. I kept this idea in mind with the rooftop space of the mosque, but here you can also go inside. We used a marble called Gebze from a nearby quarry for the construction and concrete as well. Originally there was no minaret in the design, and I imagined that a tree could fulfill that function, an idea that I took from the Mosque of the Grand National Assembly in Ankara [Behruz and Can Cinici, 1989]."

Although mosque architecture is not entirely codified, given the very texts of the Quran which provide that any clean place can be used for prayer, Arolat has dealt in detail with a number of significant issues raised by spaces of prayer in his new building. Contrary to his fears, the religious authorities reacted to his ideas with a certain enthusiasm. "When we did the first presentation of this project for the client," he explains, "we were surprised to discover that the director of religious affairs for the area also was present. As it is, when we present a project for the first time, I always think of Álvaro Siza's statement that even a successful architect has only a 20 percent chance of getting his ideas built. As I often do, I spoke a long time, perhaps one and a half hours, before showing them anything. When we finally did show them our proposal, everyone looked to the mufti to see what he thought before anyone else could express themselves. The religious people liked the project so much that I was shocked. They accepted the whole building, but they said I needed to add a symbolic element that would signal the presence of a mosque. So we did add a tower. I knew very well that minarets usually serve no real purpose since the call to prayer is issued by the muezzin who is actually sitting comfortably inside the mosque and not in the minaret. He uses a microphone. I said I would create a tower only if the muezzin would go up. I added an elevator to the minaret, which is very simple and does not resemble a traditional minaret. The mosque has a separate space for women; it also has a mihrab [niche in the wall of a mosque that indicates the *qibla*, which is the direction of the Kaaba in Mecca] and the *minbar* [raised platform from which an imam addresses the congregation]. I have placed women's prayer areas on almost the same level as that for men, just one and half meters above the men's space. I call this positive segregation."

FANCY FOR THE WORKERS TOO

One project that has marked the recent career of Arolat is his Ipekyol Textile Factory (Edirne, Turkey), which won a 2010 Aga Khan Award for Architecture. The jury citation expresses clear enthusiasm for this building:

> The intelligent and imaginative design and engineering of the Ipekyol Textile Factory make it a role model of an efficient and pleasant working environment for any industry, and exceptionally so for the textile industry where such qualities are rare. . . . Made mostly from local materials, it sits lightly on its plot. The high ceilings and internal courtyards maximise the flow of daylight and encourage natural ventilation, making the work spaces more agreeable as well as reducing energy usage and improving thermal performance. . . . Production and administration are housed within the same building, and are visible to each other, improving internal communications and fostering team spirit. At a time when the Muslim world is industrializing rapidly, and many countries, including Turkey, need to develop higher quality products to counter rising labor costs, the Ipekyol Textile Factory demonstrates how enlightened design can create a replicable blueprint of a cleaner, safer, more efficient workplace that can also achieve higher productivity and profitability. [2]

Arolat explains this project in typically personal terms. "When I quit my parents' office, I was worried about not having work. My very first client asked me to design a fancy factory. I agreed, but I said I had one condition, which was that it should be fancy for the workers as well. (My grandfather had a textile factory, but whenever I went, I was shocked by the condition of the building that was behind what I would call the showcase space, the part that was visible from the road.) The client agreed. I worked on gardens and ceiling height and sunlight and he accepted my ideas, even saying that he thought the factory would increase his income because the workers would be happy. It is a well-organized and well-run factory for the moment. What influenced the Aga Khan jury the most was an interview with a lady who works in the factory who said she liked the factory so much she didn't want to go home."

In general, Arolat maintains what might be called a healthy distance from architectural awards. "Awards are problematic for me," he says, "but some, such as the Aga Khan Award, are important. Fifteen years ago, I was very much against the Aga Khan prize. I felt that it promoted the idea of religious segregation, but I realized that this was not its real basis. It is not about architecture in Islam that is formed by faith, unless mosques are involved. The question is how they benefit Muslim communities. The Aga Khan Award gave me the feeling that people can accept my ideas, and that is why it was significant for me. Our office has decided, however, not to submit to any more awards, especially those where you have to pay to participate, which is of course not the case of the Aga Khan prize."

BEING INVISIBLE

Another more recent project by Arolat, the Vicem Bodrum Residences, again reveals aspects of his work related to landscape but also to the process of convincing clients and authorities of his approach. He decided that, contrary to local custom, he could not build white houses on a prominent site but rather intended to have the entire complex blend in with the existing shoreline. Begun in 2010, these luxurious houses are located on the Bodrum Peninsula on the Aegean Sea. Arolat explains that the complex was built on a highly visible rocky peninsula, not too far from Bodrum Castle, a fifteenth-century monument built by Crusaders. "Being invisible was one of the most important aspects of this project," he explains. "We had to build a number of houses that were to be sold at high prices, and, obviously, nobody pays a million dollars for something that is invisible! Rich people want to express their wealth. I had to work hard to convince the client of my idea, which was to blur the distinction between the site and the architecture. We used the stone similar to that found on the site to better integrate within the landscape. We even selected the same trees that grow in the area. There was another problem, which is that most of the houses in Bodrum are white, and we used only stone and earth colors. Normally, the municipality imposes the use of white. I made two presentations to the mayor, and I managed to convince him. I told him that building twenty-five white cubes on that site would be a disaster. Sometimes, I have to be 'arrogant' with a client and tell him that if he does things the way he wants, people will not like him! That was how I got my way."

I WANT TO BE AN ARCHITECT

Arolat began the interview that was the basis for this text with a description of his early years in the office of his parents. Quite logically, he concludes on a note of continuity, explaining that his daughter Zeynep has just begun her architectural studies at Pratt Institute in New York. Very much in character, he emphasizes the "hard" aspect of being an architect and attempts to rectify what he regards as an error of the previous generation, which is to say undertaking architectural education in his own country. "It is not my idea to have a family run an architectural firm. I never told my daughter that she should be an architect. Zeynep's mother, my ex-wife, is also an architect who was a classmate at the university. We always talked about architecture, so the subject was quite naturally familiar to Zeynep. Her grandfather and grandmother were also architects. Until two years ago, she said that she disliked my way of working because I am always in the office. Once I realized that Zeynep wanted to be an architect, I told her that we had to talk. I explained all of the realities to her. I told her that

if you want to be a real architect, you have to work a lot. If you think that you
can have a social life that is separate from your work in architecture, that is a
problem. One day she came to me and said, 'I have changed my mind, I want to
be an architect.' I told her not to study in Turkey, because my parents made that
mistake with me. I am often in the architecture schools in Turkey. The best one
is the Middle East Technical University (METU). The level of the students even
there is unfortunately very low. There is an annual competition for one million
students in Turkey. Once they have been admitted to a school, they feel that
they have arrived and that they have no more work to do. I spent nine days with
my daughter at Pratt Institute. At Pratt, she is reading about Peter Zumthor,
but in Turkey, even the professors know nothing about him."

MODEST STAR

Arolat's thoughts about his daughter's education are certainly not to be classi-
fied as negative or pessimistic. Rather, he continues, as he always has, trying to
learn from past mistakes and, in this instance to pass on what he has learned to
his daughter. Hard work and openness to change are two hallmarks of his own
career, as is a deep involvement in the tradition and reality of Turkey. Having
started with superficial and largely foreign postmodern influences, in more
recent years Arolat has sought his inspiration in different layers of reality. The
light and space of Islamic architecture inspire him, as does the need to convince clients—be they businessmen, politicians, or religious authorities—that
his approach is the correct one. This approach justifies and explains his feeling
that architecture is and must remain a local profession. The size and current
success of Turkey's economy make this "local" approach propitious for an architect who certainly has a talent that can be measured on an international scale.
And yet, Arolat consciously rejects the model of the peripatetic "star" architect.
As he says about Islamic architecture, it is necessary to understand a society
before attempting to sublimate its architecture in ways that subtly connect
past and present. Above all, it is necessary, according to him, to think carefully
before drawing and building. He aims, within what might be called a range of
modest ambition, to reduce the size of his office and to apply his energy even
more fully to an approach that has been manifestly successful, anchoring his
work in function while taking into account larger concerns such as urban life
or the meaning of prayer in a modern society. The lessons that Emre Arolat has
learned might well be applied to architects in many other countries.

Philip Jodidio

GRIMENTZ, SWITZERLAND
NOVEMBER 26, 2012

1

See https://www.cia.gov/library/publications/the-world-factbook/
geos//tu.html#documentContent; accessed November 25, 2012.

2

See http://www.akdn.org/Architecture/project.asp?id=3725;
accessed November 26, 2012.

Emre Arolat as Curator of Istanbul Design Biennial

In 2012 Emre Arolat was named cocurator, with Joseph Grima, of the Istanbul
Design Biennial. Organized by the Istanbul Foundation for Culture and Arts
(IKSV), the inaugural design biennial coincided with the foundation's fortieth
anniversary. IKSV was founded in 1973 by Nejat Ferit Eczacıbaşı and today
operates under the leadership of his son Bülent Eczacıbaşı.

The theme of the biennial, "Imperfection," was approached in two different
ways by the curators. The exhibition curated by Arolat was titled Musibet,
which translates as "disaster" or "calamity." It was held at the Istanbul Museum
of Modern Art, where Arolat displayed a wide array of urban situations and
proposals that addressed the insumountable transformations happening in
cities not just in Turkey but worldwide. Upon the success of the biennial, IKSV
decided to expand the scope of the biennial by embracing architecture in 2014.
The success of this venture owes a substantial debt to Arolat.

Emre Arolat at Istanbul Design Biennial, 2012

Projects

Dalaman International Airport Terminal

Built between 2004 and 2006, this airport facility of 130,000 square meters (nearly 1.4 million square feet) was designed beginning in 1999. The architects sought to deal with the "boredom and feeling of emptiness" created by standard terminal buildings. They found their inspiration in the local climate, the surrounding landscape, and specific tourist activities. The structure's exterior masses are fragmented, creating gaps between interior spaces that are filled with references to the Turkish landscape.

The terminal was designed to accommodate a capacity of five million passengers who use the facility mostly in summer. The flow of arriving and departing passengers is handled on different floors, although "visual fluidity" between the levels has been maintained.

The steel roof and concrete frame structure are separated, and the terminal is equipped with a brise-soleil system that reduces energy consumption by 40 percent. Exposed concrete, natural wood, and matte finishes signal an intentional rejection of the use of "shiny materials and glittering forms." An unusual feature of the project is the build-operate-transfer (BOT) contract, which required that design and construction advance simultaneously.

LOCATION / **Muğla, Turkey**

YEAR / **2006**

STATUS / **built**

TOTAL AREA / **130.000 m²**

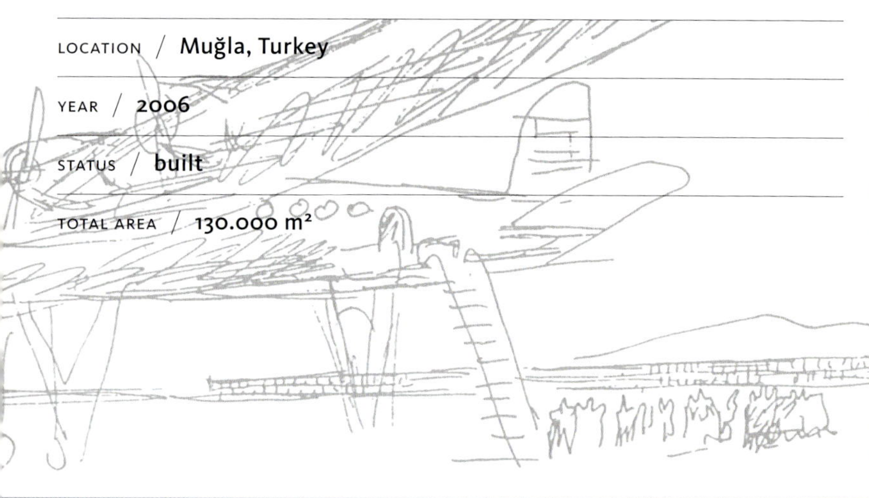

LEFT
Le Corbusier's sketch of a naked airport

ABOVE
Approach to the departure entrance

LEFT
View from the apron

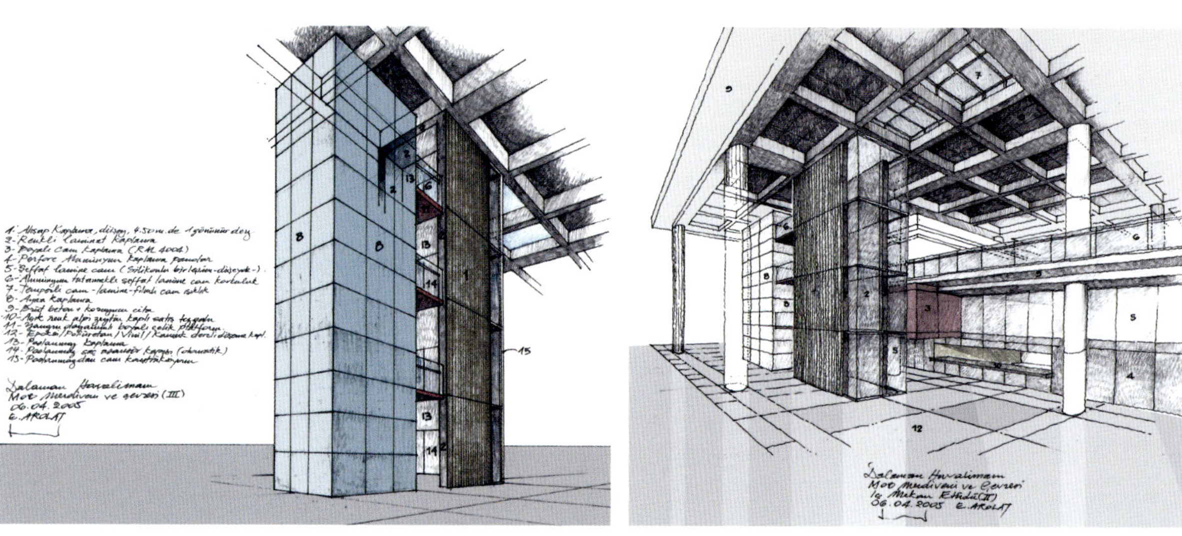

ABOVE
Sketch for the vertical circulation elements

RIGHT
Sketch for the volumetric composition

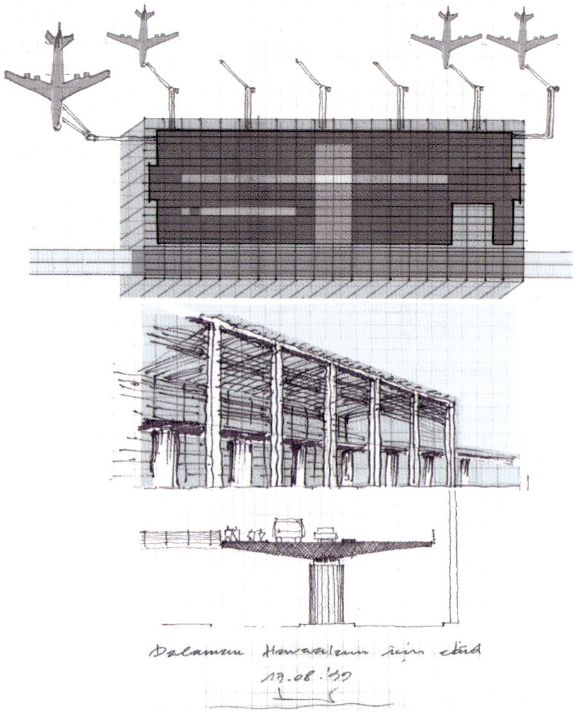

BELOW
Conceptual diagram of the building

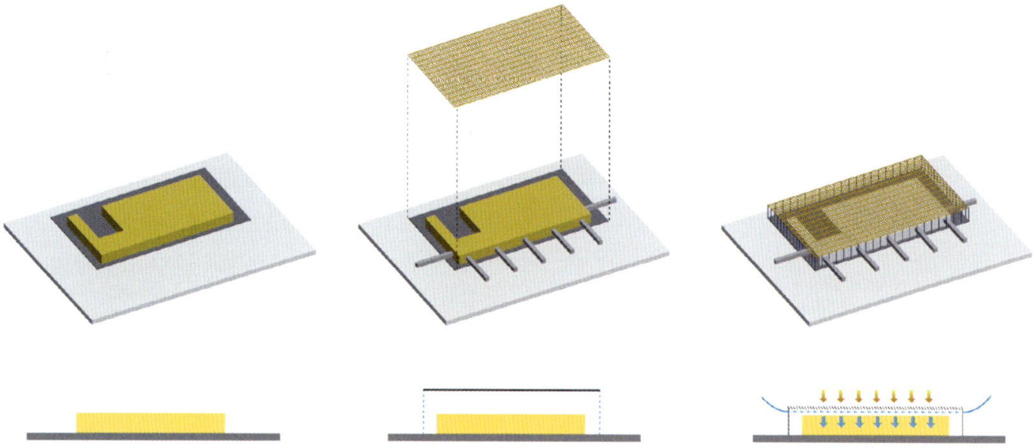

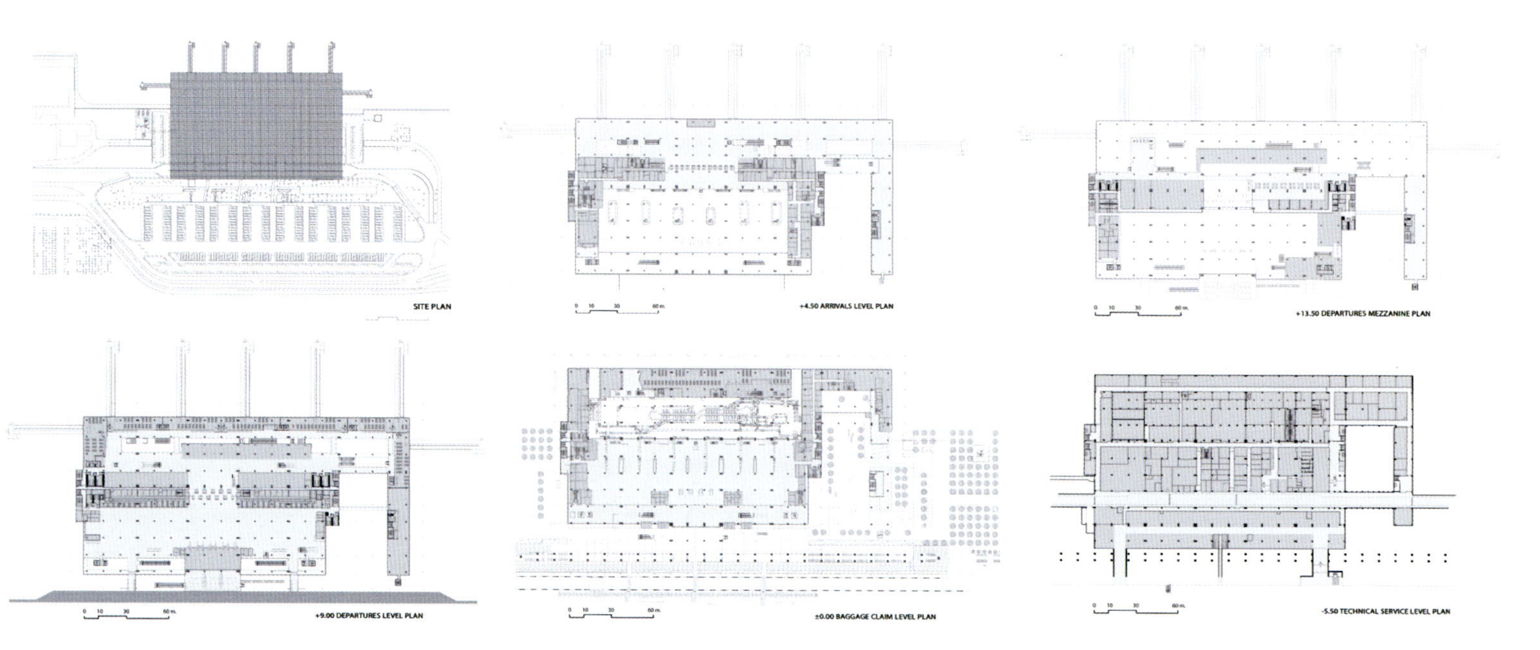

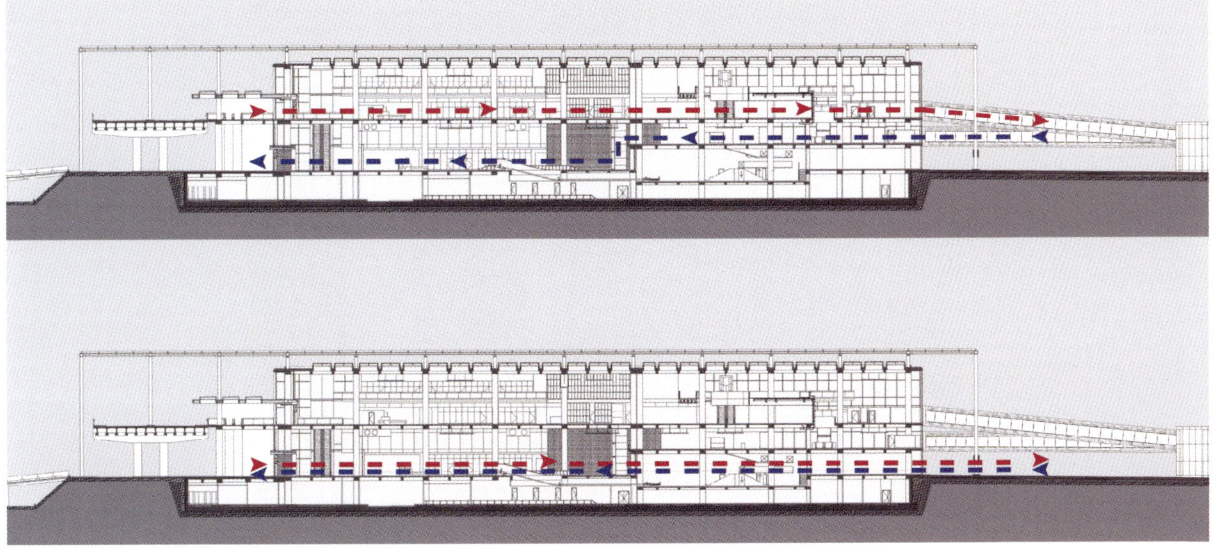

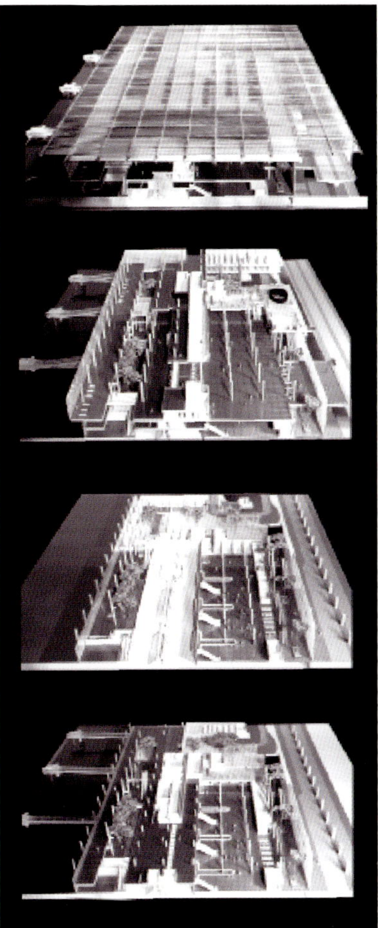

ABOVE
Passenger flow inside the building

RIGHT
Model showing different layers of
the building

LEFT
Sections

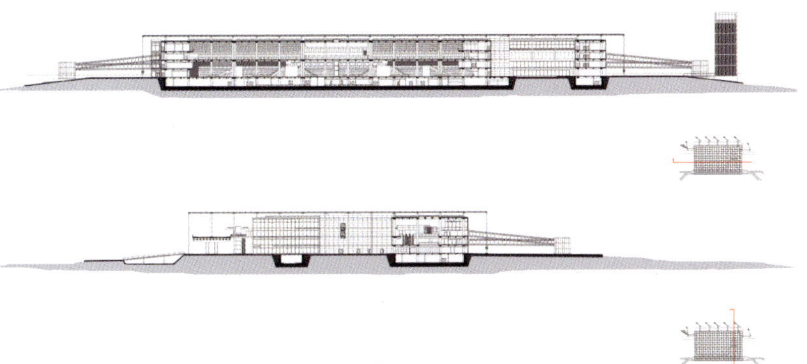

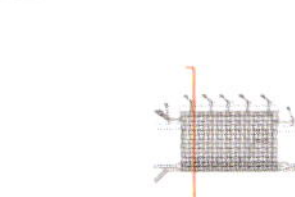

RIGHT
Model from the aerial view

BOTTOM, RIGHT
Section model

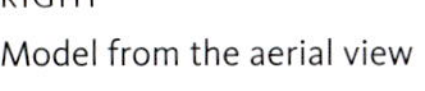

OPPOSITE, TOP
View from the northeast

OPPOSITE, MIDDLE
View from the southwest

OPPOSITE, BOTTOM
View of the canopy from the south

LEFT
View from the apron

BELOW
View from the apron on the northeastern side

BOTTOM
Walking ramps

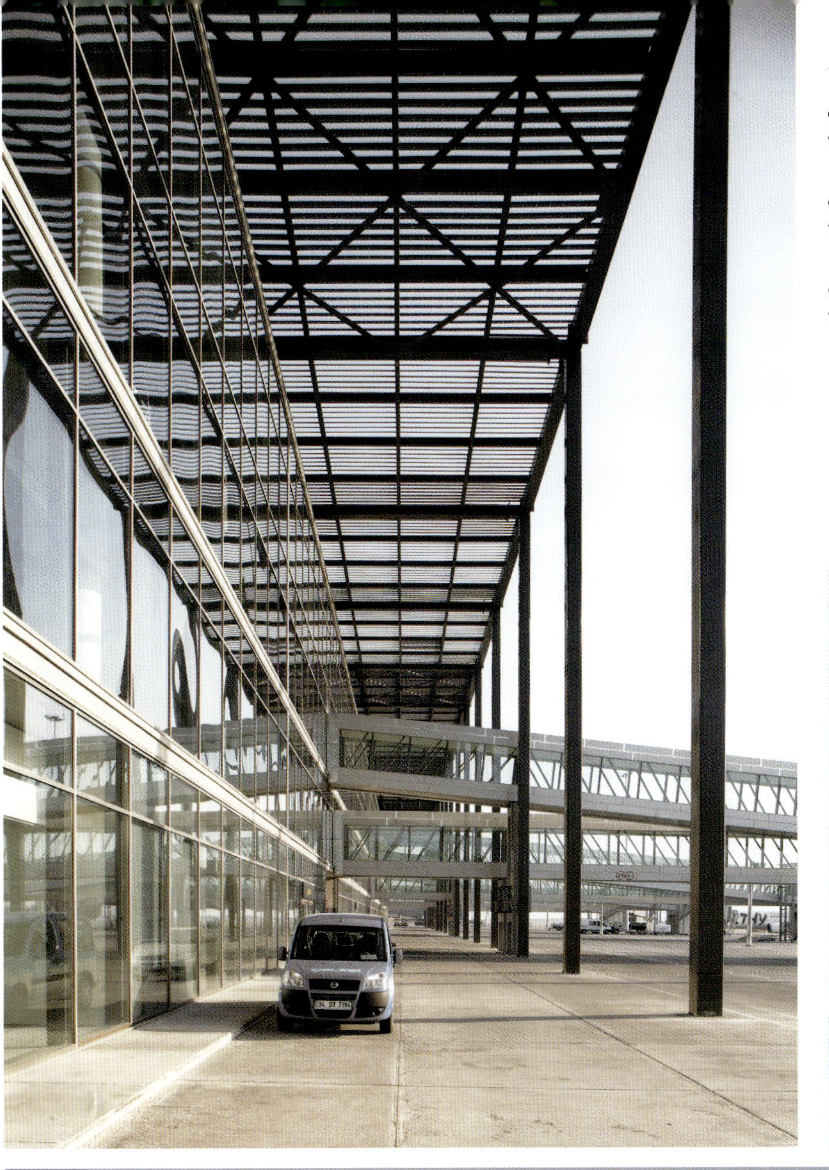

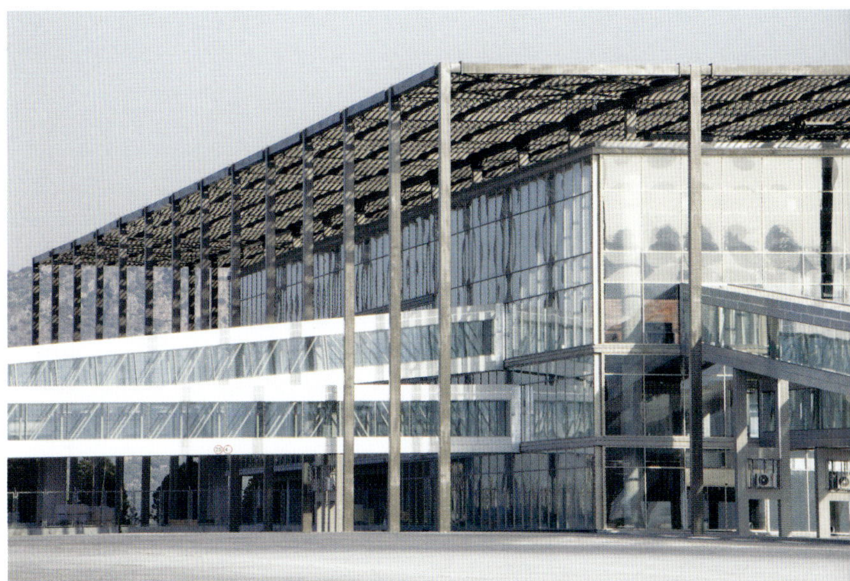

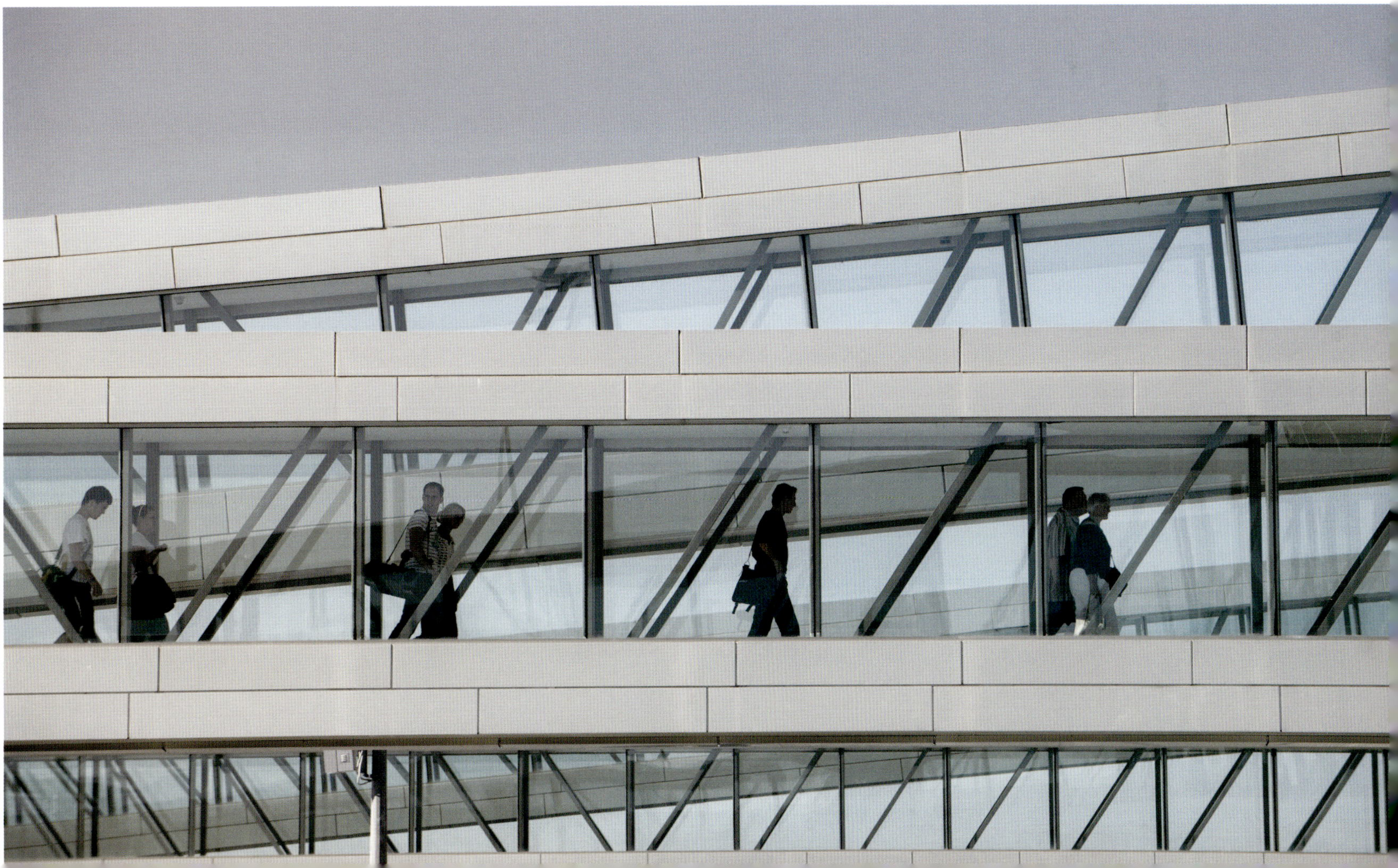

OPPOSITE
Waiting lounge in the departure hall

ABOVE
Counters in the departure hall

BELOW
View from the departure hall

RIGHT
View from the departure hall

BOTTOM
View of the shaded courtyard in
the office area

Lara Kervansaray Hotel and Conference Center

LOCATION / **Antalya, Turkey**

YEAR / **2002**

STATUS / **built**

TOTAL AREA / **87.000 m²**

Completed in 2002, this 87,000-square-meter (936,460 square foot) complex is located in Antalya, a city on the Mediterranean coast of southwestern Turkey. The site is perpendicular to the well-known Lara beach.

The overall form of the building was determined by local regulations concerning its height and width, but the architects ensured that all rooms have a view of the sea. The waterfront facade assumes a semicircular shape that unites the two bars of guest rooms, which are separated by a semipermeable ceiling covering indoor recreational areas. Partial shading creates varied light patterns within the central area, while careful attention to color schemes accentuates the impression of spatial variety generated despite the essentially rectilinear plan. Landscaped gardens create a transition between interior and exterior spaces. A simple load-bearing system was used, allowing for rapid, relatively low-budget construction.

BELOW
View from the south

RIGHT
View from the northeast

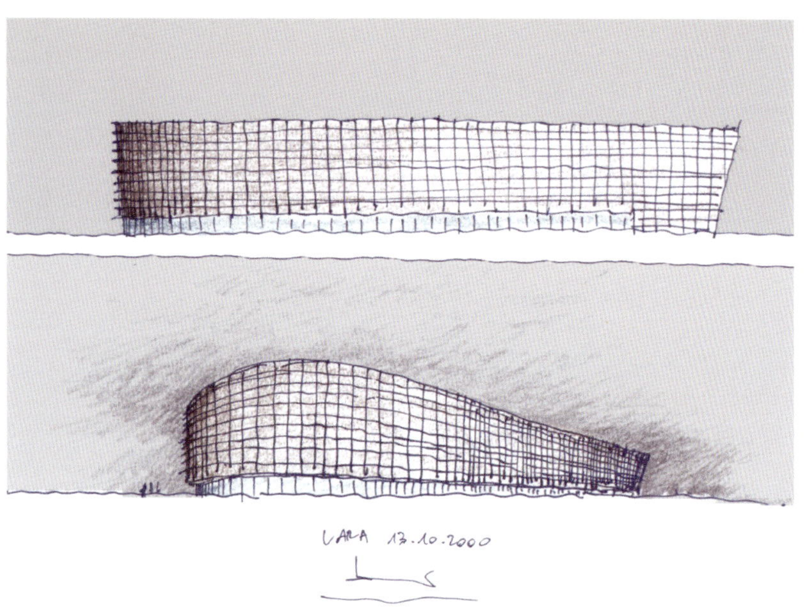

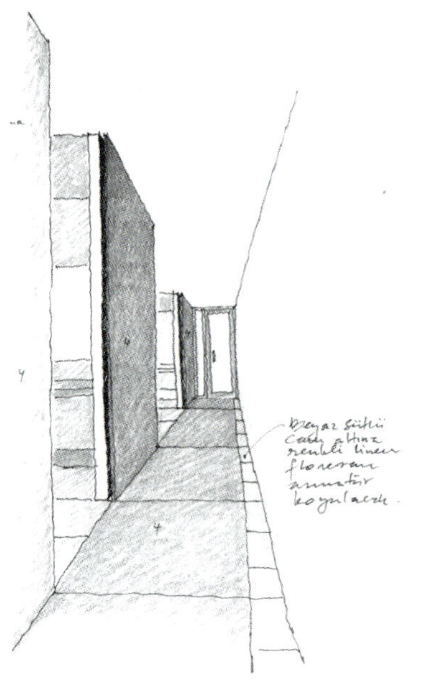

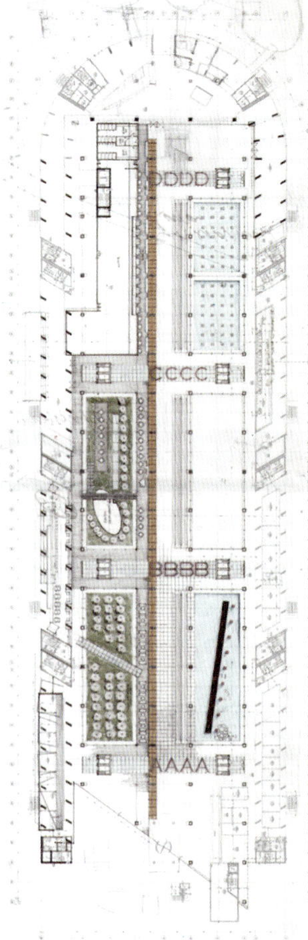

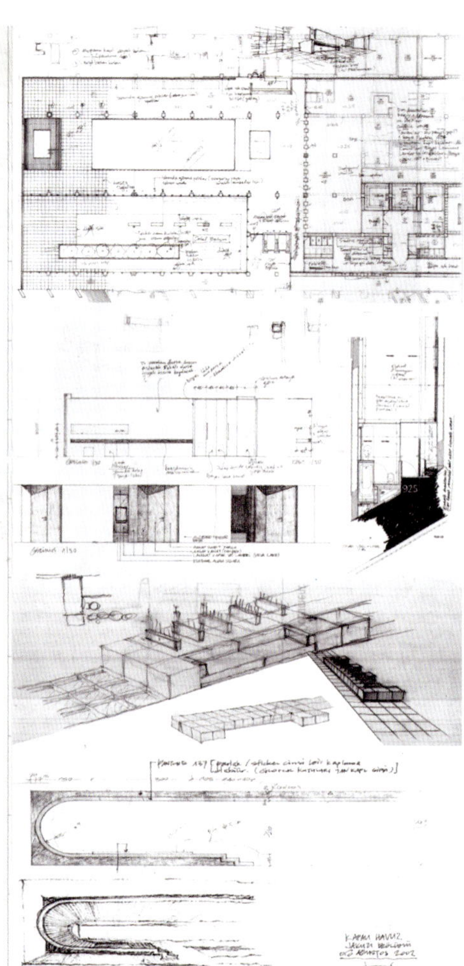

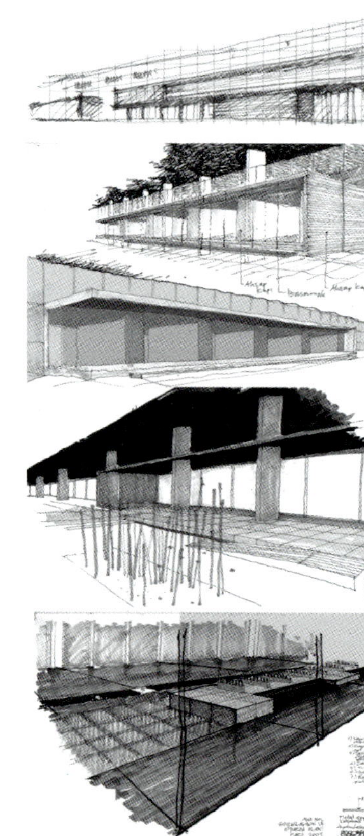

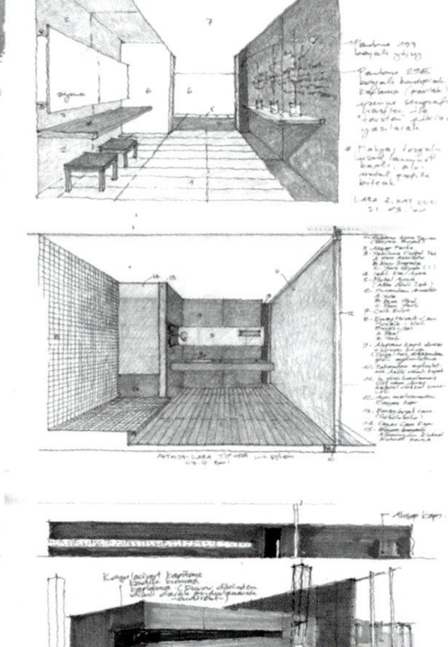

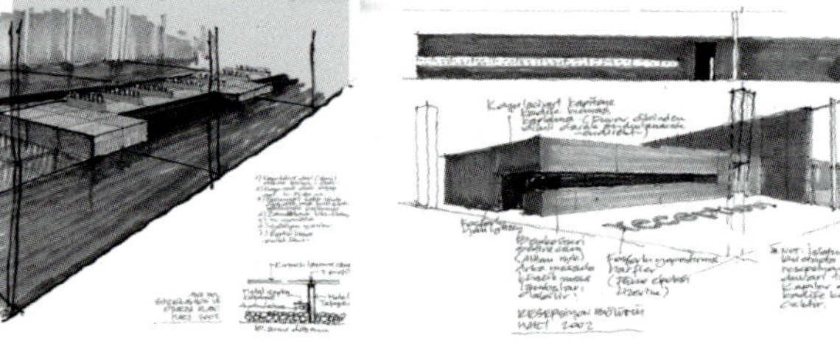

ABOVE
Sketches for the indoor pool area

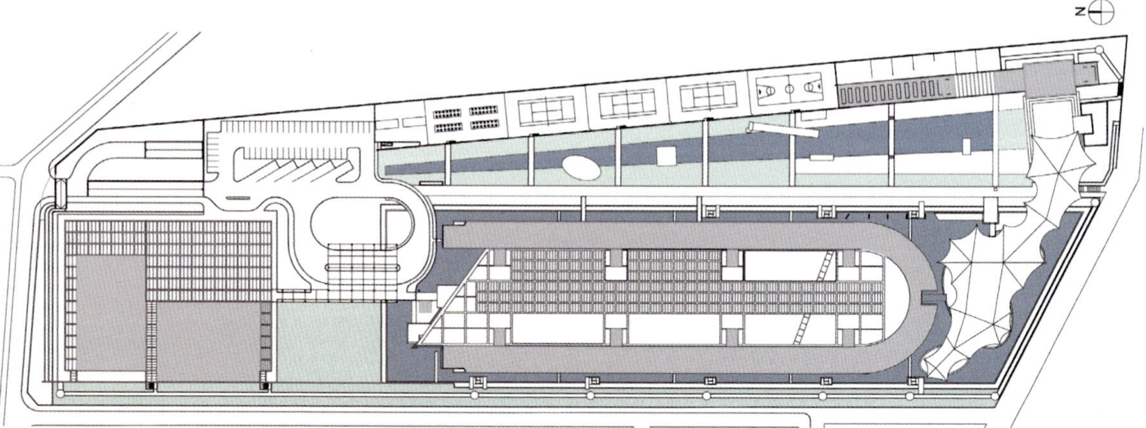

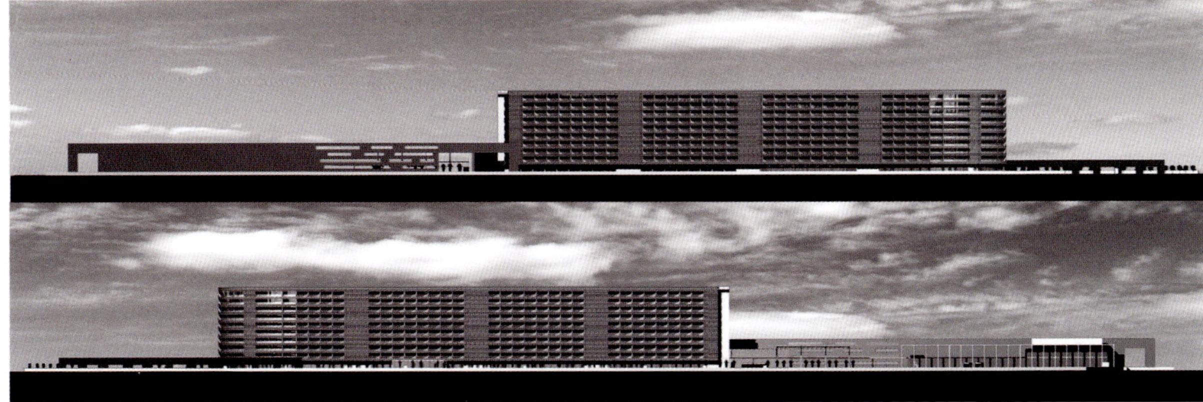

LEFT
East, west, and south facade views

BELOW
Abstraction of the mass among the
surrounding buildings

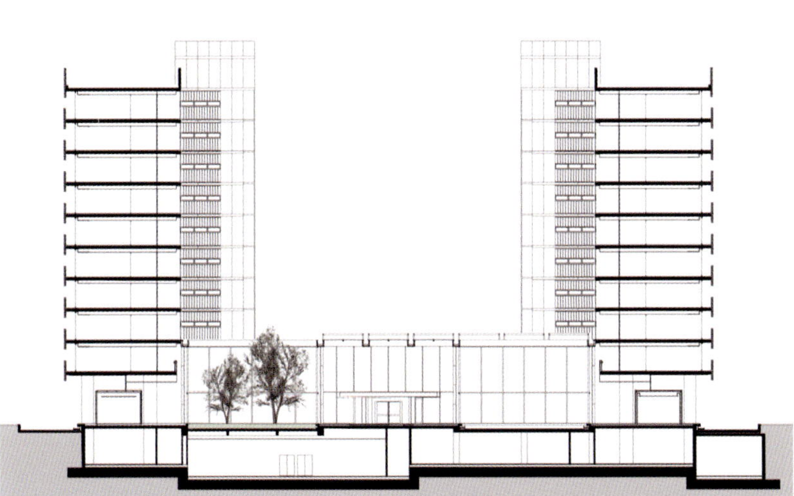

ABOVE
Typical section

RIGHT
Aerial view from the northeast

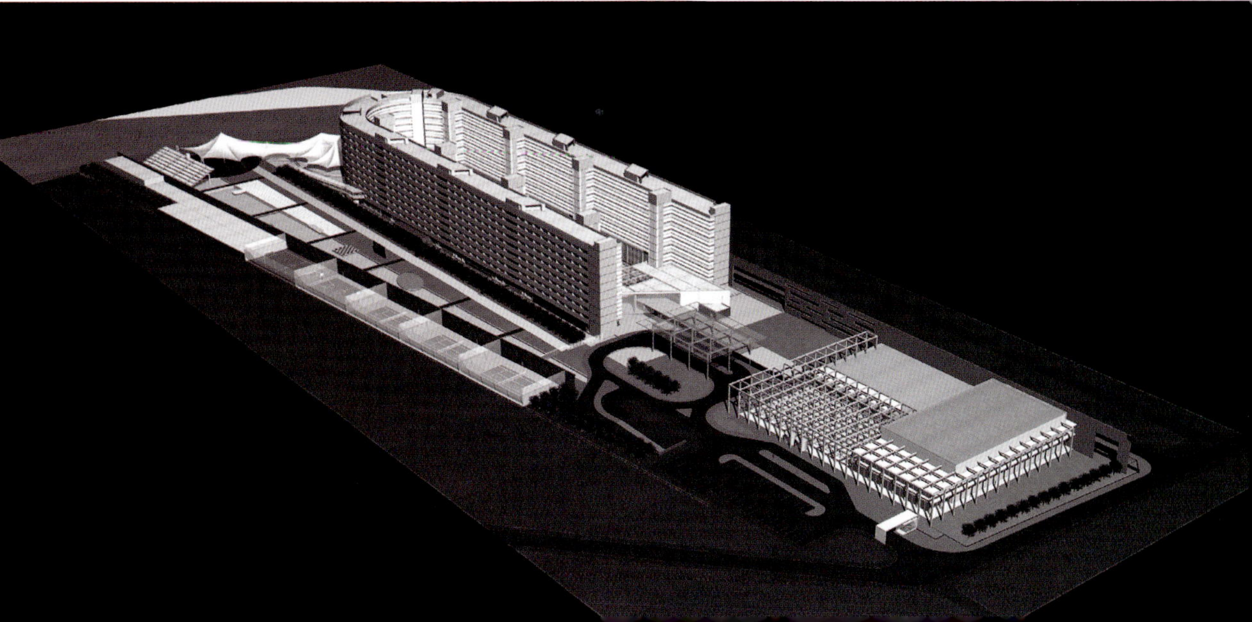

OPPOSITE, TOP LEFT
View of the eastern facade and
the convention center

OPPOSITE, TOP RIGHT
View of the western facade

OPPOSITE, MIDDLE
View from the eastern facade

OPPOSITE, BOTTOM
View of the inner courtyard

RIGHT
Circulation hall leading to
the hotel rooms

ABOVE
Outdoor dining

ABOVE, RIGHT
Indoor dining

RIGHT
View of the inner courtyard

LEFT
Resting area in the indoor pool

BOTTOM
View from the entrance on
the northern side

BELOW
Café at the indoor pool

BELOW
Circulation hall leading to
the hotel rooms

BOTTOM
Indoor pool

RIGHT
Lounge

MIDDLE, RIGHT
Typical room

OPPOSITE, TOP LEFT
View of the entrance canopy

OPPOSITE, TOP RIGHT AND BOTTOM,
RIGHT
Views from the entrance hall

BELOW, RIGHT
View from the entrance hall
toward reception

Minicity Theme Park

LOCATION / **Antalya, Turkey**

YEAR / **2004**

STATUS / **built**

TOTAL AREA / **55.000 m²**

Completed in 2004, the Minicity Theme Park building is a 55,000-square-meter (592,015 square foot) facility that serves an exhibition of 1:25 scale models of buildings from different regions of Turkey. A requirement of the client was that the building not allow visitors to see the models from the outside.

A fragmented, angular plan is faced on the south side by a long, high wall, which fulfills the client's desire to separate the commercial and recreational functions of the building from those of the theme park. The architect describes the building as a "series of shells that constitute their own specificity." Broken or "torn" at several points, the rear of the building allows for terraces on the side, where the scale models are located. On the western side, the building is "detached from the ground, somewhere between dividing and not dividing the interior and exterior."

This project was one of the works short-listed among the finalists and featured in the traveling exhibition in 2005 for the **EUROPEAN UNION PRIZE FOR CONTEMPORARY ARCHITECTURE/MIES VAN DER ROHE AWARD.**

OPPOSITE, TOP LEFT
Entrance view from the interior

OPPOSITE, TOP RIGHT
View from the southeast

RIGHT
Entrance view from the road

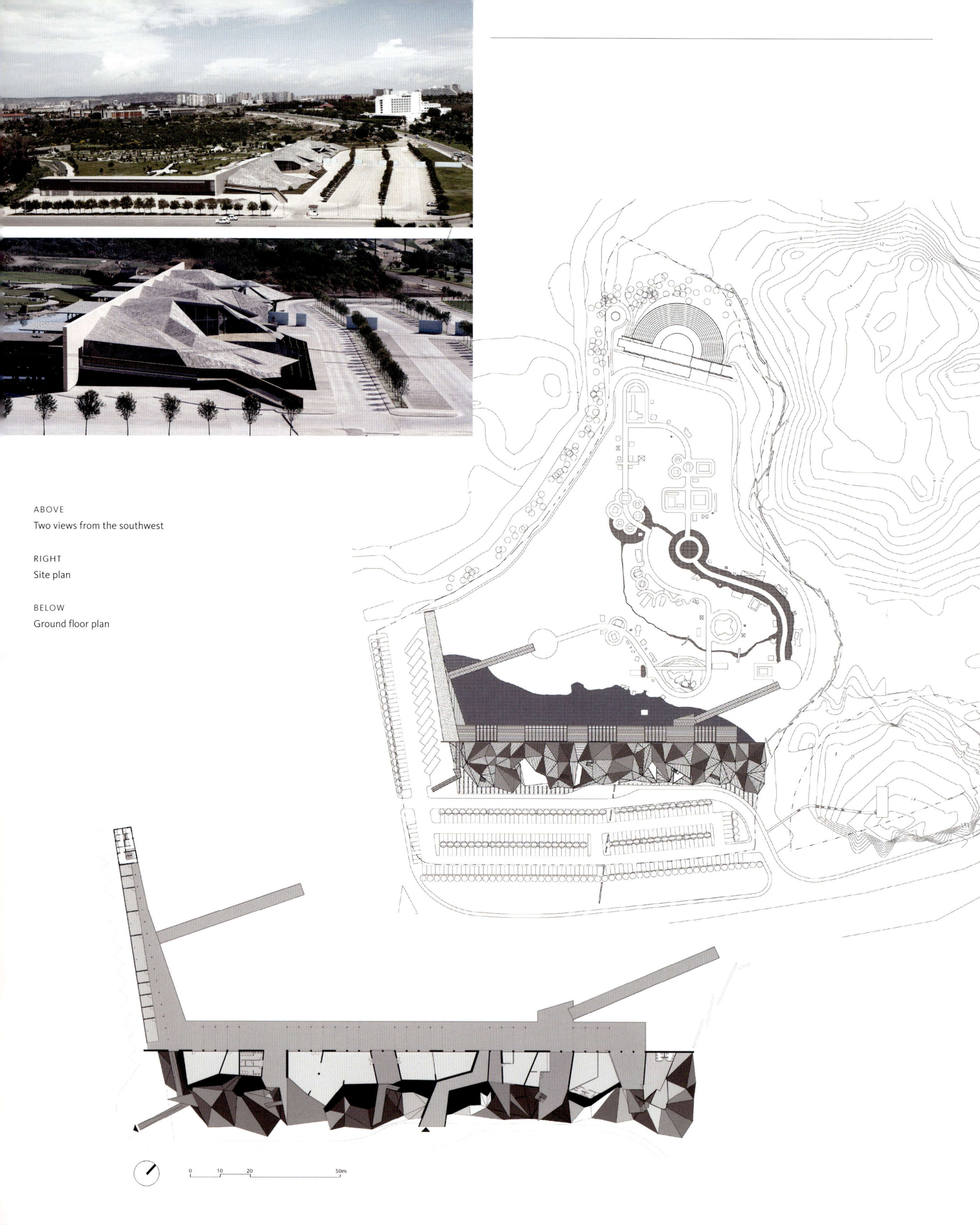

ABOVE
Two views from the southwest

RIGHT
Site plan

BELOW
Ground floor plan

RIGHT
Sections

BELOW
Model

BOTTOM
View from the pool on
the northwest

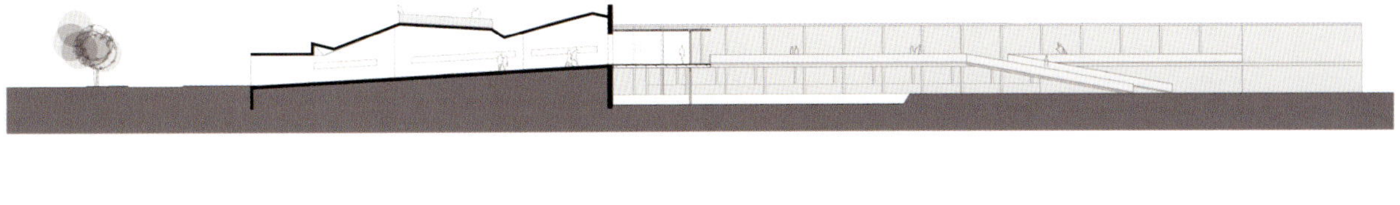

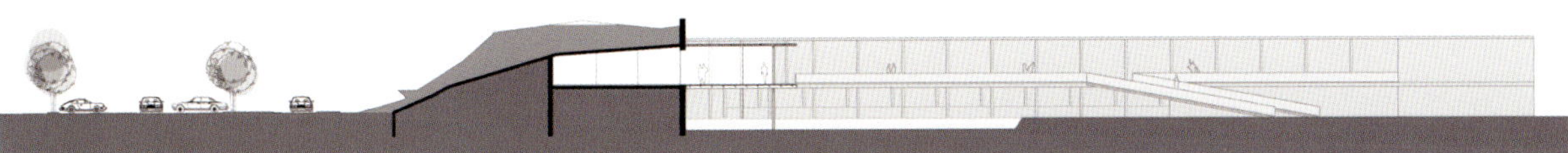

LEFT
Interior view

BELOW, LEFT
View from the walls on the northwest

BELOW
View from the northwest

BOTTOM
Texture of the natural stone

OPPOSITE
View from a slit

OPPOSITE
Stair on the northern side

BELOW
View from the north

Maksimum Houses

LOCATION / **Istanbul, Turkey**

YEAR / **2004**

STATUS / **built**

TOTAL AREA / **5.500 m²**

Building regulations in the Bosphorus area of Istanbul have generated a pattern of construction that has little to do with the site and is essentially without character. This 5,500-square-meter (59,200 square foot) housing complex was designed in 2001 and built in 2004. The principle behind the project was to respect every aspect of the existing building codes in order to see if it was possible to create interesting residences in spite of regulations.

The solution chosen was that of a small gated community consisting of just three buildings, a feature that distinguishes it from its surroundings. Each building is different, though on all three structures folding, sliding panels are used to shield residents from the sun and noise of a nearby road.

Taking advantage of rules that allow temporary buildings to disregard the aesthetic regulations imposed on more permanent structures, the architects created a sales office for the complex that is still in use as a social gathering place for residents.

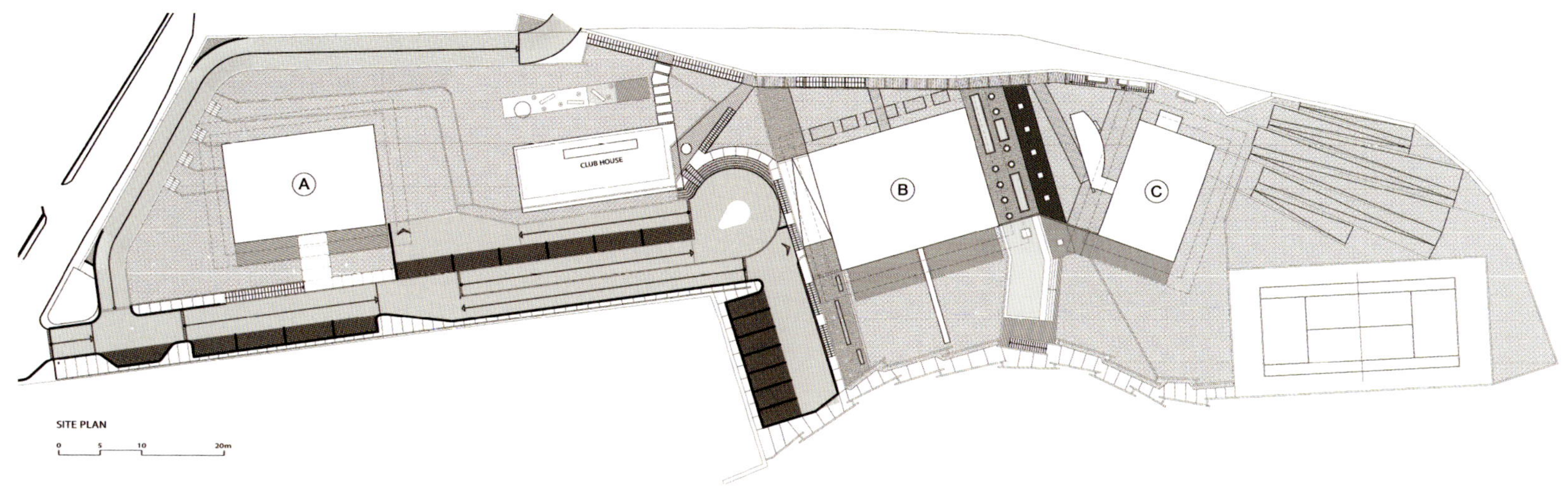

SITE PLAN

0   5   10   20m

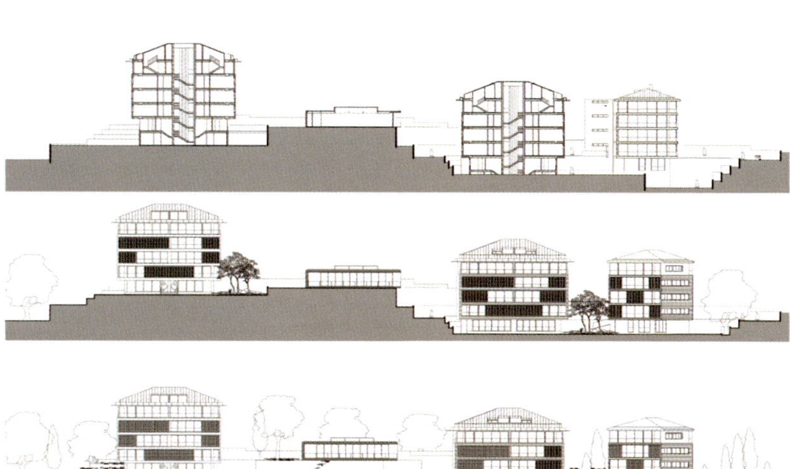

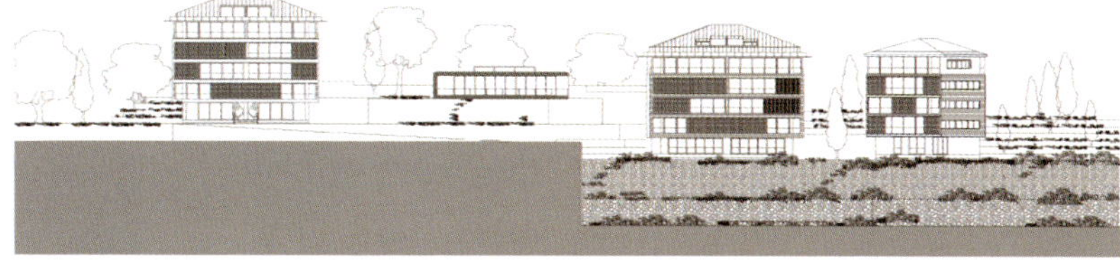

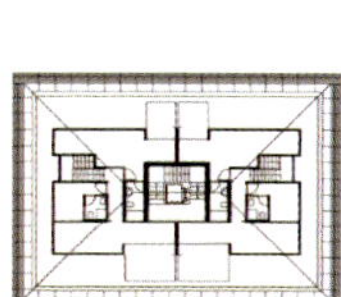
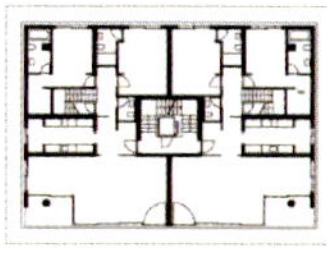
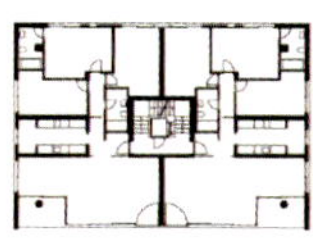
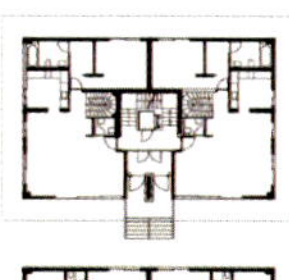
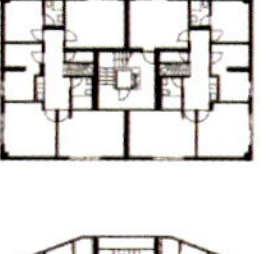
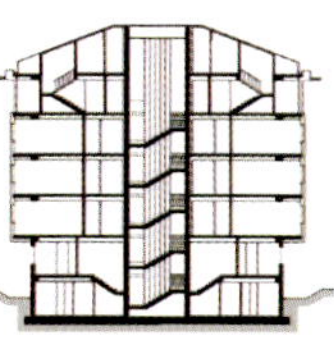
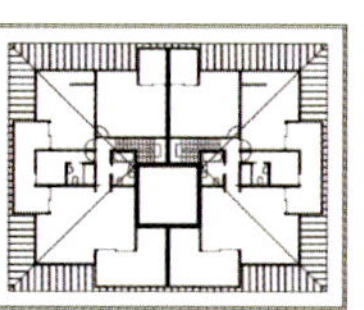
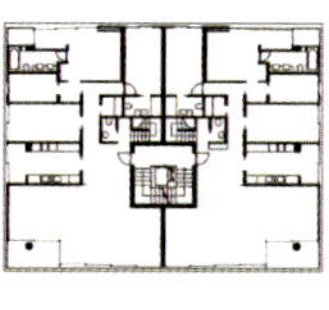
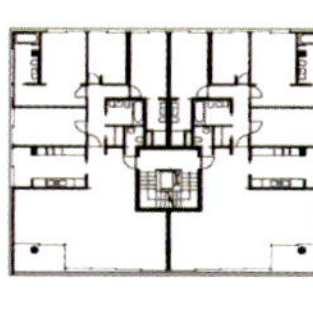
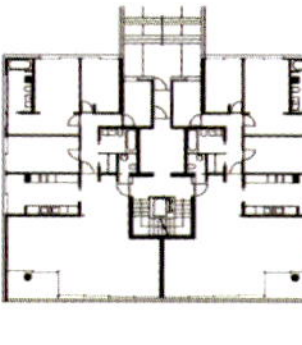
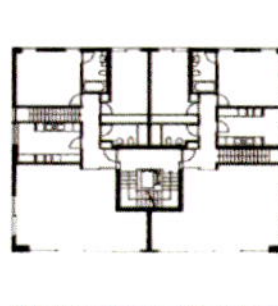
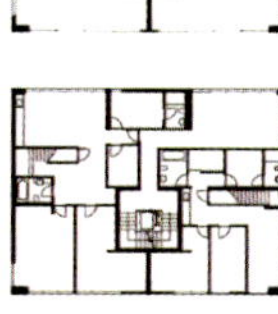
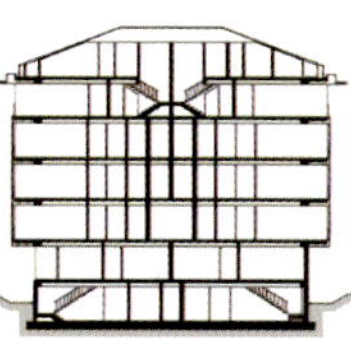
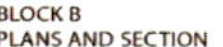
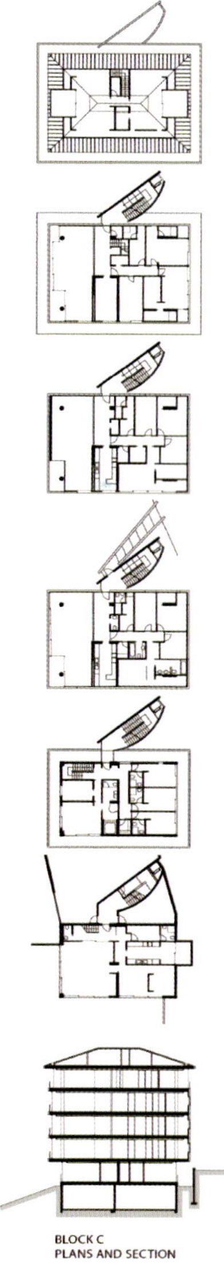

BLOCK A
PLANS AND SECTION

BLOCK B
PLANS AND SECTION

BLOCK C
PLANS AND SECTION

0   5   10   20m

TOP
Site plan

MIDDLE
Sections and elevations
from the site

LEFT
Sketch for the environmental
design of the site

ABOVE
Typical plans and sections

RIGHT
Front facade with wooden sliding panels

BELOW
View of the block from the northwest

ABOVE
Sales office building

LEFT
View from the circulation area at
the back of the blocks

BELOW, LEFT
View of the site from the south

BELOW
Close view from the south

OPPOSITE
View of the pool area
between blocks

Kemerlife XXI

LOCATION / Istanbul, Turkey

YEAR / 2005

STATUS / built

TOTAL AREA / 40.000 m²

This 40,000-square-meter (430,556 square foot) complex is made up of 206 units of thirteen different types. Terrace-house duplexes in the lower section open onto private gardens that are distinct from the neighboring public garden. A shift in the axis of the structure allows terraces above the duplexes to serve as private gardens for the apartments on the ground floor.

Making use of the sloped site, the architects placed recreational facilities in the basement and connected them to the public garden on the same level. The rest of the basement is used for parking and service functions. The architects explain that "the fragmentation achieved both horizontally and vertically provided a loose and permeable layout by blurring the norms of typical five-story apartment buildings."

The overall layout and load-bearing system allowed for rapid construction, while the use of wood and stone cladding was meant to contribute in a positive way to the appearance of the building as it ages.

BELOW
Sketches for the general layout
and the entrance canopy

RIGHT
Site plan and floor plans

BELOW
Section and elevations

BOTTOM
Aerial view of the site

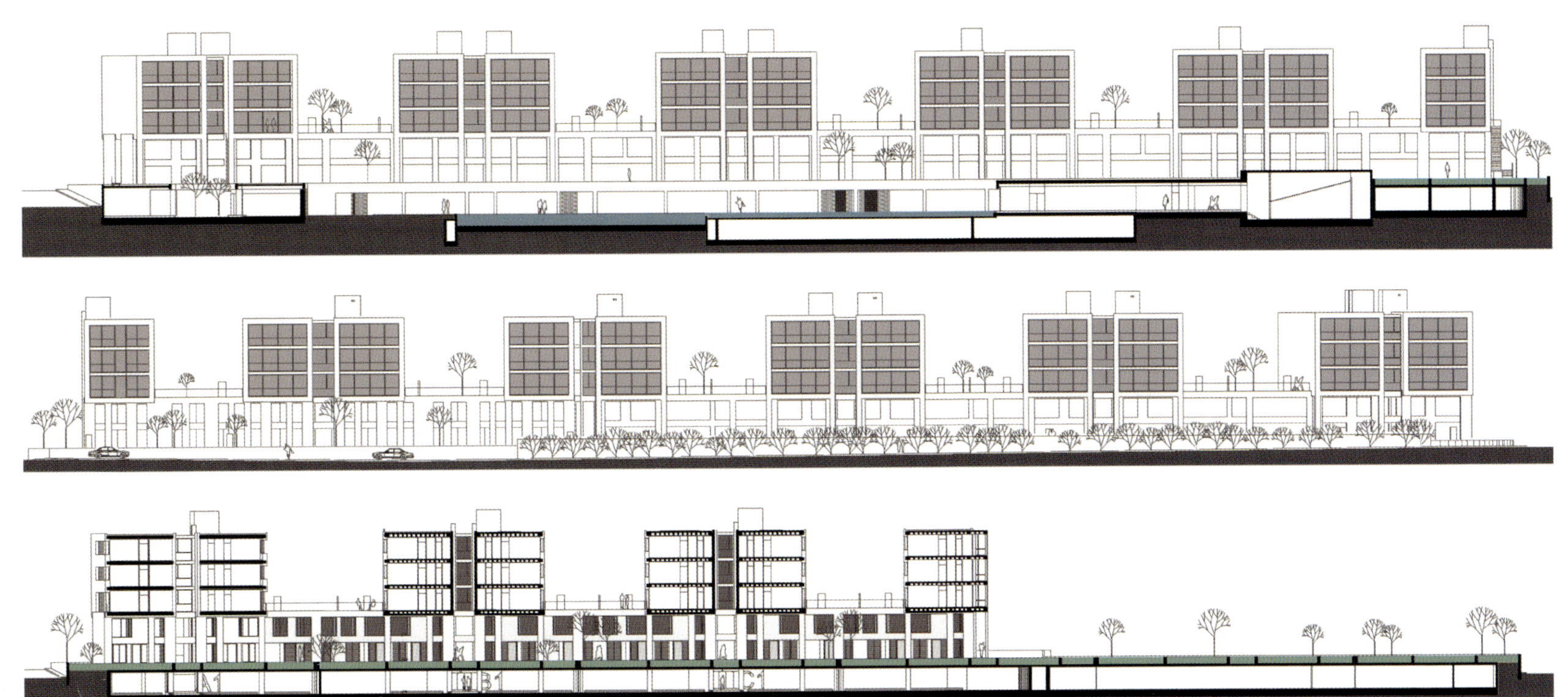

OPPOSITE TOP
View of the facade of a block from
the courtyard

OPPOSITE BOTTOM
View from the exterior southern side

RIGHT
View from the northwest

BELOW, RIGHT AND FAR RIGHT
Views of the circulation space
in between rows

BOTTOM LEFT
View of the back gardens
in between rows

BOTTOM RIGHT
View from the social area
in the courtyard

Evidea Housing

LOCATION / Istanbul, Turkey

YEAR / 2006

STATUS / built

TOTAL AREA / 100.000 m²

BELOW, LEFT
View of the exterior facade

BELOW
View of the courtyard

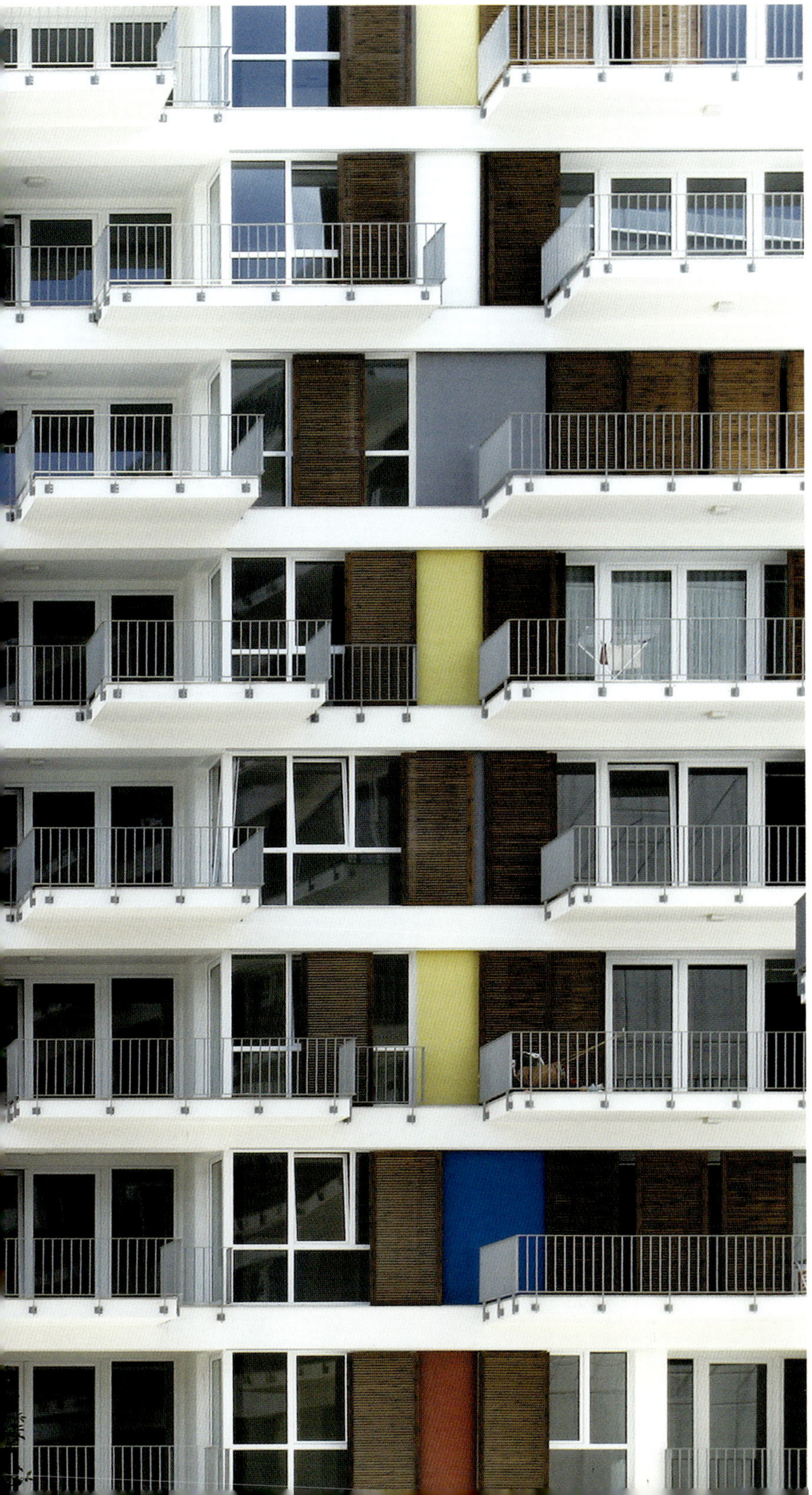

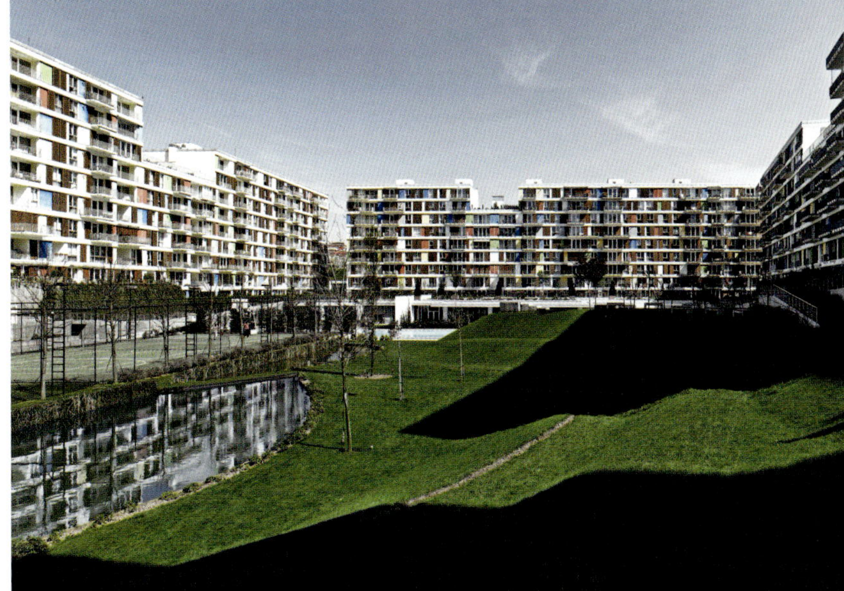

Çekmeköy is a rapidly developing area of Istanbul that has recently been opened to new construction. Local building regulations were drawn up, taking into consideration projects that would be carried out by large construction firms. Municipal zoning rules detail restrictions to the total construction area, a height limited to nine stories, and the methods for defining elevations and proportions. In a rather clear, irrevocable way, the firm investing in the project determined matters related to the market and terms of sale. These included the distribution of housing units according to their size, the number of rooms, size of service areas per square meter, types of materials that could be used and their details, as well as cost limits. The main purpose of this 100,000 square meter (nearly 1.1 million square foot) project was to interpret architecturally these strictly defined rules.

The design took shape as an inward-turned, homogenous structure, rather than the scattered and staggered individual apartment buildings typical of the conventions within Turkey's construction sector; the project was completed in 2006. A large area in the middle of the housing blocks includes private areas on the peripheries and communal space in the lowered middle portion. All vehicular circulation was confined to the road outside the housing blocks and to the garage below.

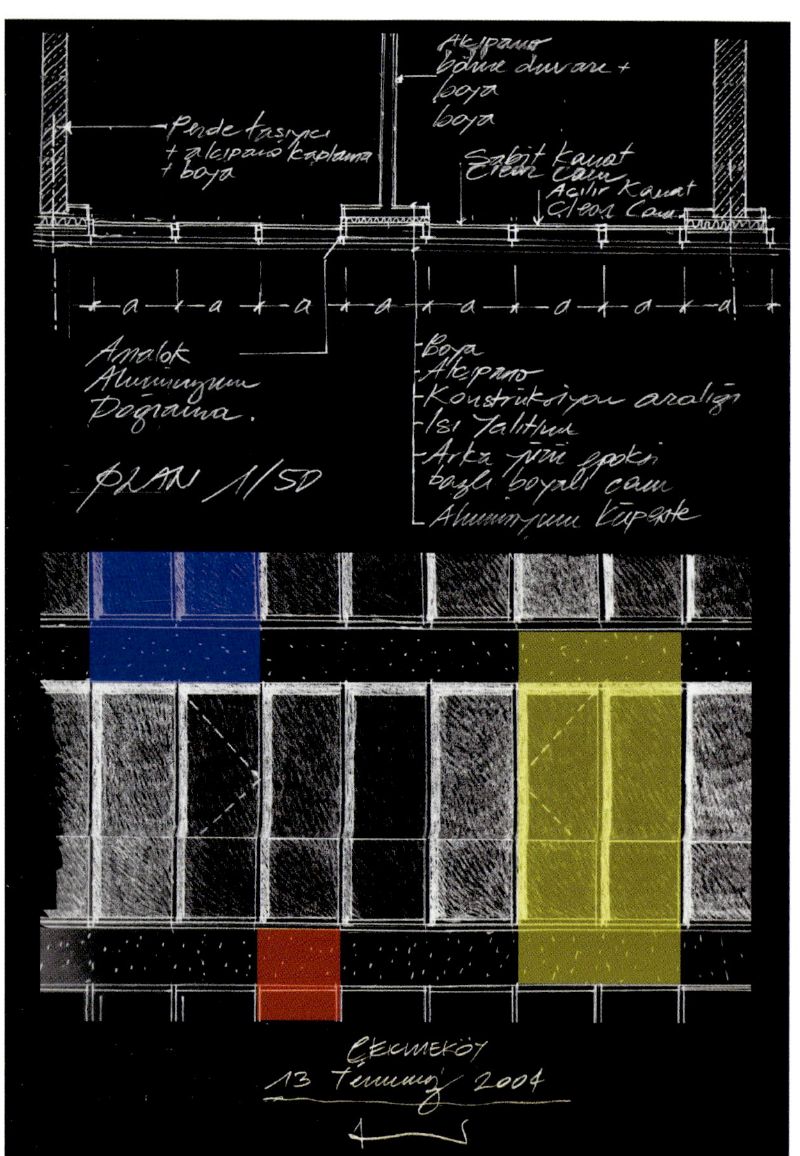
Pde taşıyıcı
+ alçıpan kaplama
+ boya
Alçıpan
bölme duvarı +
boya
boya
Sabit Kanat
Clear Cam
Açılır Kanat
Clear Cam
Amalok
Alüminyum
Doğrama.
Boya
Alçıpan
Konstrüksiyon aralığı
Isı Yalıtımı
Arka yüz epoksi
bazlı boyalı cam
Alüminyum Küpeşte
PLAN 1/50
ÇEKMEKÖY
13 Temmuz 2004

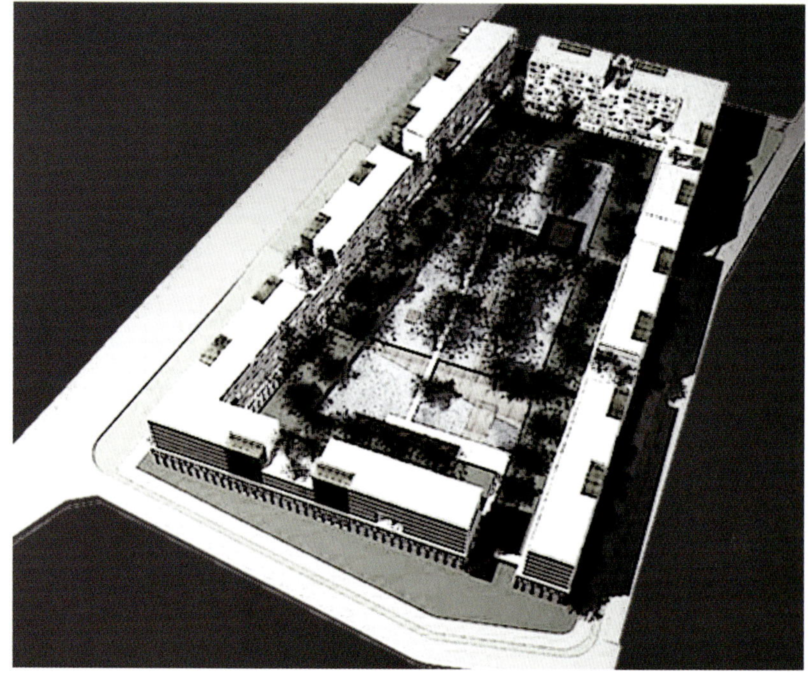

A
B1
B2
C1
C2
D1
D2
E1
E2

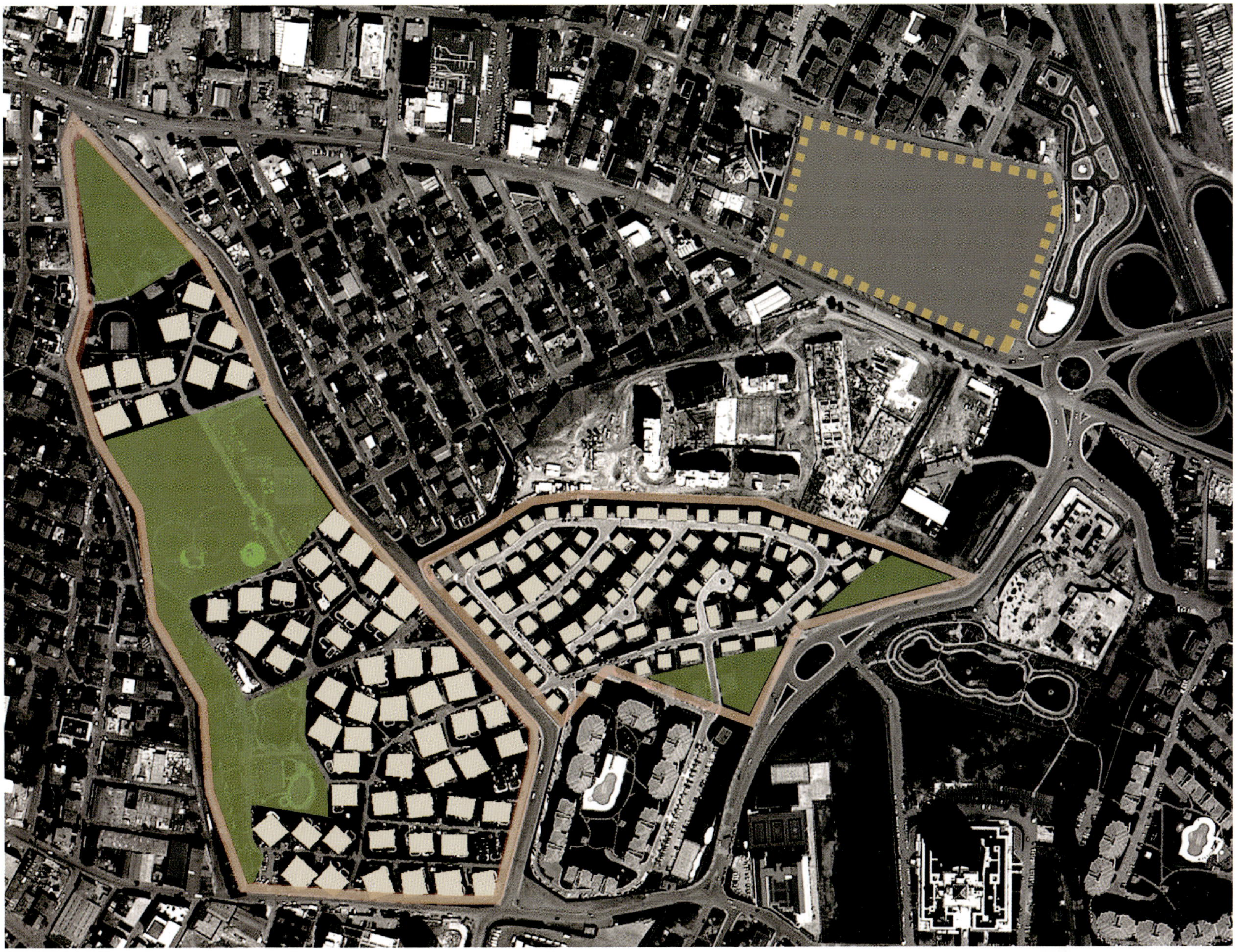

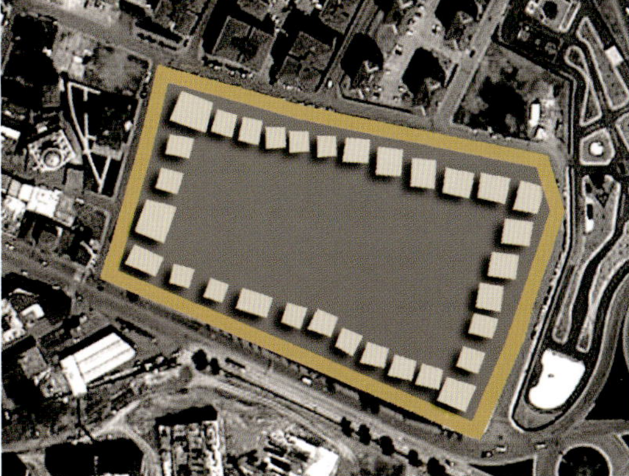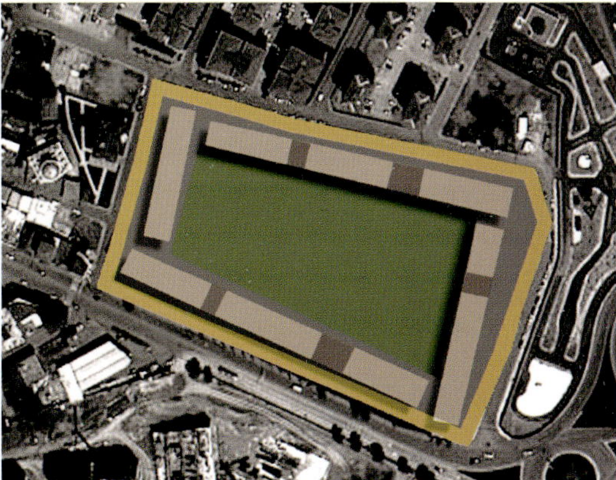

OPPOSITE, TOP LEFT
Sketch for the facade

OPPOSITE, TOP RIGHT AND MIDDLE
Site plan and aerial view of the site

OPPOSITE, BOTTOM
Typical plans

ABOVE
Conceptual layout diagrams

ABOVE AND LEFT
Facade facing the inner courtyard

FAR LEFT AND MIDDLE
Exterior facade

TOP AND ABOVE, LEFT
Exterior facade at night

ABOVE
Inner courtyard at night

SantralIstanbul Contemporary Arts Museum

LOCATION / **Istanbul, Turkey**

YEAR / **2006**

STATUS / **built**

TOTAL AREA / **7000 m²**

View of the Contemporary Arts Museum together with the existing buildings of the power plant

This 7,000-square-meter (75,347 square foot) project was completed in 2006 and opened in 2007. The Istanbul Bilgi University developed the idea of renovating the Silahtaraga power plant, a typical modern industrial complex built between the early 1900s and the 1950s, converting it into a museum and recreational and educational center.

The site is at the end of Golden Horn, a former center of Istanbul that was progressively abandoned but has again come into fashion. The architects studied the history of the power plant and sought to understand the layered construction that transformed the site over the course of its industrial existence. The renovation and conservation scheme was developed on the basis of this history and included such elements as the role of two large boiler houses long since demolished. According to the architects, "Just like the old buildings, the new structures are composed of a dense and heavy inner core and a light, semitransparent exterior sheathing that covers the core without touching it to the greatest possible extent." Metal mesh placed over a concrete base was used.

In addition to EAA, architects such as Nevzat Sayın (public library) and Han Tümertekin (energy museum) were involved in the overall project.

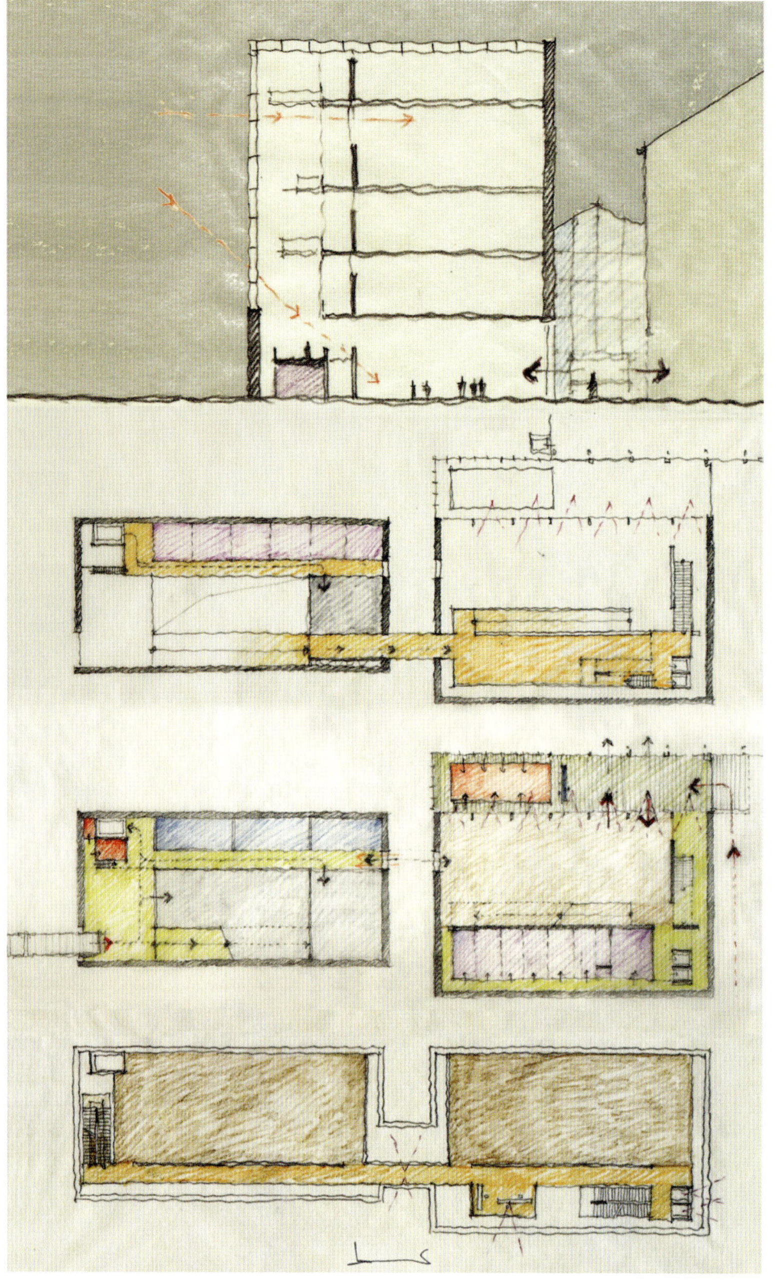

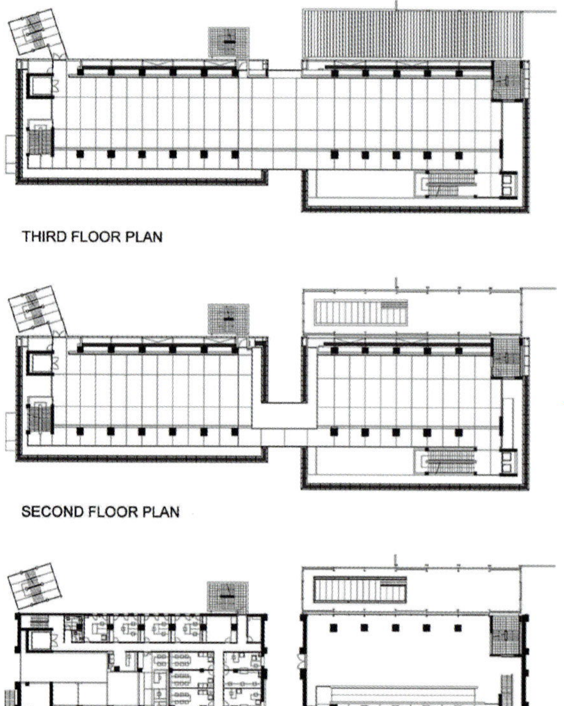

THIRD FLOOR PLAN
SECOND FLOOR PLAN
GROUND FLOOR PLAN
0 5 10   20m

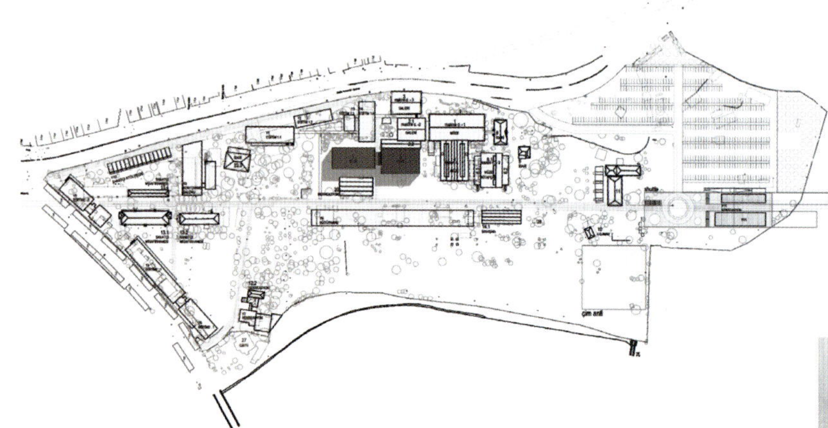

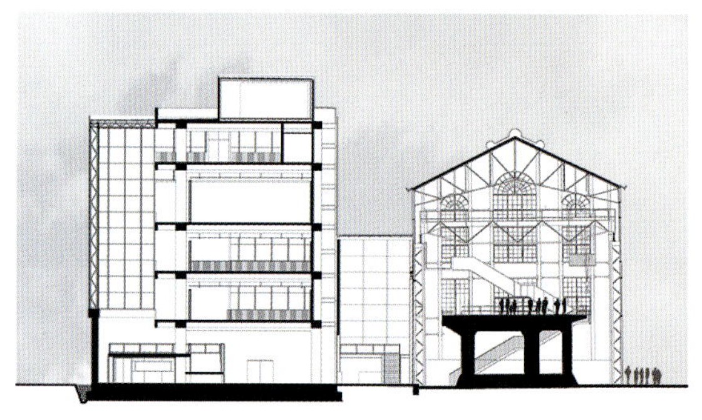

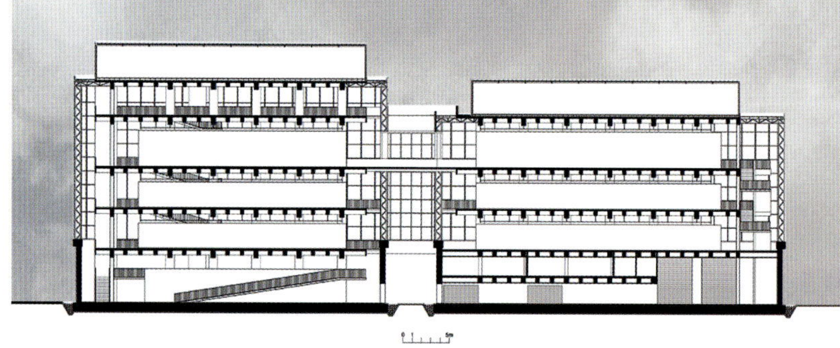

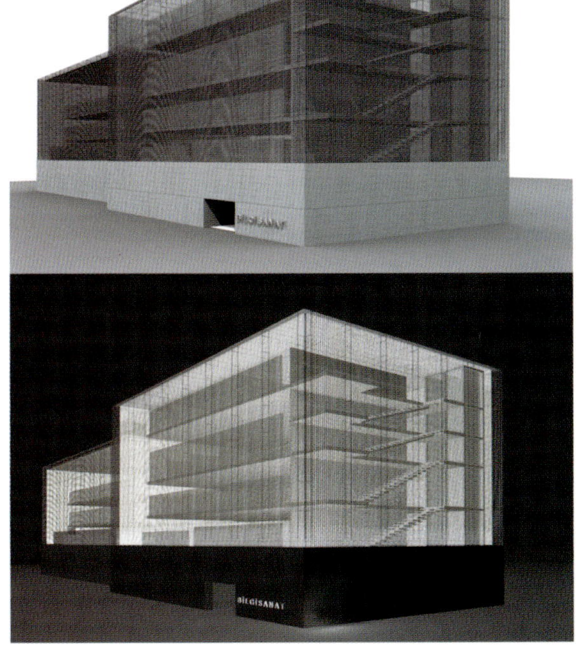

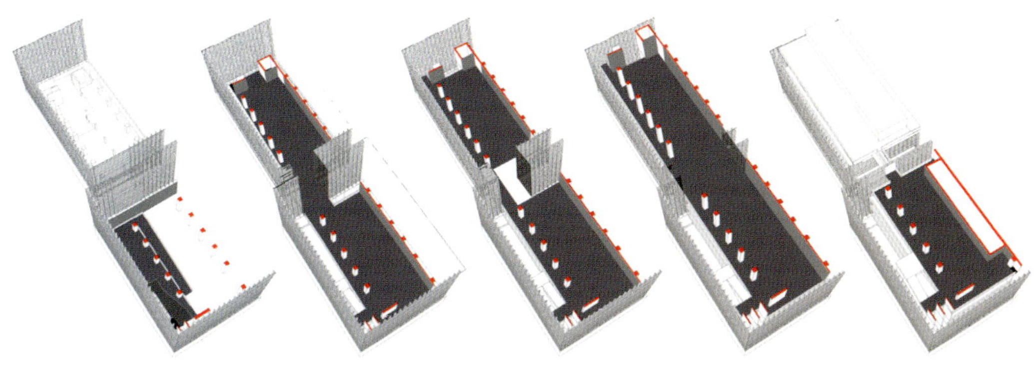

OPPOSITE, TOP LEFT
Sketch for general planning of the blocks

OPPOSITE, TOP RIGHT
Former boiler house in construction

OPPOSITE, MIDDLE
Floor plans

OPPOSITE, BOTTOM
Sections

OPPOSITE, BOTTOM LEFT
Site plan of the complex

LEFT
Volumetric assembly of the building

ABOVE
Axonometric floor diagram

BELOW, LEFT AND RIGHT
Aerial views of the site

BOTTOM
Aerial view of the general layout

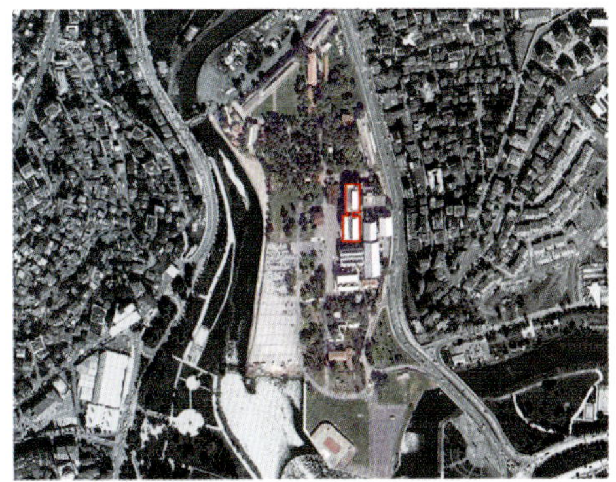

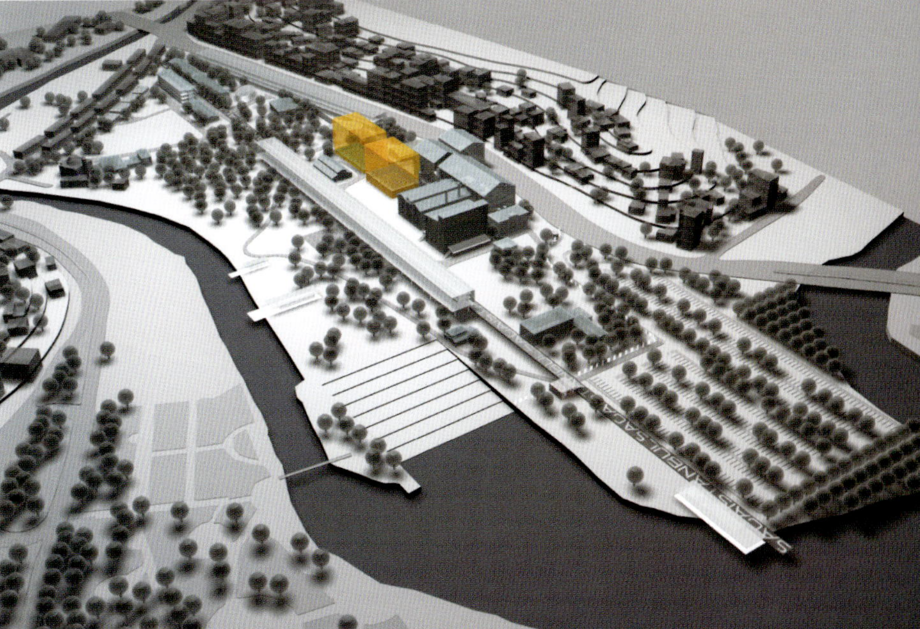

LEFT
View from the southwest

BELOW, LEFT
View from the west

BOTTOM
Night view of the museum

OPPOSITE, TOP
Exterior sheathing in daytime

OPPOSITE, BOTTOM
Museum among the
existing buildings

ABOVE
View from the front gallery

ABOVE, RIGHT
View toward the neighborhood
through exterior sheathing

BELOW
View from the gallery in the entrance

OPPOSITE, TOP LEFT
Circulation gallery

OPPOSITE, TOP RIGHT
Stair in the gallery

OPPOSITE, BOTTOM RIGHT
View from the inner gallery

OPPOSITE, BOTTOM LEFT
View of the front gallery

NIMI TOPLULUGU

İpekyol Textile Factory

LOCATION / **Edirne, Turkey**

YEAR / **2004**

STATUS / **built**

TOTAL AREA / **15.000 m²**

Winner of the **2010 AGA KHAN AWARD FOR ARCHITECTURE**, this 15,000-square-meter (161,459 square foot) project was undertaken in 2004. The design is strictly related to its site and to the functions of the factory.

Located on a limited plot on the road to Kırklareli and near the E5 highway, the structure links administrative and factory functions in a single large mass rather than separating them, as local traditions would have implied. Linear gardens are located between the different sections of the factory, serving as space for staff rest breaks and also bringing natural light and air into the building.

Given the nature of the project and an understanding of local building techniques, the architects chose to avoid "innovative experiments in building materials and production methods," preferring to use "vertical reinforced concrete load-bearing elements, a lightweight steel structure cover placed on top of them, and a coffered system for the facades." The exterior surfaces of the factory employ a grammar determined by the clear distinction between areas that are respectively open or closed to the outside.

BELOW
View from the south

RIGHT
Close-up view from the
southwest facade

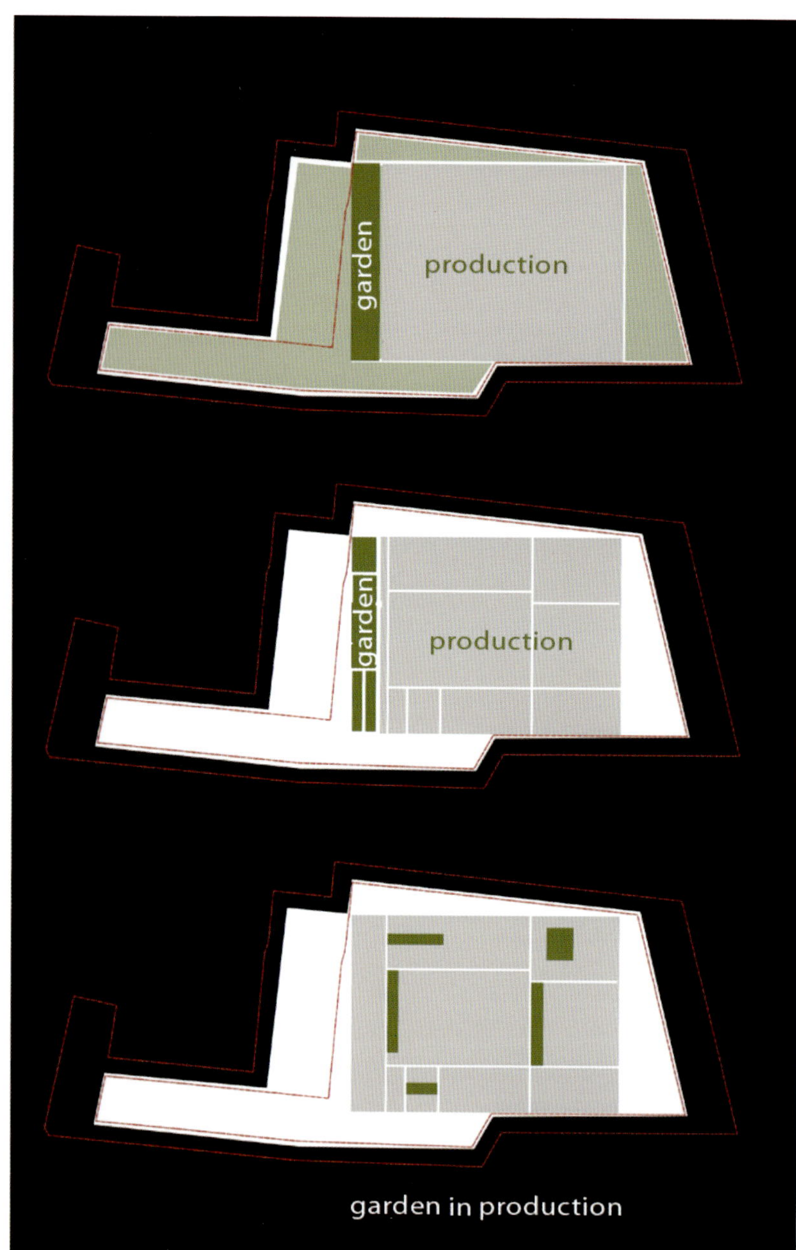

garden
production
garden
production
garden in production

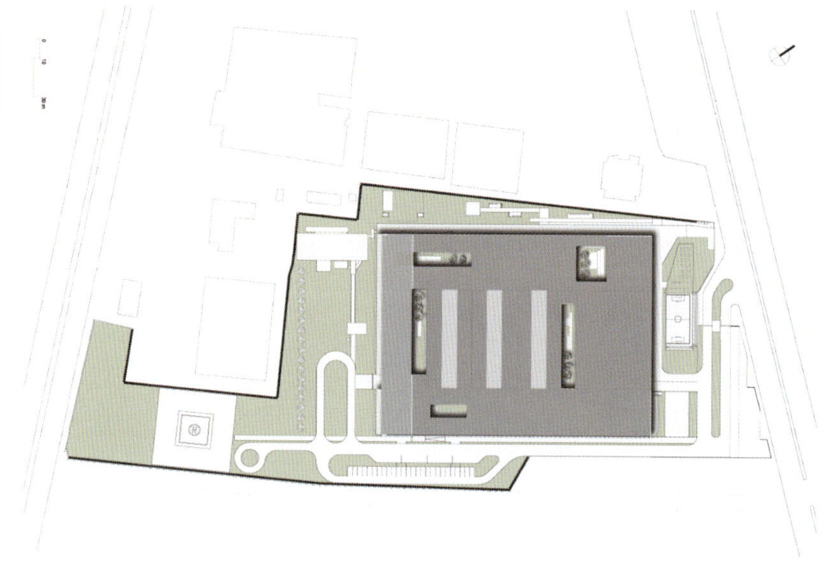

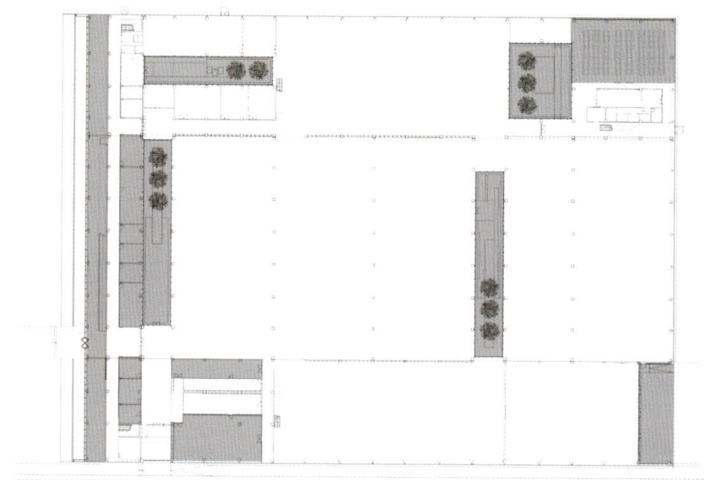

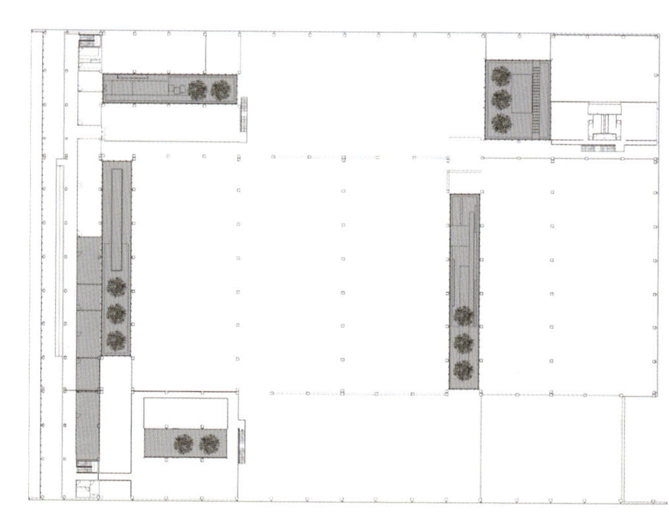

ABOVE
Conceptual scheme of the layout

ABOVE, RIGHT
Site plan

RIGHT
Floor plans

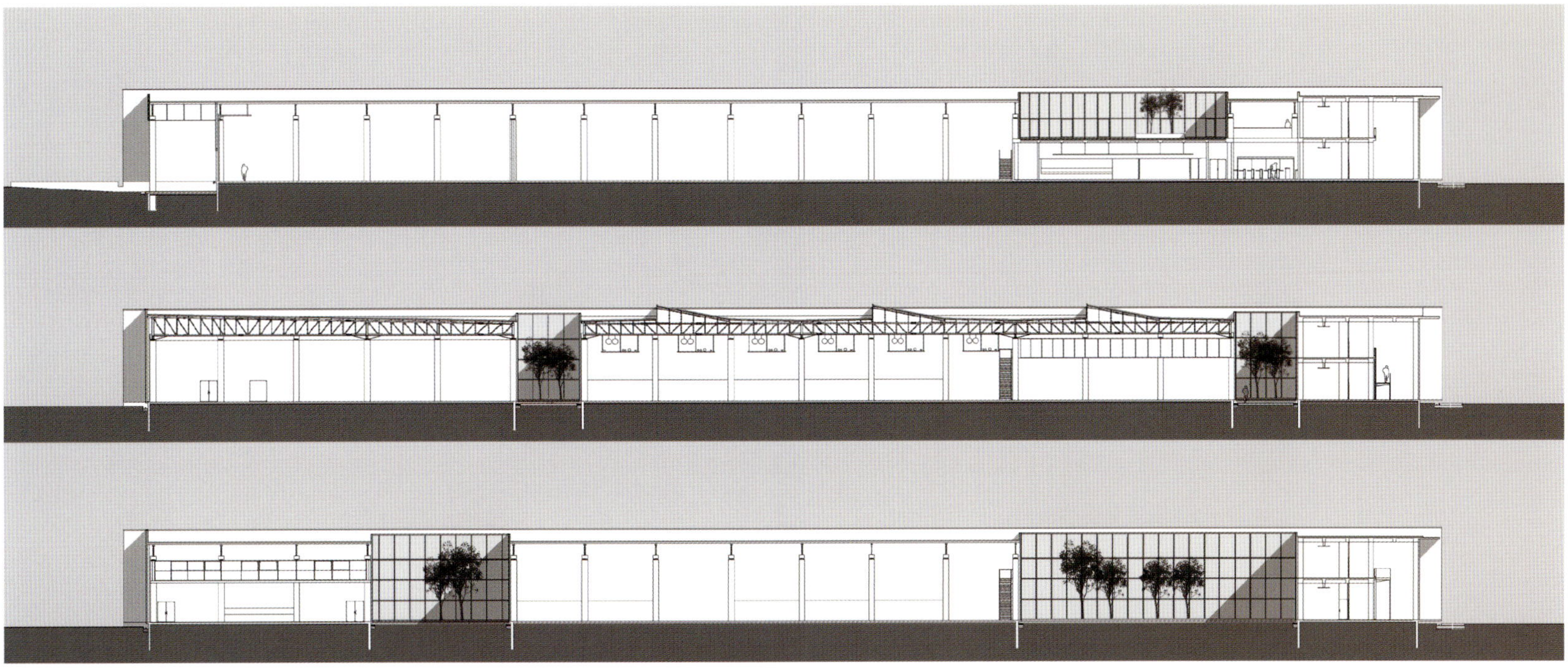

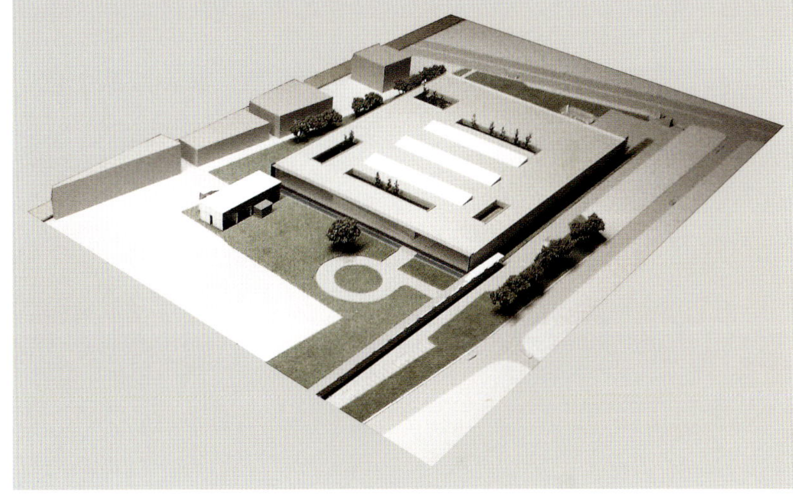

ABOVE, TOP
Sections

ABOVE, LEFT AND RIGHT
Aerial views from the model

BELOW, LEFT
View from the inner courtyard

BELOW
View from the social spaces in the garden

OPPOSITE, TOP
View from the southwest

OPPOSITE, BOTTOM
View from the north

ABOVE
Border walls on the northern side

BELOW
View from the south

LEFT
Entrance on the northwestern facade

OPPOSITE
View from the inner courtyard

ABOVE
Southern facade

ABOVE, RIGHT
View from the south

RIGHT
Close-up view of the
southwestern facade

BELOW AND OPPOSITE
Southwestern facade at dusk

RIGHT
Entrance on the northwestern facade

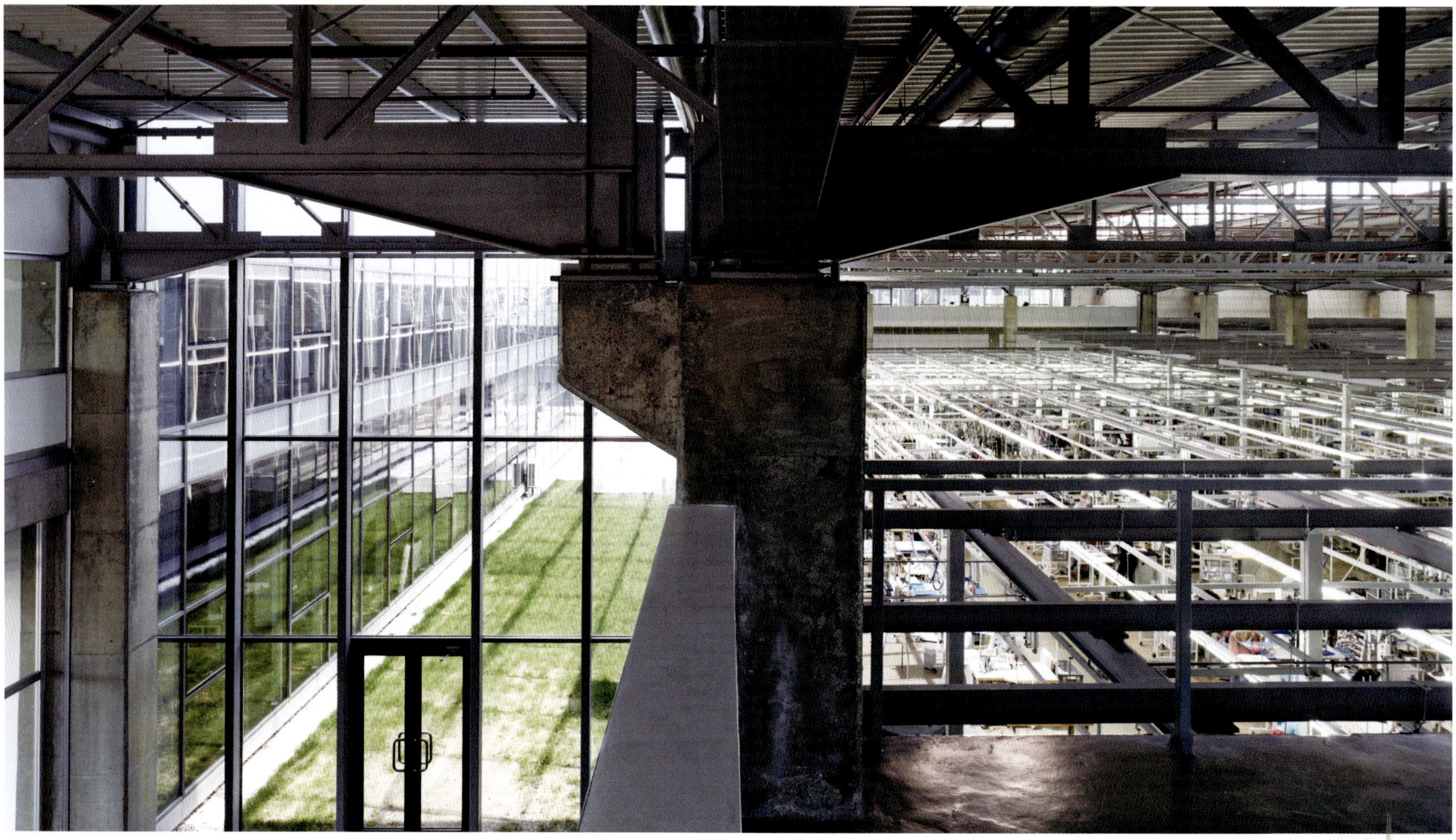

TOP
View of the inner courtyard and production space

ABOVE
View from the production space

LEFT
View of the gallery inside the southwestern facade

OPPOSITE, TOP
The dining hall

OPPOSITE, BOTTOM LEFT
Different views from the inner courtyard and gallery at dusk

OPPOSITE, BOTTOM RIGHT
View of the gallery

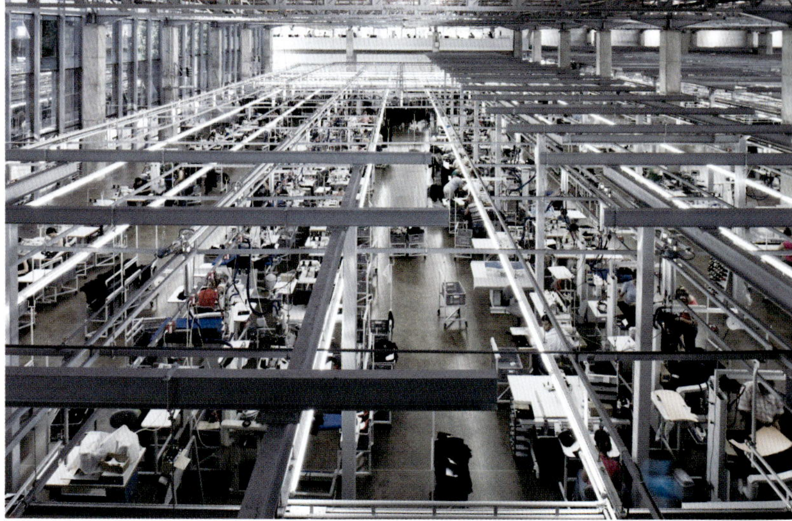

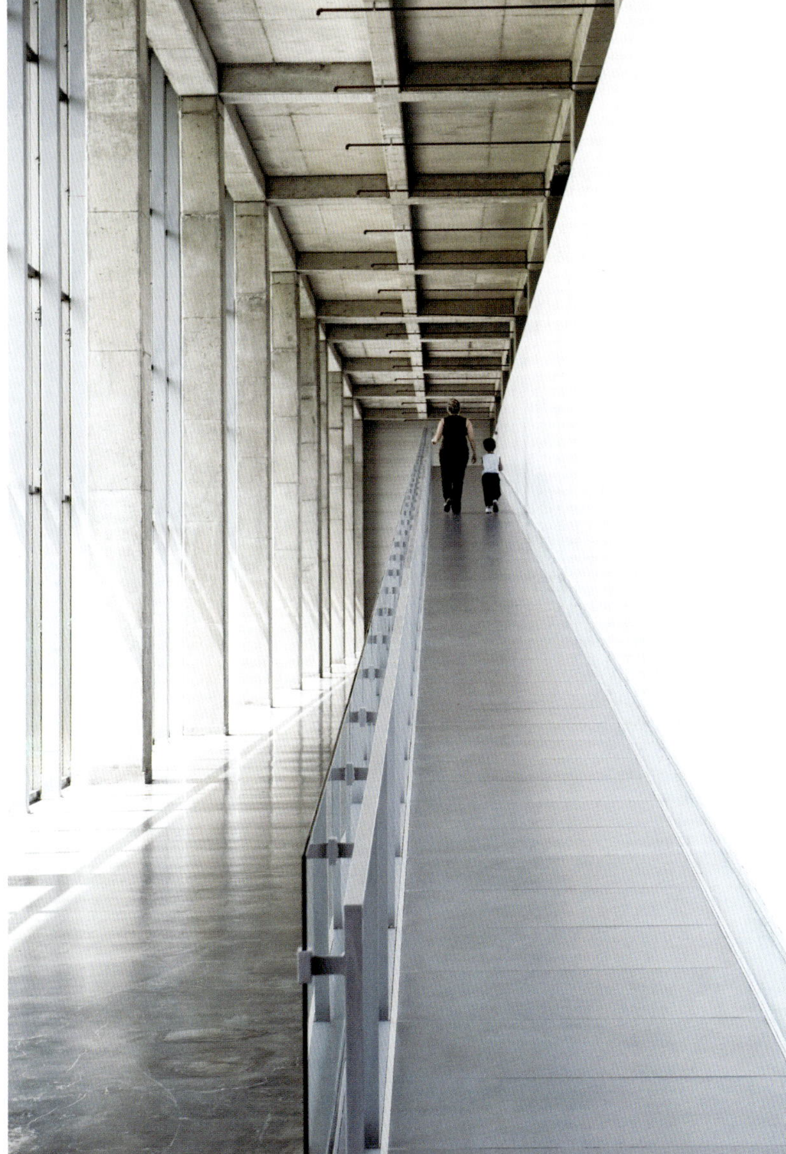

Çubuklu Vadi Homes

LOCATION / **Istanbul, Turkey**

YEAR / **2009**

STATUS / **built**

TOTAL AREA / **40.000 m²**

Built on a sloped site with an overall area of 1.5 million square meters (370 acres), this 40,000-square-meter (430,556 square foot) project took the place of a design that had been developed by another firm and abandoned for legal reasons in 2005.

The decklike terraces are detached from the ground, replacing gardens deemed too difficult to create because of the inclination of the landscape. Articulated terrace roofs form a fifth facade, while modular systems that allow for industrial-style construction made the entire project economically feasible.

Interior and exterior spaces can easily be separated or brought together with sliding systems. These characteristics were developed and used in the different types of residences and the hotel building, which is located on the highest part of the site. Existing forest roads determined the linear planning of the housing, and the hotel, which has guest room wings detached from a middle block containing recreational areas, is fragmented to take into account the topography and views.

OPPOSITE, TOP
Residence with a large terrace

OPPOSITE, BOTTOM
View of the site from the southwest

BELOW
Site plan

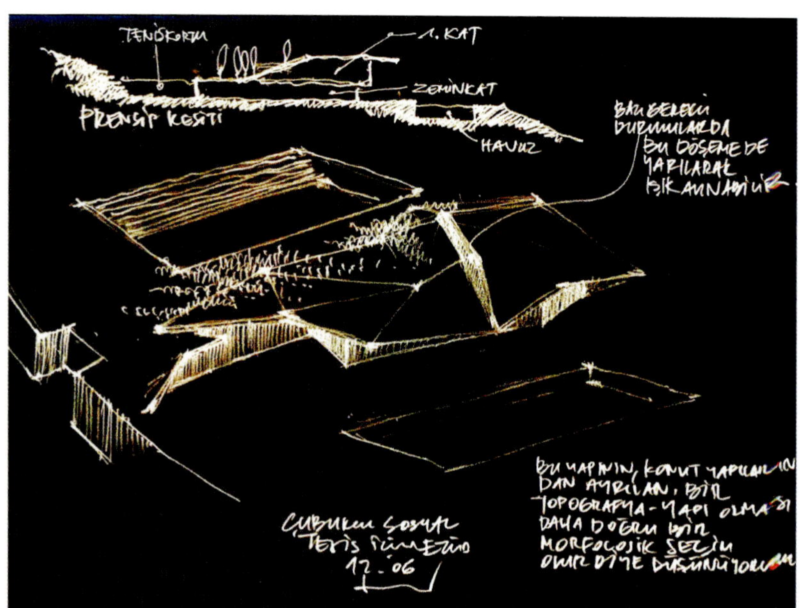

ABOVE
Study for the social club

ABOVE, RIGHT
Location

BELOW
Conceptual study for the roof
as a fifth facade

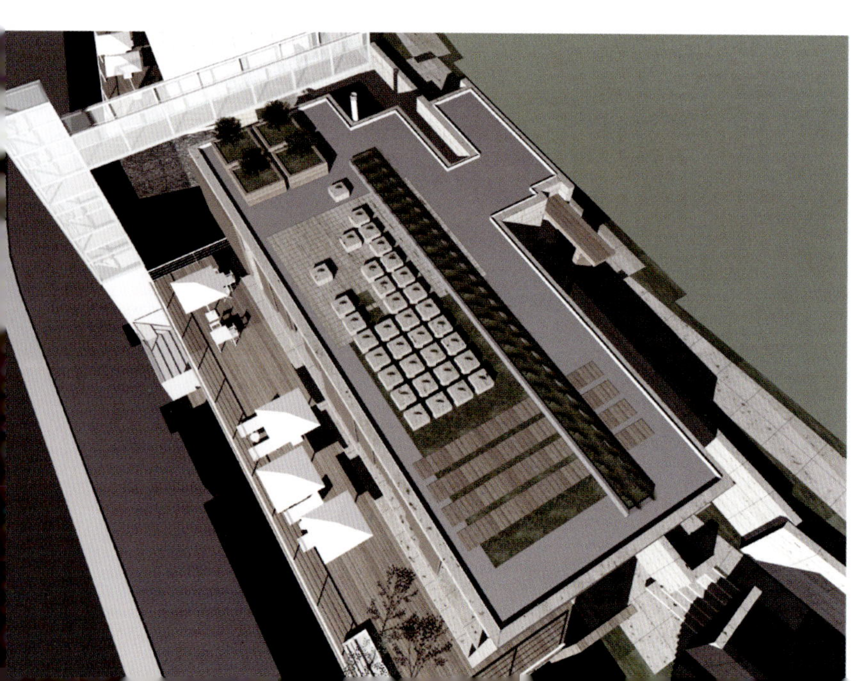

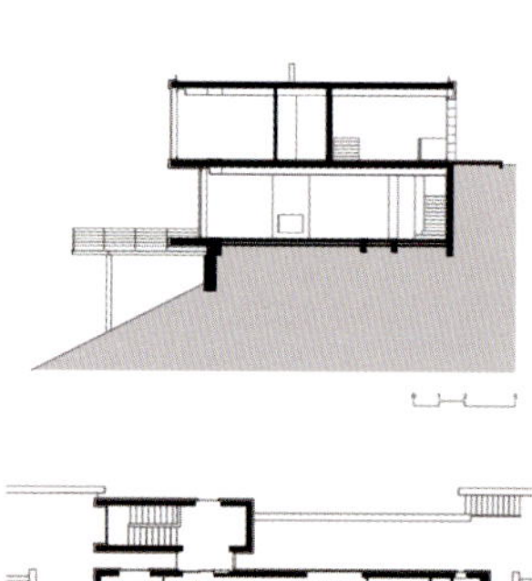

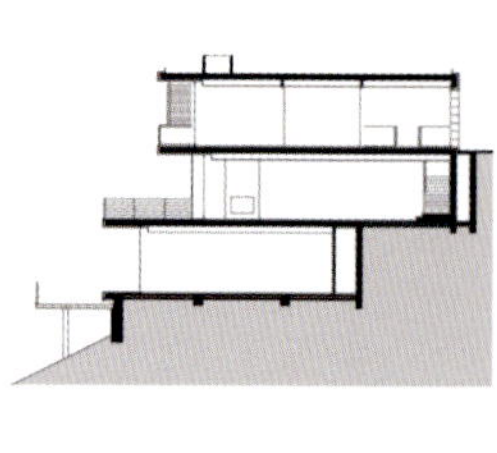

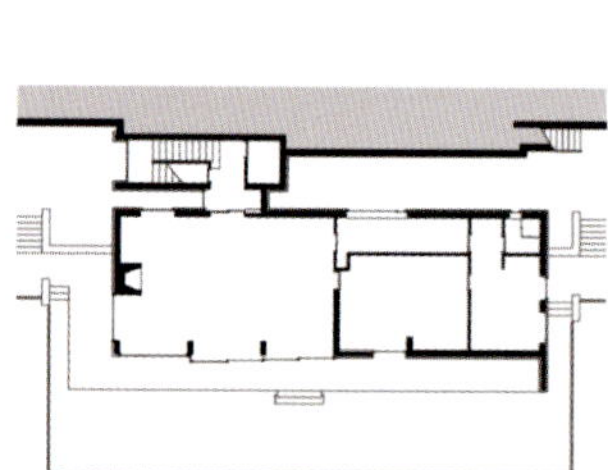

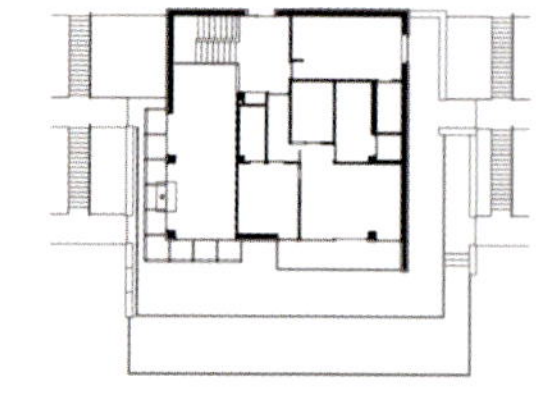

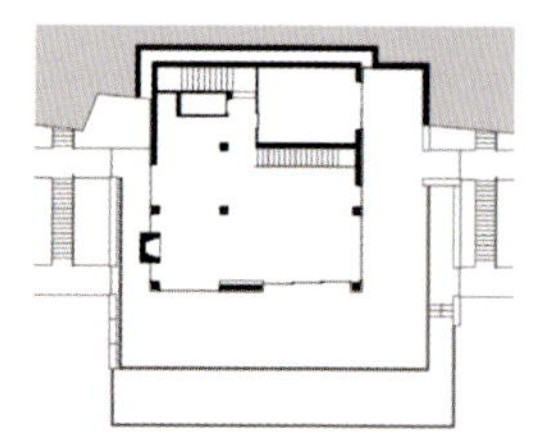

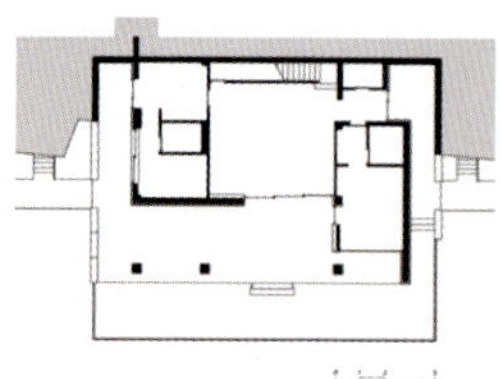

ABOVE AND LEFT
Model views

BELOW
Typical plans and sections

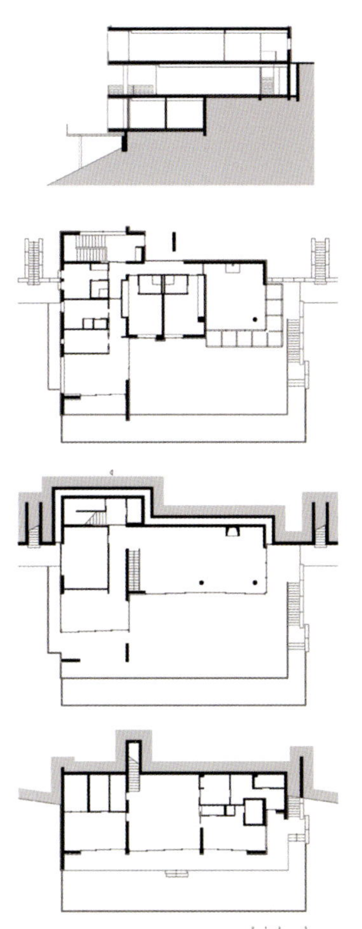

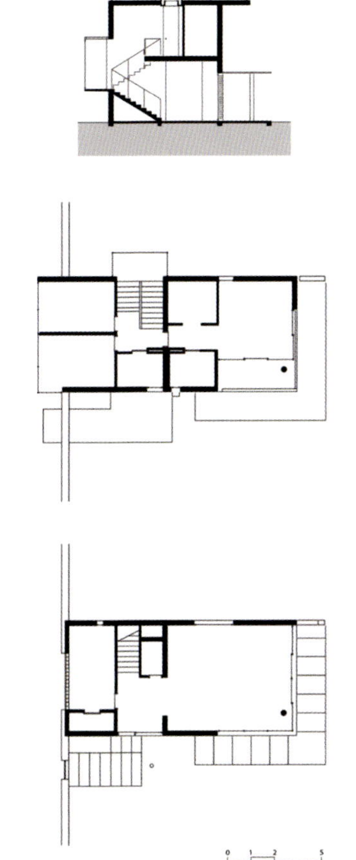
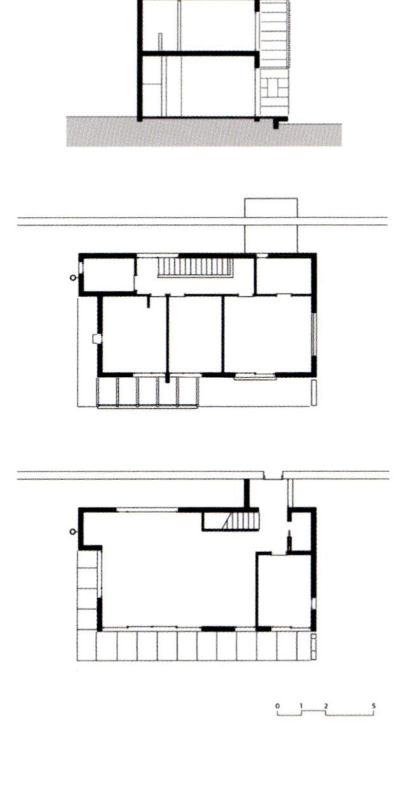

OPPOSITE, TOP
View from the southeast

OPPOSITE, BOTTOM LEFT
View from a wooden terrace

OPPOSITE, BOTTOM RIGHT
View from a terrace on
the upper floor

RIGHT
View of a residence from the southeast

BELOW
Partial view of the site

OPPOSITE
General views

BELOW
A three-story residence

Arketip Housing

View from the interior courtyard

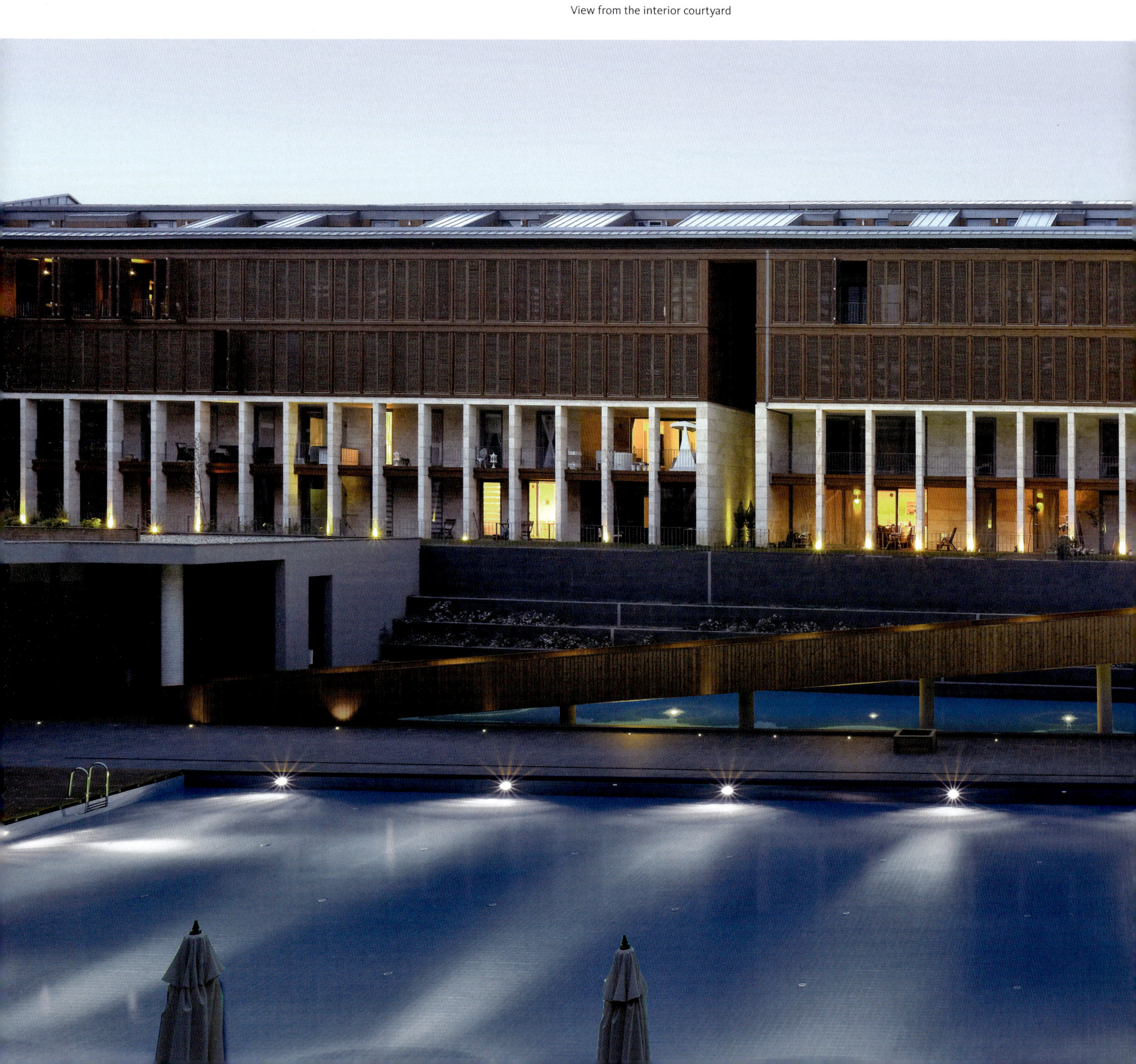

This 78,500-square-meter (844,967 square foot) housing complex was built at the same time as three other projects in the Göktürk area in northern Istanbul.

The design revolves around tensions between private and public spaces, pedestrian versus vehicular areas, the performance over time of main building and landscape materials, and the optimization of the overall expenses during the building's life.

A linear plan was developed around a shared main entry, service areas, and wet areas inside apartments. Hallways, main areas, and terraces are placed according to a regular rhythm that is repeated for each different residence type, making maximum use of natural light. The middle areas of the apartment buildings, arrayed on an east–west axis, are "loosened and detached," creating deep voids that provide attractive public spaces on the north–south axis; in addition, they form a relationship with the social facilities located below the ground grade. The voids between the building blocks form private gardens. This scheme also generates terraces on the upper levels.

The materials used in the main facade include natural stone, wood, and concrete, chosen because they age well. Some inspiration for the design comes from local traditional architecture.

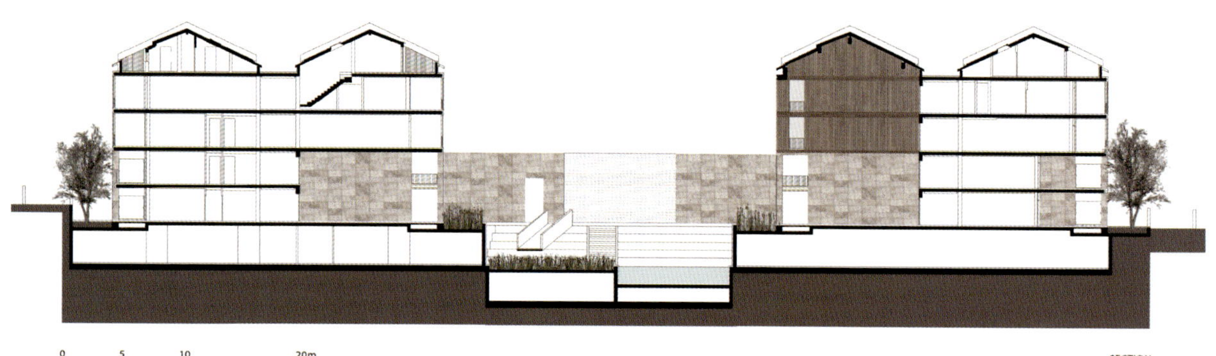

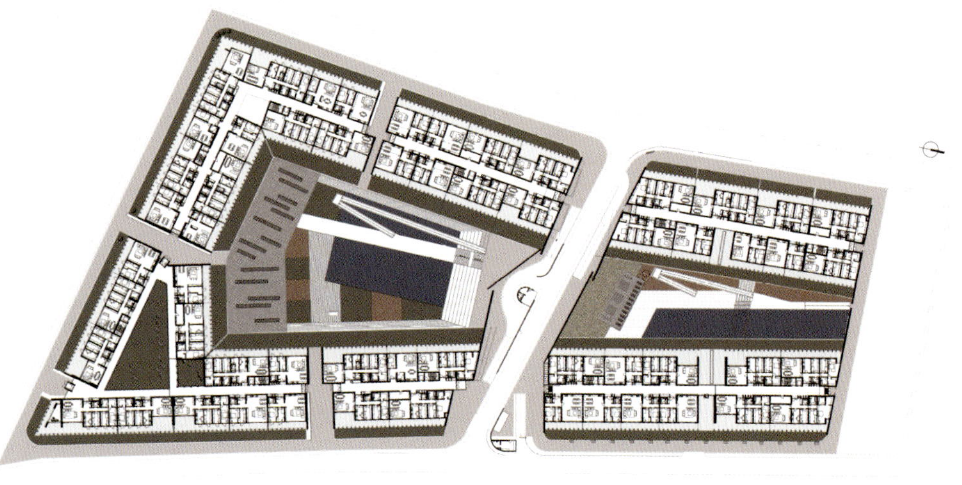

ABOVE
Ground floor plan

RIGHT
Location shots

OPPOSITE, TOP
View of the facade from
the exterior

OPPOSITE, BOTTOM
Main entrance

OPPOSITE, TOP AND BOTTOM
View of the inner courtyard

LEFT
View from the entrance

ABOVE
Views from the entrances

BELOW
View from the exterior

TOP
View from the exterior

ABOVE, LEFT
View from the entrance

ABOVE
View of the inner circulation spaces

OPPOSITE, TOP
View from the inner courtyard

OPPOSITE, BOTTOM
View from the back gardens on
the southeastern corner

OPPOSITE
View from the inner courtyard

ABOVE, LEFT
View from the pool level

ABOVE
View from the green terrace
at upper level

LEFT
View toward the inner courtyard
from the terrace

Ulus Savoy Residences

LOCATION / **Istanbul, Turkey**

YEAR / **2013**

STATUS / **built**

TOTAL AREA / **83.000 m²**

The architects faced rigid zoning restrictions for this 83,000-square-meter (893,405 square foot) housing project undertaken in 2005. Planning permission for twenty-six blocks of the same size had been granted, and the client preferred not to request a new permit. As a result, the number, location, and levels of the building blocks in the existing project were exactly preserved in the new design. The 15-by-20-meter (49 by 65.6 foot) base area of blocks was to be parallel to the slope of the lot, and the roofs were to have a 33-percent slope on all four sides.

The location of the project within the city and the client's desire to make an architectural statement were positive factors in the process. The architects used the rather complicated parking situation to their advantage, creating "occasional slits and interstices formed by the slight difference in level," thus "blurring the boundary between the underground layer and the exterior." This solution permitted connections to be made between recreational areas and the exterior and also gave the complex a presence at night, with light visible from the lower level.

Despite the fragmented nature of the overall scheme, continuity was achieved by the garages and exterior landscape acting as the link between the housing blocks.

View toward the blocks from the shell

TOP
Location

ABOVE, MIDDLE
Study for the topography

LEFT
Site plan

ABOVE
Section through the site

BOTTOM
View from the indoor pool area

BELOW, LEFT AND RIGHT
Views from the inner social spaces

LEFT
View toward the facade with wooden
battens

BELOW
View from the outdoor pool area

OPPOSITE
View toward the facade with sliding
panels

LEFT
View of the blocks

BELOW
View from the ramp on the shell

LEFT
Close-up view of the sliding panels

BELOW
Close-up view of the facade with wooden
battens

BOTTOM
View from the shell toward the blocks

LEFT
View from a block toward the site

BELOW AND OPPOSITE, TOP
View from the indoor pool area

OPPOSITE, BOTTOM
Views from the social spaces

Göktürk Hybrid Housing

LOCATION / **Istanbul, Turkey**

YEAR / **2010**

STATUS / **built**

TOTAL AREA / **27.122 m²**

For this design the architects used systems that they had previously experimented with, such as the use of a grid, the repetition of structural elements, and a modular approach.

Built between 2006 and 2009, the project deals with a site whose form is complex, a situation that resulted in the use of "masses of different sizes, which were designed by articulating each mass within itself, brought together in a disorderly fashion due to the boundaries of the lot."

The theme of plurality might best describe this residential complex, in which each building surface was selected and designed by a different architect within the office. These designs were chosen at a charrette organized at the office, and they were brought together after minor revisions and adaptations to create the overall appearance of the complex.

View from the inner courtyard

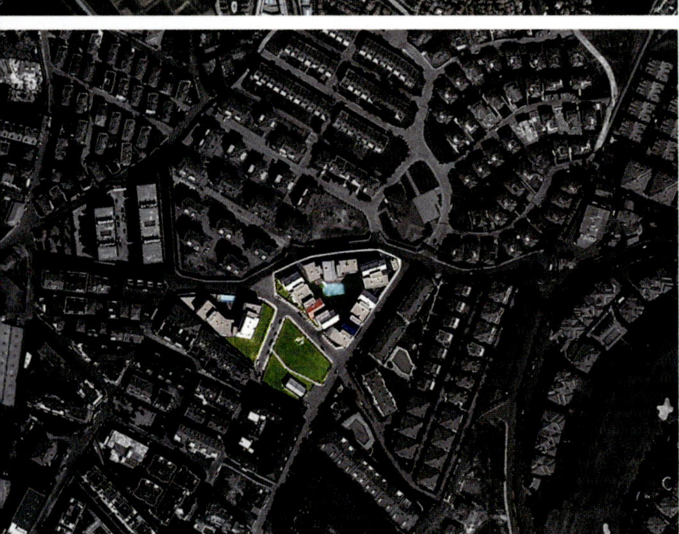

LEFT
Location

BELOW
Ground floor plan

ABOVE
Site plan

LEFT
Volumetric study model

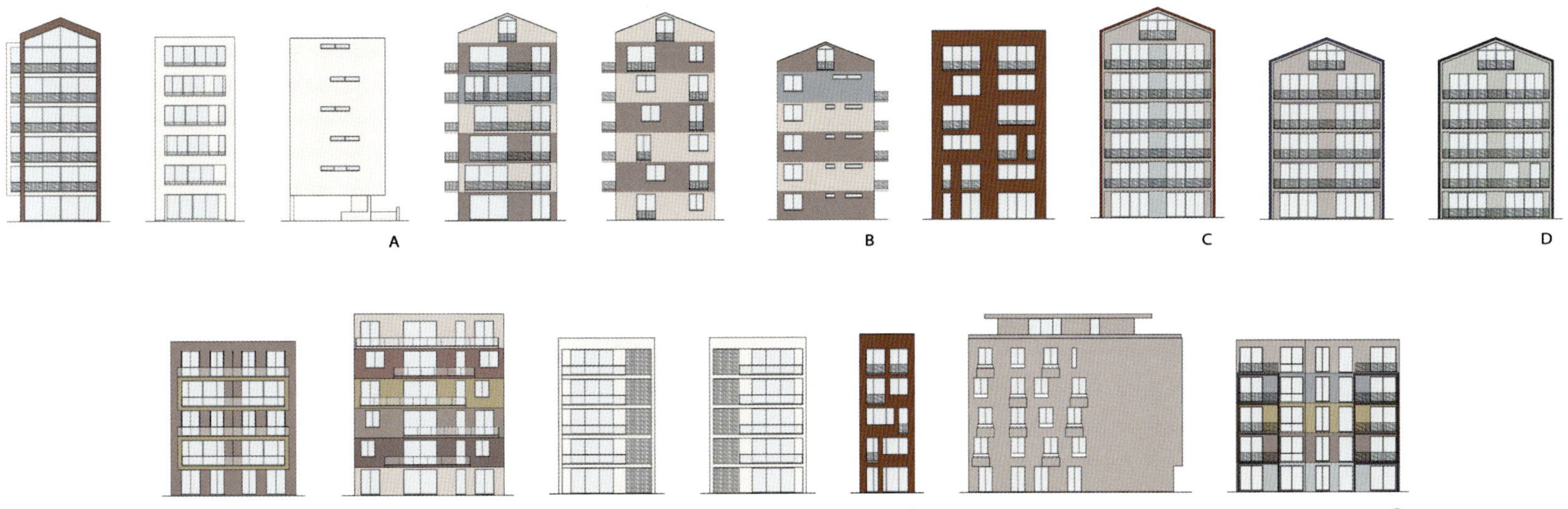

TOP
Facades of the housing types

ABOVE
Volumetric and textural specification

BELOW
View from the exterior

OPPOSITE, TOP LEFT
Close-up view from the facade
of Type B

OPPOSITE, TOP RIGHT
View from the pool area

OPPOSITE, BOTTOM
View from the inner courtyard

RIGHT
View from the inner courtyard

BELOW
View from the exterior

BELOW, RIGHT
View in between blocks

Eyüp Cultural Center and Marriage Hall

LOCATION / **Istanbul, Turkey**

YEAR / **2013**

STATUS / **built**

TOTAL AREA / **7000 m²**

This 7,000-square-meter (73,625 square foot) project was built between 2006 and 2013.

It is expressed "as a kind of structural landscape component," compensating for the differences in levels between a pedestrian path and the sea with a wooden ramp on the waterfront of the Golden Horn, in Eyüp. This ramp appears to connect the roof of the building with a basin situated in front of the structure. The site is particularly popular for weddings (one takes place every fifteen minutes during operating hours) because of its proximity to the Eyüp Sultan Tomb and Mosque, where prayer is part of the ritual after the nuptials.

The combination of cultural events and marriages guarantees a constant flow of visitors, numbering in the hundreds every day.

View from the southeast

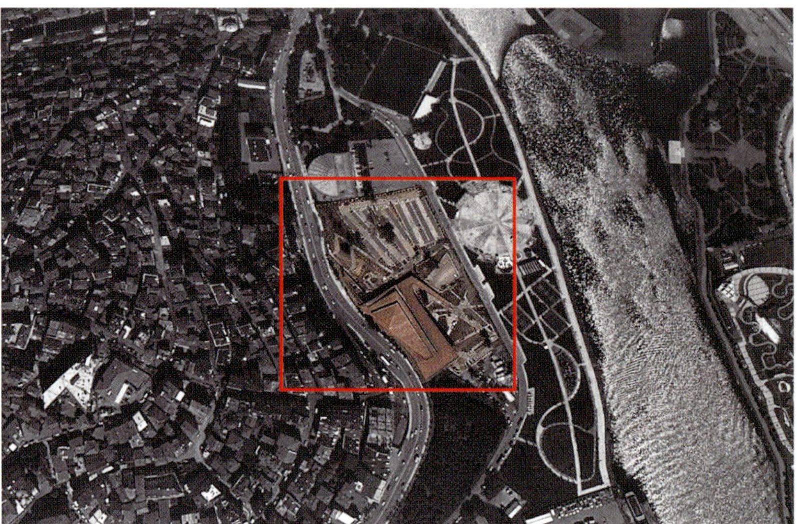

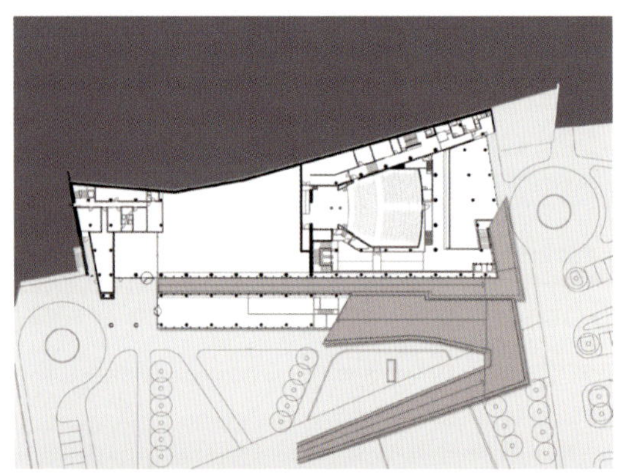

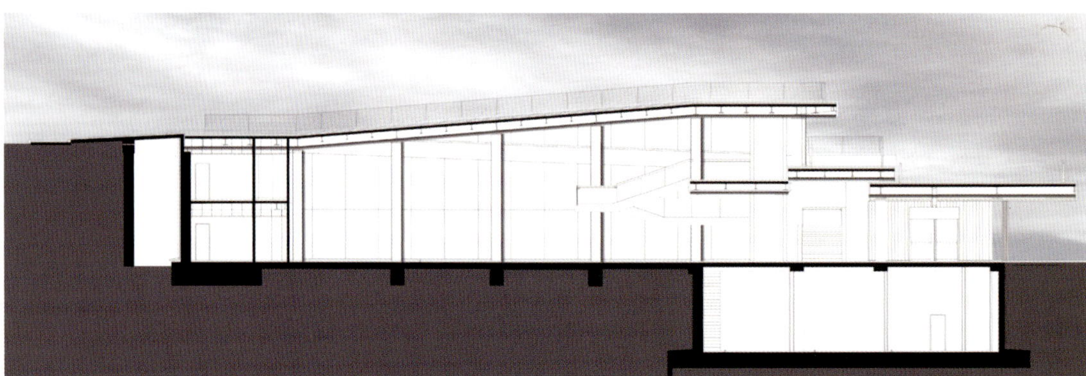

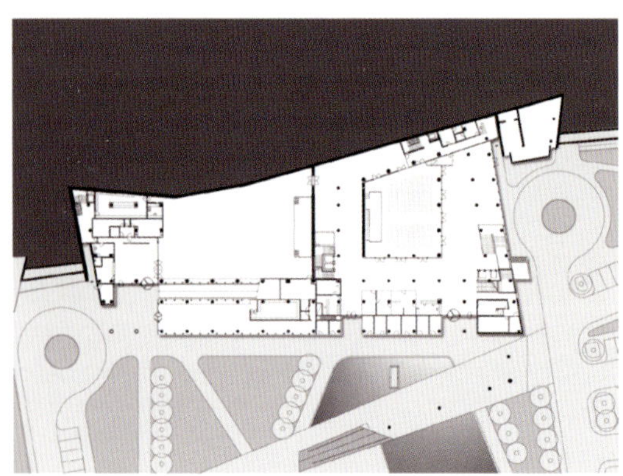

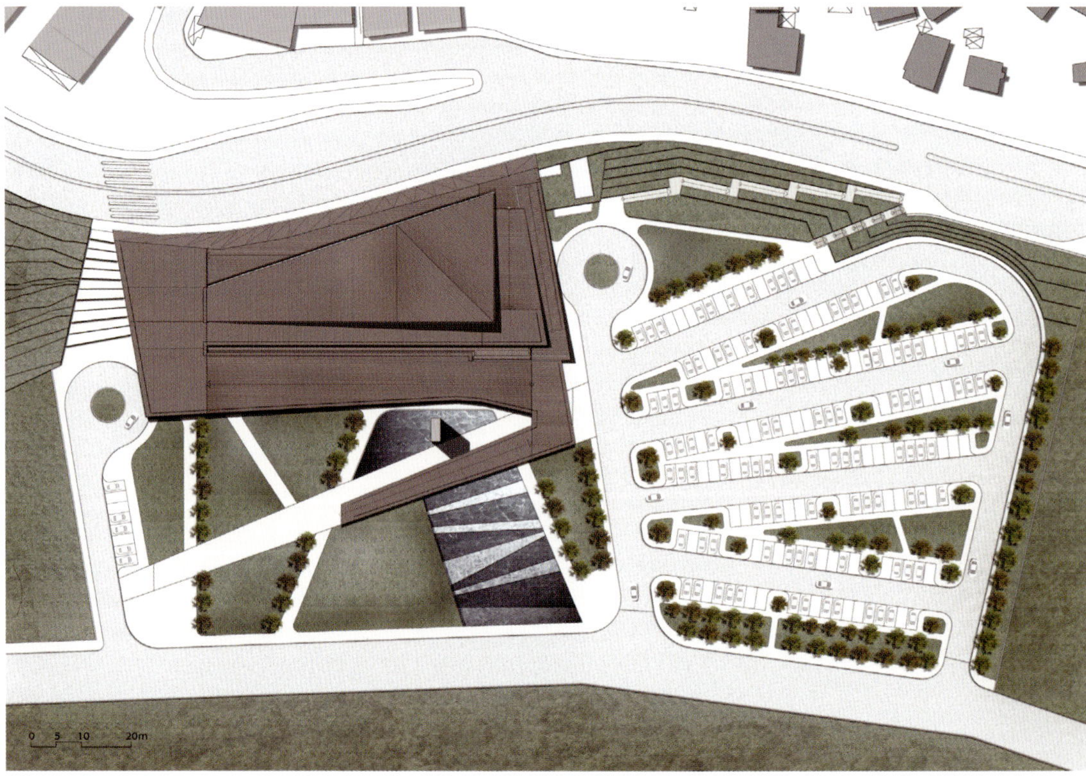

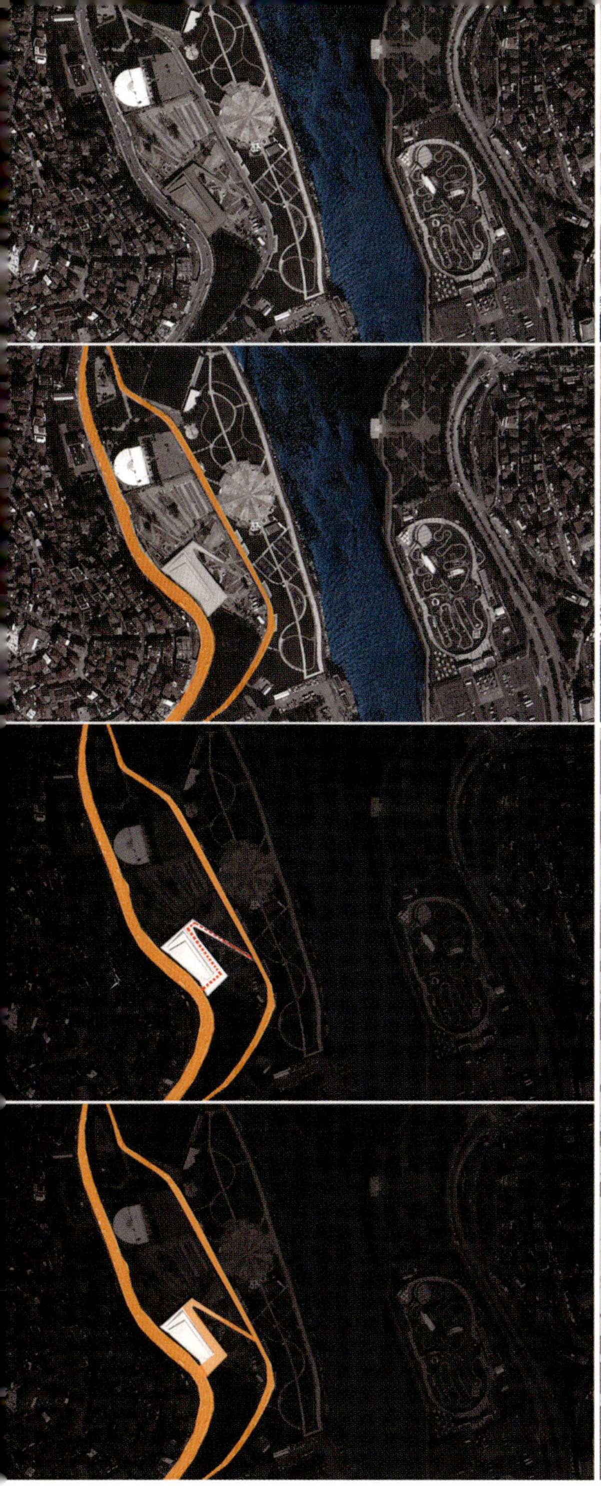

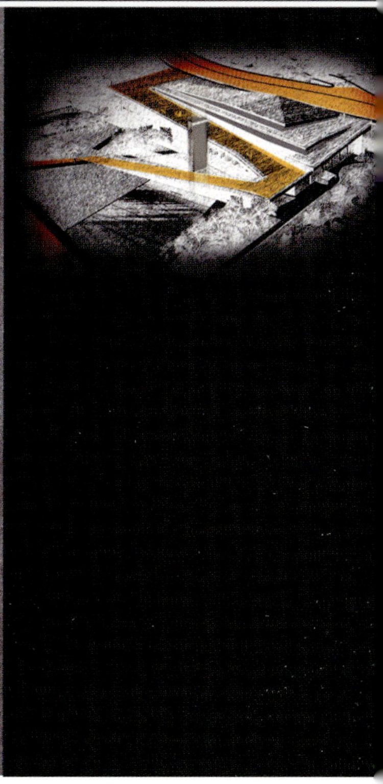

TOP
View from the upper level on the northwest

ABOVE
Views from different levels

LEFT
View from the front facade on the northeast

OPPOSITE, TOP
View from the ramp

OPPOSITE, BOTTOM LEFT
View from the ramp between the café
and main hall

OPPOSITE, BOTTOM RIGHT
View from the ramp

LEFT
View toward the café

BELOW, LEFT
View toward the small hall

BOTTOM, LEFT
View from the main hall interior

BELOW
View from the main hall interior

OPPOSITE, TOP
View toward the neighborhood from
the main hall interior

OPPOSITE, BOTTOM
View under the canopy

Folkart Narlıdere Housing

LOCATION / İzmir, Turkey

YEAR / 2009

STATUS / built

TOTAL AREA / 70.000 m²

Built between 2006 and 2009, this 70,000-square-meter (753,474 square foot) housing project involved careful study of the topography of the site, the existing structural pattern of the area, transportation, construction density, and the sociological balances of the region.

The architects analyzed the relationship of target users to the environment and used this information as the "distinguishing feature of the project." Large amorphous terraces were oriented toward views from the site, while promenades offering horizontal circulation were separated from the main masses and lined with rosebays (rhododendron).

Inner spaces, which replace apartment hallways, feature a light roof skin that allows improved air circulation and microclimatic effects generated by cooling pools placed within these spaces. Wood, stone, and exposed concrete were used for exterior surfaces with the conviction that these materials will age gracefully in this climate and context.

View from the north toward the site

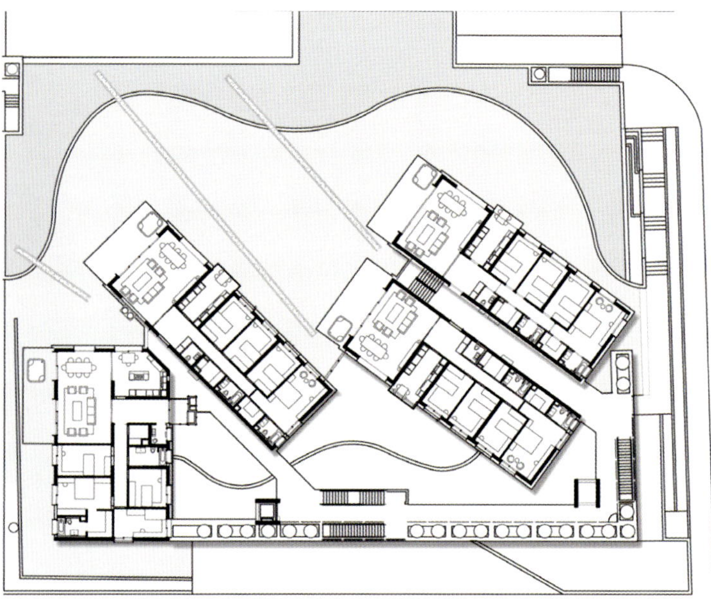

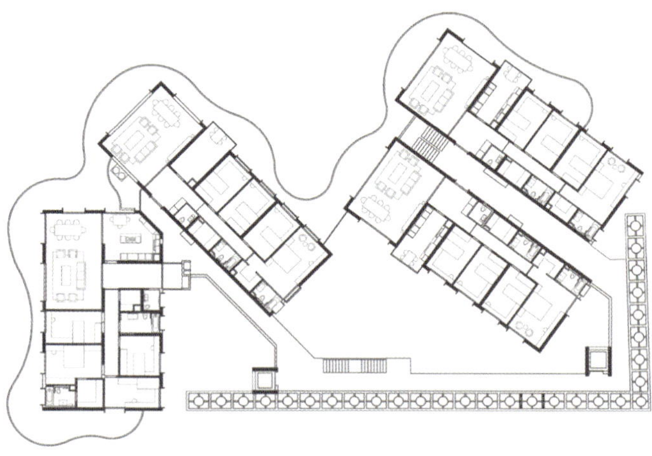

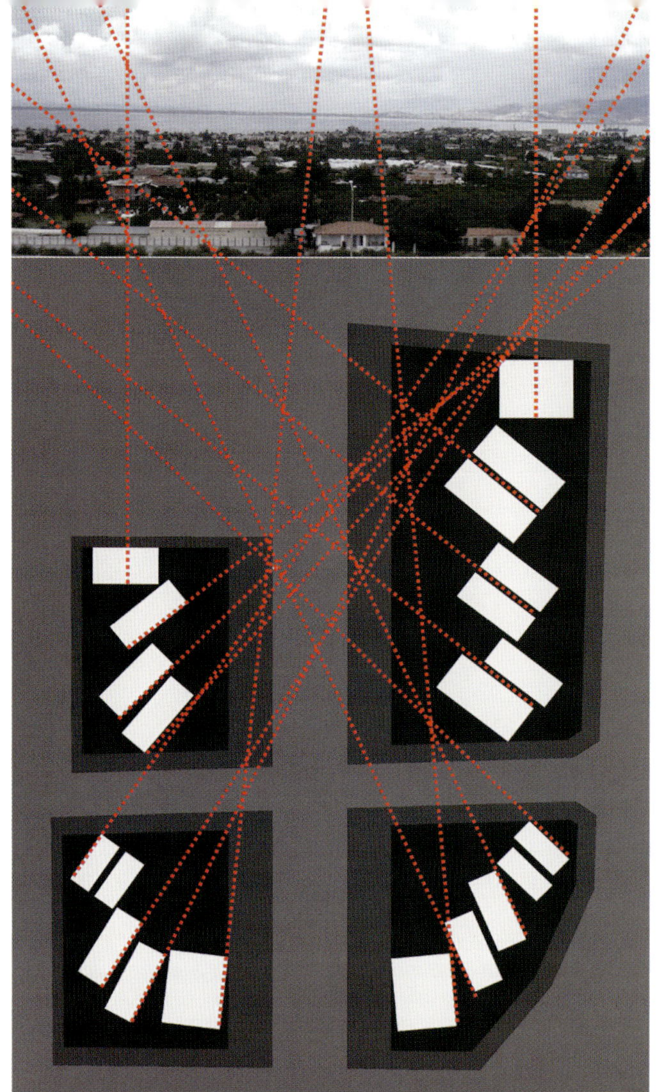

TOP LEFT
Partial plan, ground floor

ABOVE
Partial plan, upper floors

TOP RIGHT
Vista analysis

RIGHT
Site plan

TOP
Section through the site

ABOVE
Model photo from the exterior

RIGHT
Model photo from the interior
gallery space

OPPOSITE, TOP AND BOTTOM
View from the south

ABOVE
View from the pool area

BELOW
View toward the amorphous terraces

ABOVE
View from the gallery

RIGHT
View from the garden on
the ground floor

Sabiha Gökçen International Airport Terminal

LOCATION / **Istanbul, Turkey**

YEAR / **2006**

STATUS / **unbuilt**

TOTAL AREA / **225.000 m²**

Designed in 2006, this facility has a floor area of 225,000 square meters (2.4 million square feet).

The architects considered the commission to be an "important cultural responsibility." Restaurants and hotels related to the complex were treated as elements that could be used in the everyday life of the neighborhood in which the terminal is located.

Voids allow daylight into all levels, and multiple bridge connections within the structural system, which is articulated by a repetitive broad vault system, contribute to the interior landscape. Indeed, the architects describe the project in terms of a "handmade topography." Multistory car parks serve the reinforced concrete frame structure. A vast landscaped roof that requires minimum maintenance is part of the scheme, in the hope that the roof and its environment will be "blurred over time and gradually become one with nature."

LEFT
View of the building from the apron

BELOW
Facade facing the apron

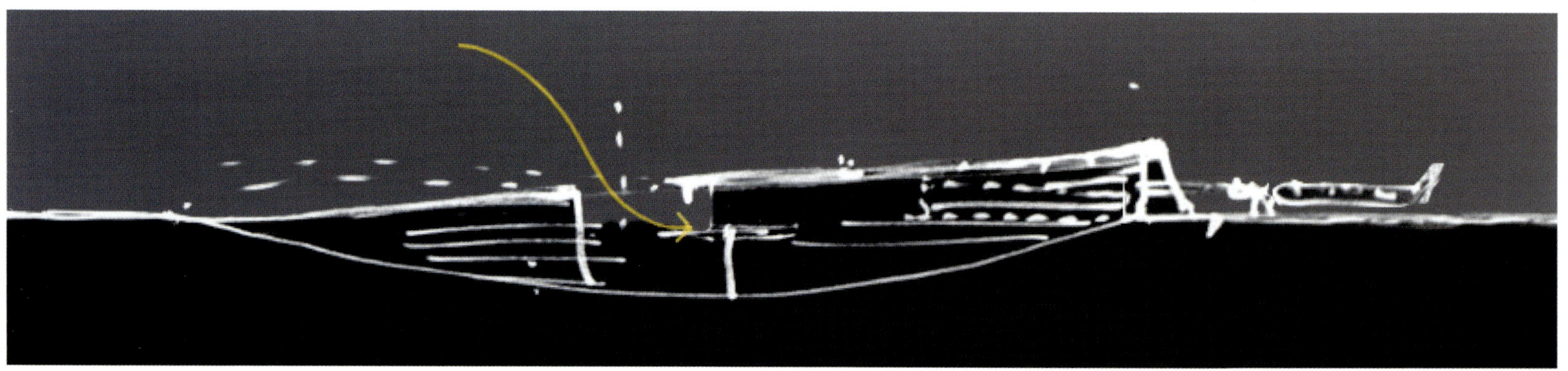

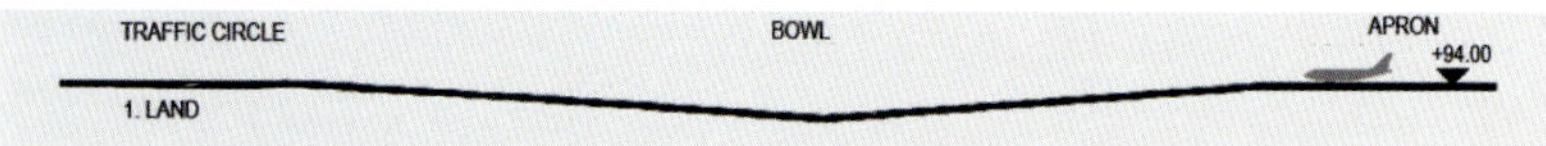

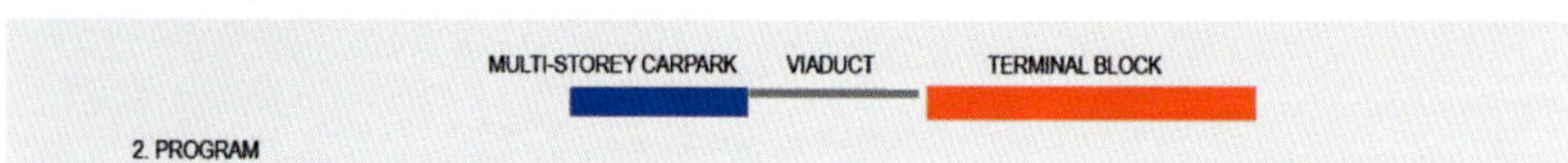

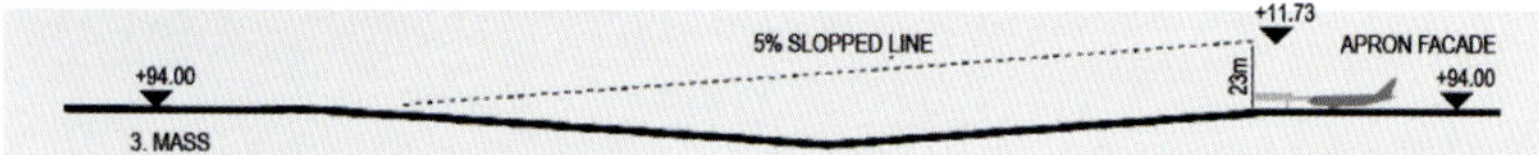

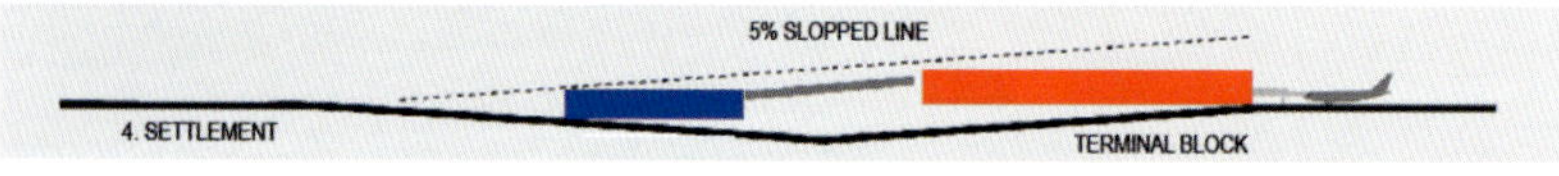

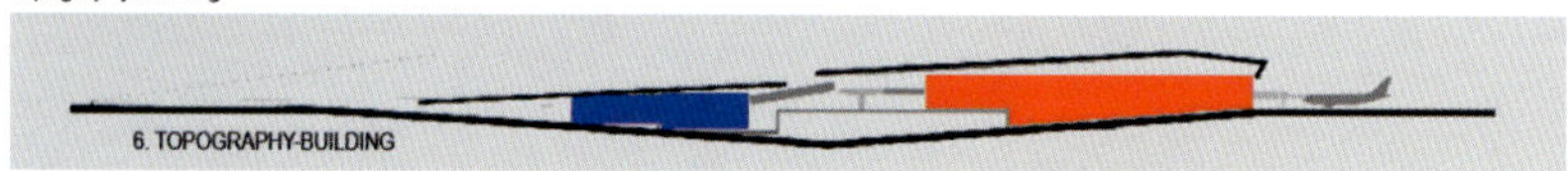

TOP
Conceptual sketch

RIGHT
Floor plans

ABOVE
Sectional diagram of the building
as a topography

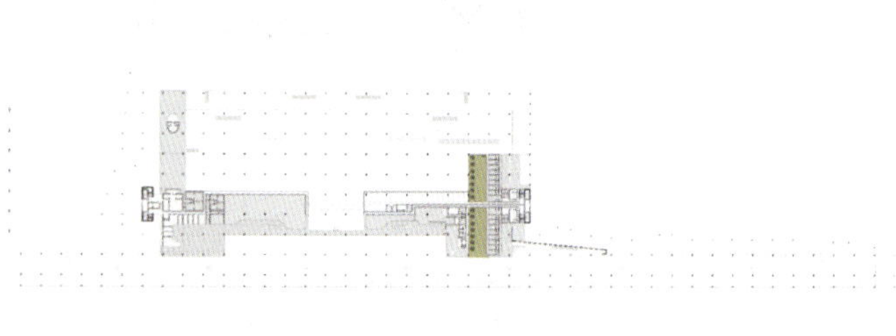

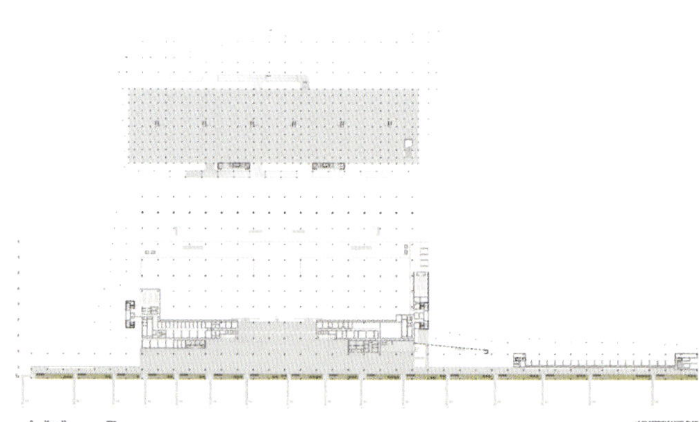

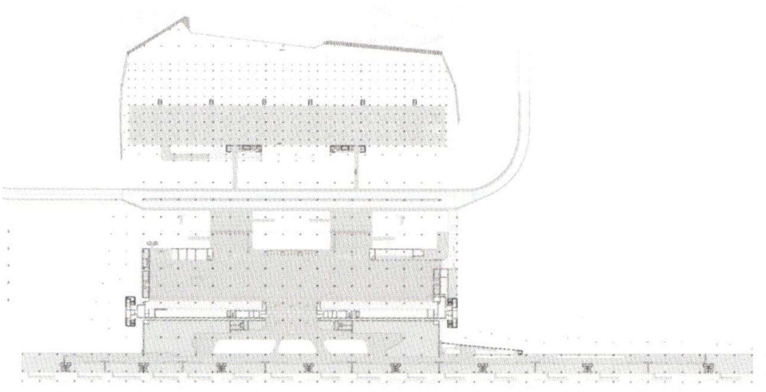

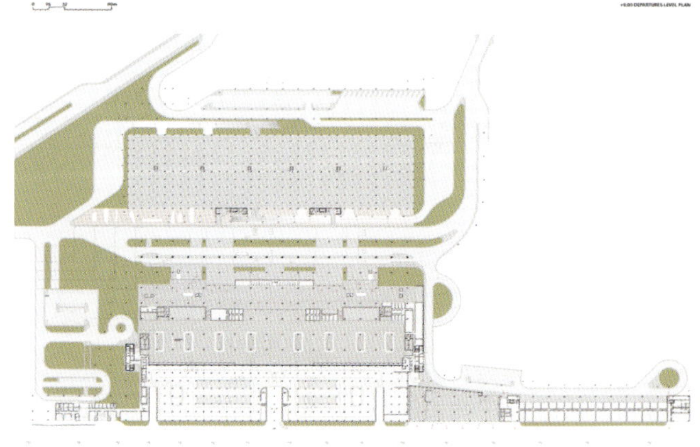

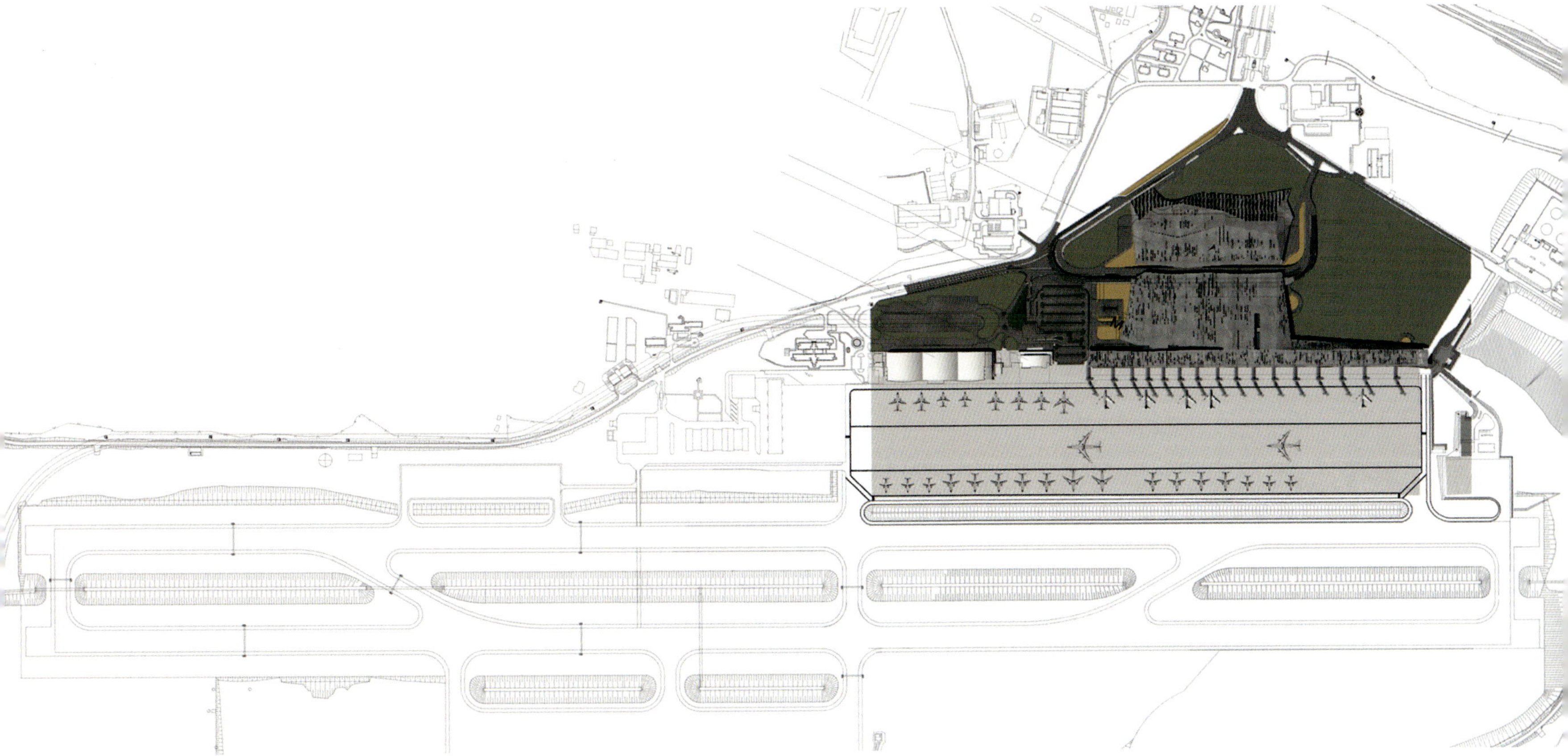

ABOVE
Site plan

BOTTOM
Section perspective

BELOW
Section

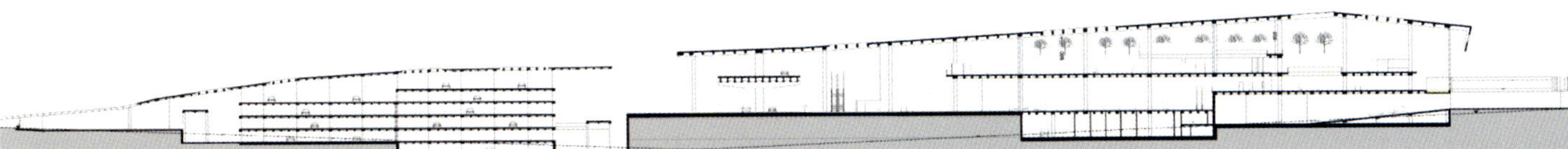

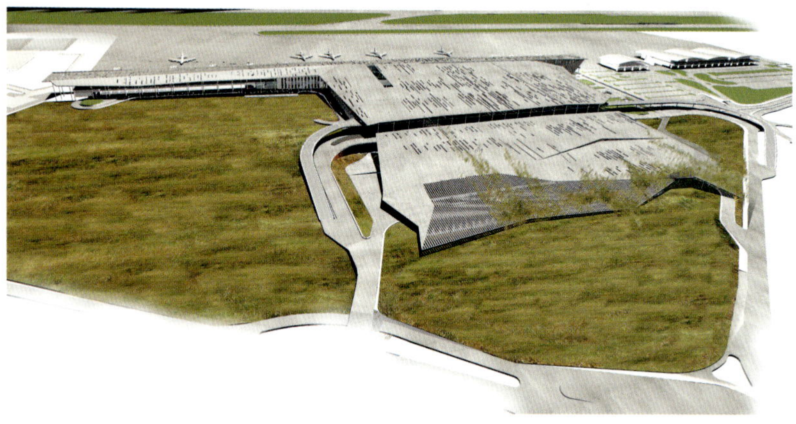

TOP
Aerial view

ABOVE
Landscape creeping over the concrete shell

BELOW
View toward the shell

LEFT
Approach to the departure entrance

RIGHT AND BELOW
Views from the departure hall

7800 Çeşme Residences and Hotel

LOCATION / **Izmir, Turkey**

YEAR / **2008**

STATUS / **built**

TOTAL AREA / **10.000 m²**

Çeşme is located 85 kilometers (53 miles) west of Izmir on the Aegean Sea. A summer resort that has seen considerable development over the past decade, Çeşme offered another opportunity for the architects to show how their approach differs from that of other Turkish firms.

The main five-story mass of this 10,000-square-meter (107,640 square foot) project was completed in 2008 and is placed close to a road, leaving the beach side as free as possible. An internal street facilitates both vertical and horizontal circulation within the complex. The presence of landscaping is privileged to alleviate the burden of "concepts that might be defined as style, taste, and genre of architecture."

Two special blind systems for the north and south sides were imagined as important elements of the appearance of the complex, intended to shield residents from the sun and wind. The superposition of the housing units allows the creation of large garden terraces, which form the basic external landscape. Interior design was conceived as being "transparent and flowing."

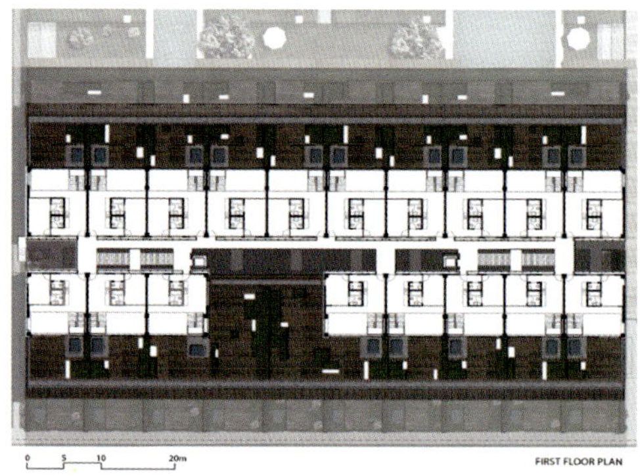

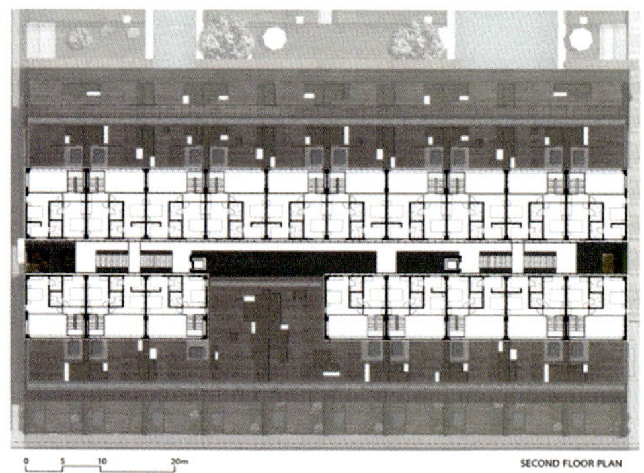

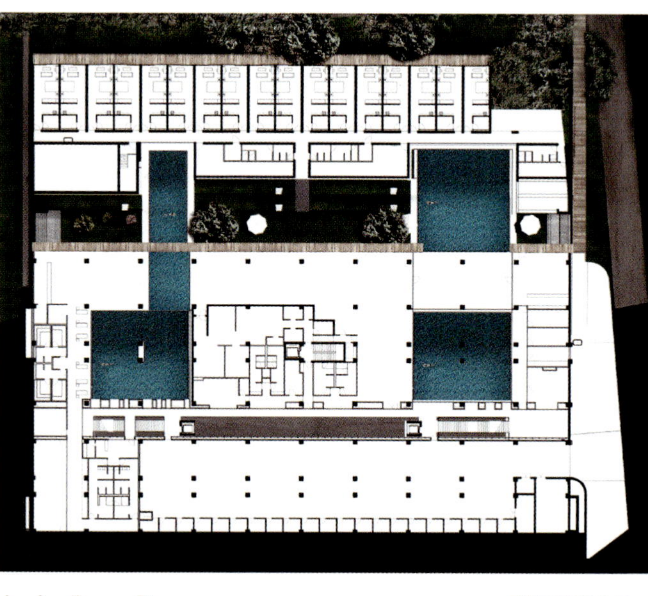

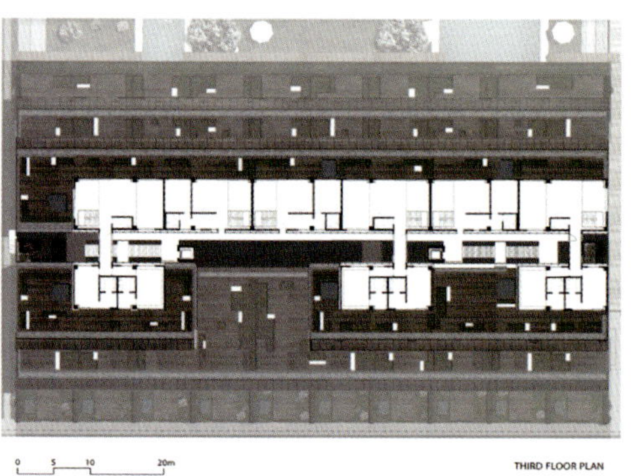

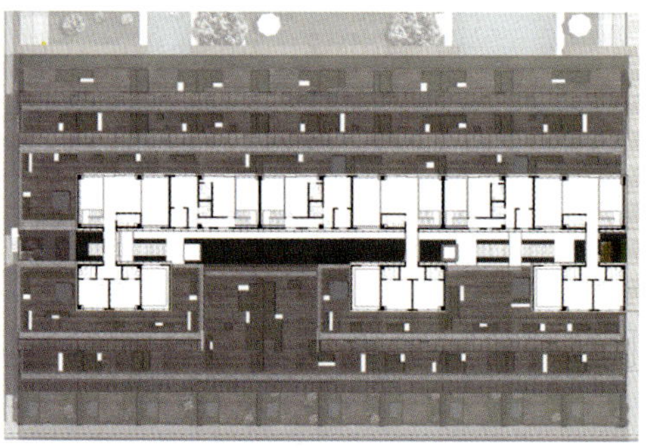

GROUND FLOOR PLAN

FIRST FLOOR PLAN

SECOND FLOOR PLAN

ENTRANCE LEVEL PLAN

THIRD FLOOR PLAN

FORTH FLOOR PLAN

OPPOSITE, TOP LEFT
Site plan

OPPOSITE, BOTTOM LEFT
Entrance level plan

OPPOSITE, RIGHT
Floor plans

ABOVE
Section

RIGHT
View from the south

BELOW, RIGHT
View from the sea on
the northern side

OPPOSITE
Views from the social spaces

ABOVE, LEFT AND RIGHT
Views from the southern facade

BELOW
View from the east

BELOW
Views from the inner street

OPPOSITE
Views from the upper levels of
the inner street

OPPOSITE
Inner circulation hall on the level of
the social spaces

ABOVE
View from the entrance level

RIGHT
View from the top of the landscape

Raif Dinçkök Cultural Center

Yalova is located in northwestern Turkey near the Sea of Marmara. A city of about 100,000 residents, it is known for its industry but also its arboretums and rich variety of endemic plants. The client for the 7,000-square-meter (75,347 square foot) project completed in 2007 was Akkök, the largest industrial company in Yalova, which planned to hand it over to the municipality. The city intends to create a garden in front of the complex.

Perforated weather-resistant steel with a rusty surface was chosen for exterior surfaces, in a kind of homage to industry and the resilient forces of nature. Air and light penetrate this steel skin.

A multipurpose room with a capacity of 600 persons, a workshop for up to 150 people, wedding and exhibition rooms, and an office and cafeteria are part of the scheme within specific volumes that are disconnected from the building facade. These functional volumes are connected to one another by a ramp that forms a sheltered inner street. Recreational and service areas are situated between the functional volumes.

LOCATION / **Yalova, Turkey**

YEAR / **2011**

STATUS / **built**

TOTAL AREA / **7.000 m²**

BELOW
View from the east

RIGHT
View from the south

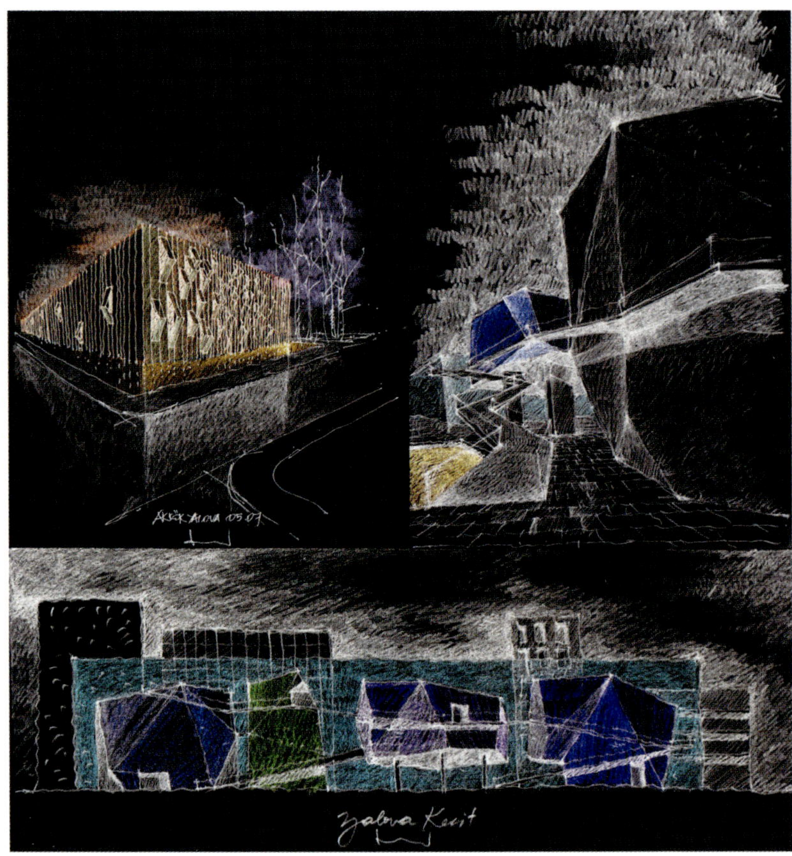

ABOVE
Conceptual sketches

BELOW
Site plan

LEFT
Industrial-natural-historical
textures of the place

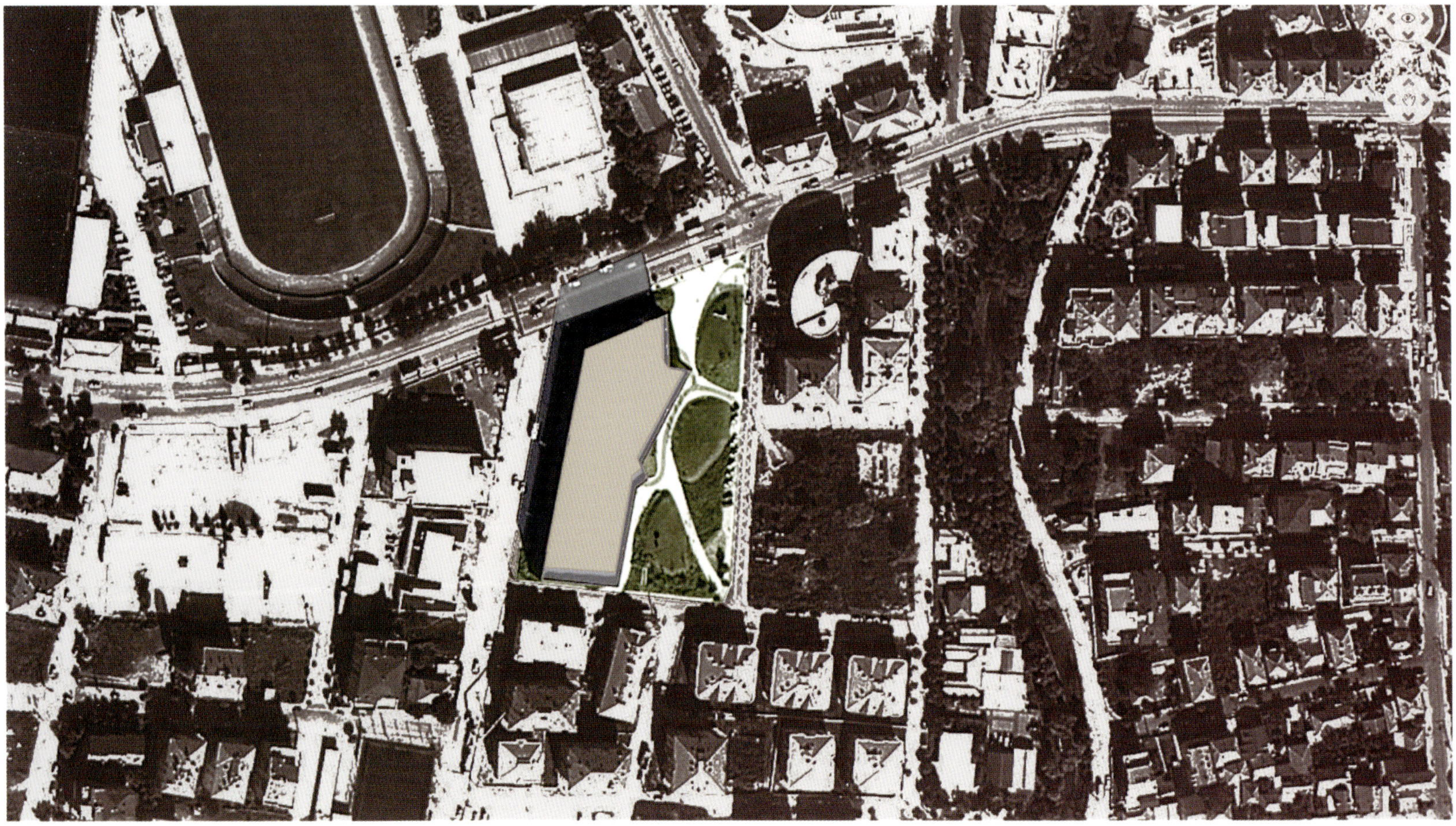

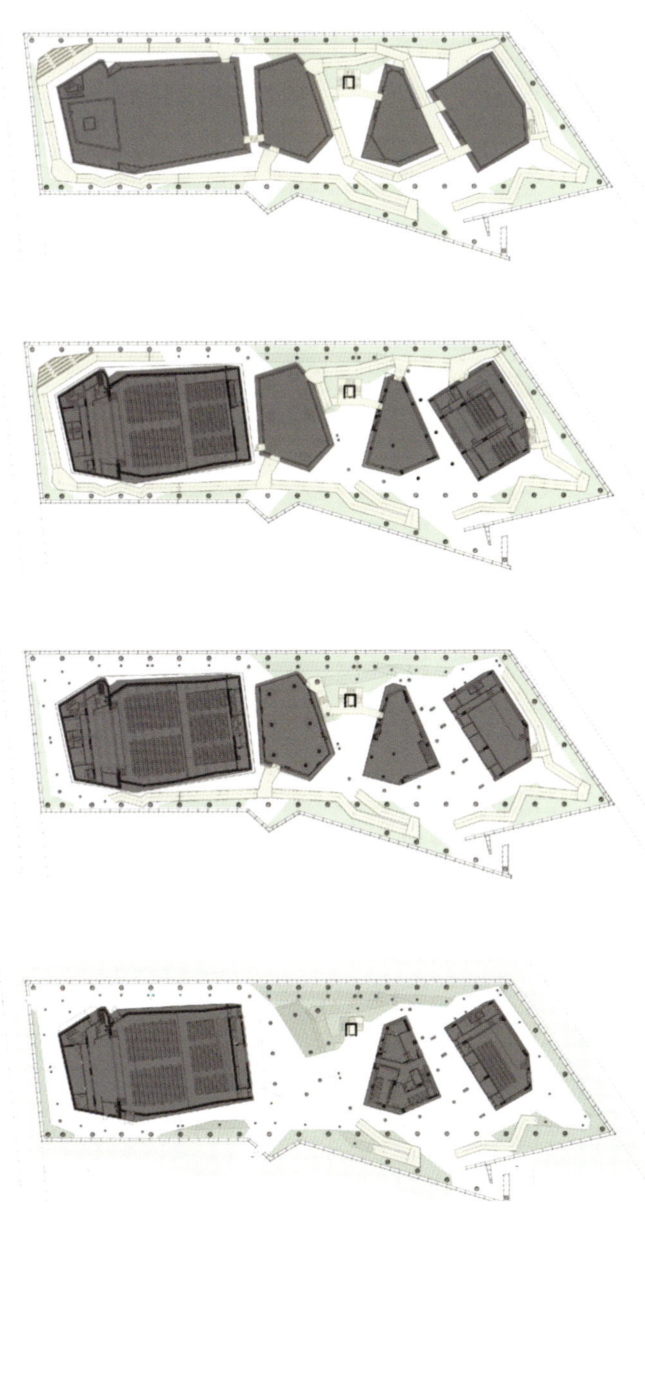

LEFT
Floor plans

BELOW
Masses and skin

BOTTOM
Longitudinal section

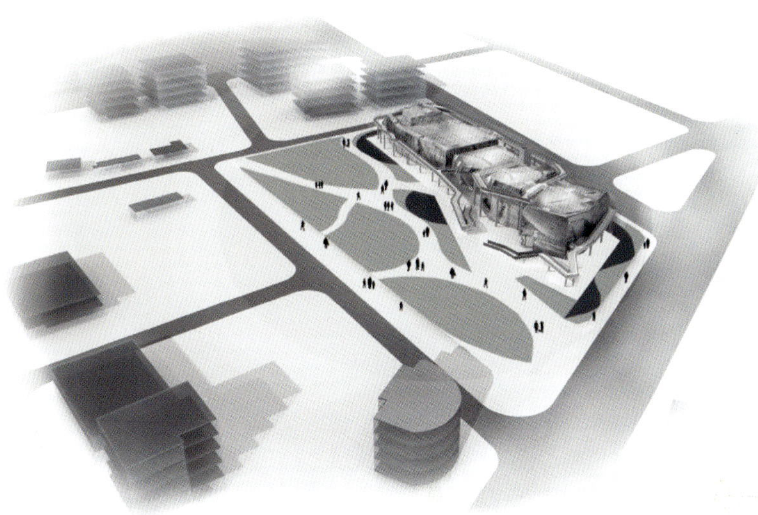

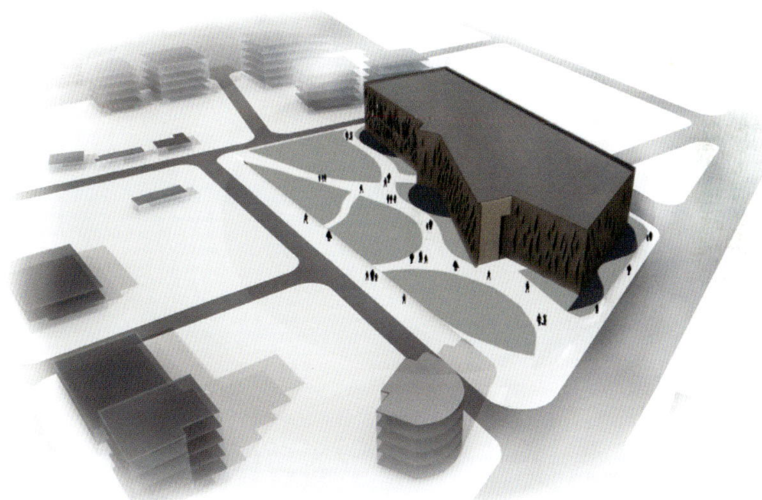

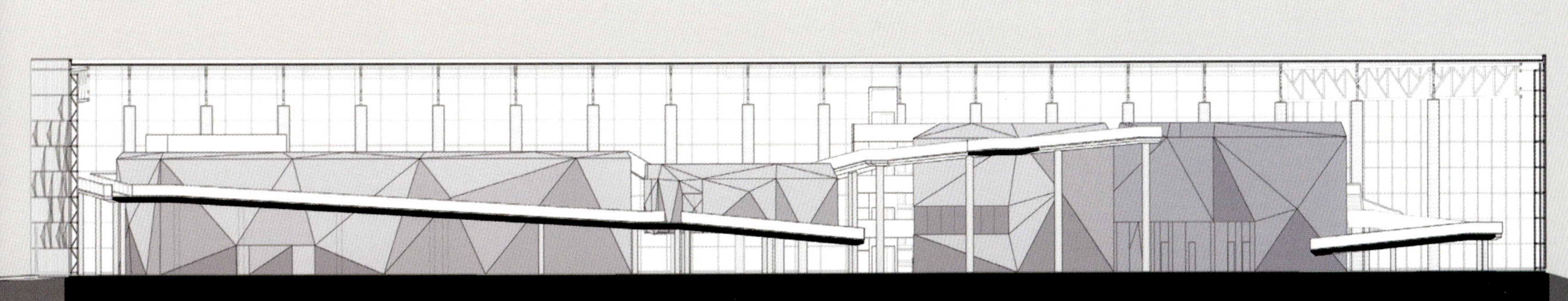

ABOVE
View from the east

LEFT
View from the northeast

BELOW
View from the southwest

OPPOSITE
Close-up view of the facade

NEXT SPREAD
View from the ramp in
the inner space

ABOVE
View from the inner space

ABOVE
View from the inner space

ABOVE, RIGHT
View toward the multipurpose room

RIGHT
Entrance of the multipurpose room

ABOVE
View from the upper level toward the
circulation elements

ABOVE, RIGHT
The facade becoming transparent with
the effects of daylight

RIGHT
View of the terraces on top of
the masses

BELOW
Interior of the multipurpose room

Le Méridien
Hotel
Istanbul

Built between 2005 and 2012, this prestigious hotel has an area of 65,000 square meters (699,654 square feet). It is located in the sloping Etiler tourism area, near the toll booths of the TEM highway and the Fatih Sultan Mehmet Bridge.

The architects sought to take advantage of local zoning regulations but chose not to contradict the district's relatively homogenous architectural style. They achieved the desired effect by proposing a "vertical fragmentation" of the three volumes of the building. Large terrace gardens created between these masses were given different exterior treatments. Careful attention was paid to the visibility of the complex from a distance, guaranteeing that it is nearly invisible from the Anatolian side of the district.

The entrance is located on the lowest part of the site, offering direct access to the social spaces of the hotel. A cafeteria is accessible without entering the main building. According to the architects, "The hotel building, which was designed within the Le Méridien Hotel, is assertive about its situation, its function, and its management's motivations. This complex, which stands in front of the most important and newest gate of Istanbul, aims to project an image of modern Istanbul and its architectural characteristics."

LOCATION / **Istanbul, Turkey**

YEAR / **2012**

STATUS / **built**

TOTAL AREA / **65.000 m²**

BELOW
View from the northeast

OPPOSITE
View from the east

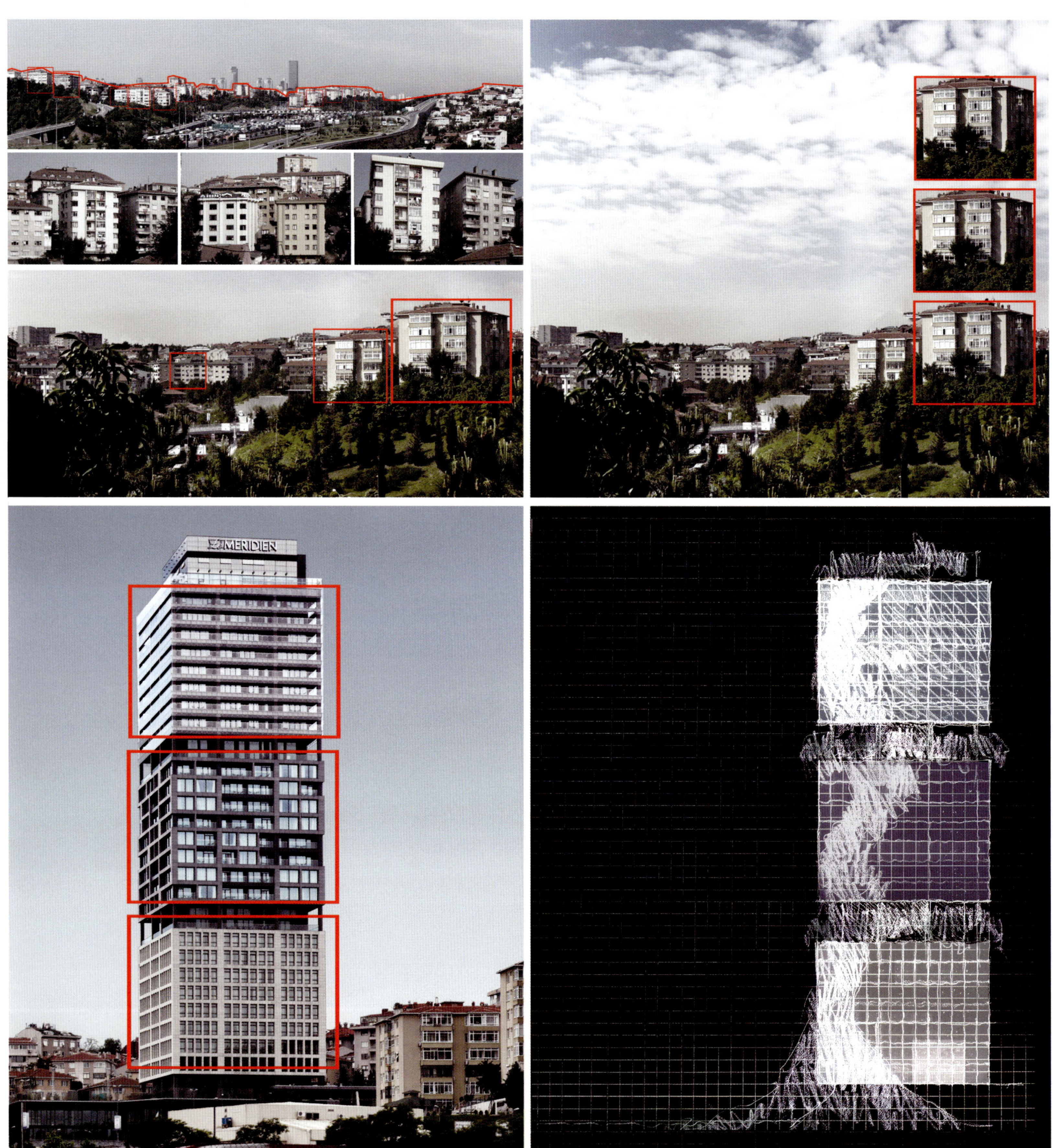

ABOVE
Facade detail

BELOW
Section

ABOVE
Detail of the terraces

BELOW
Typical plans

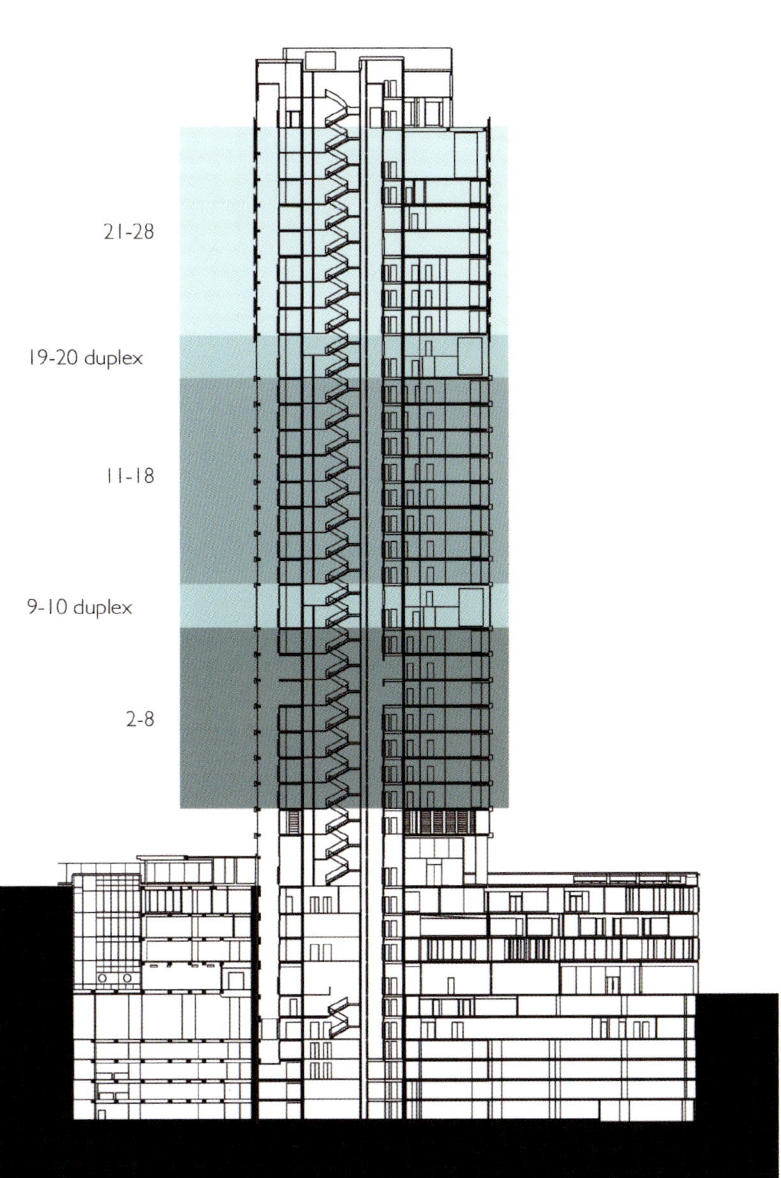
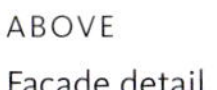

21-28
19-20 duplex
11-18
9-10 duplex
2-8

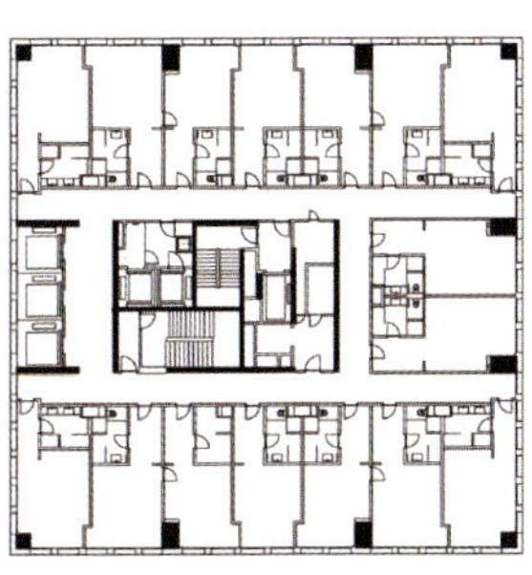

2nd-8th floor plan

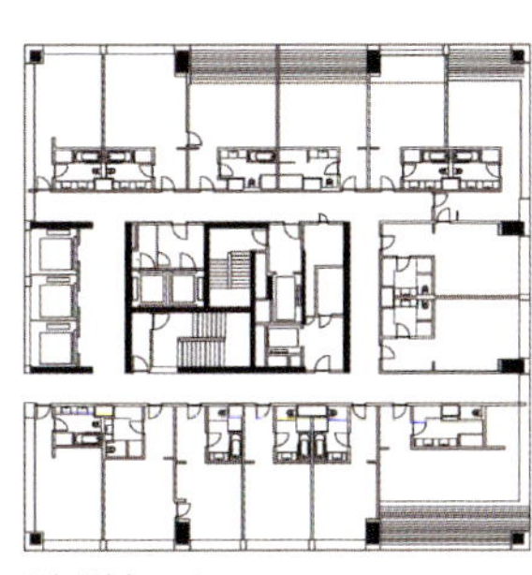

11th-18th floor plan

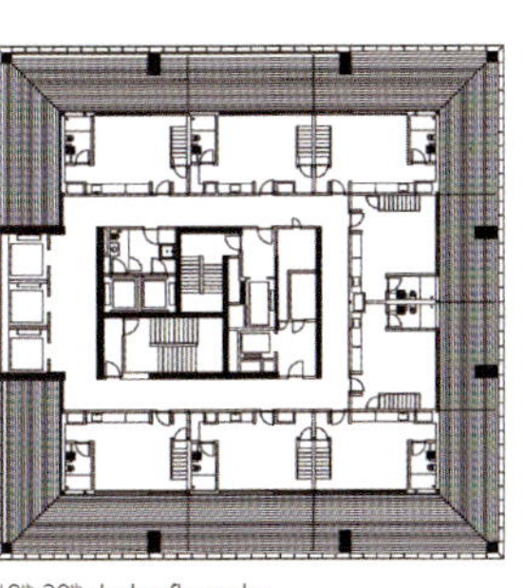

19th-20th duplex floor plan
level 1

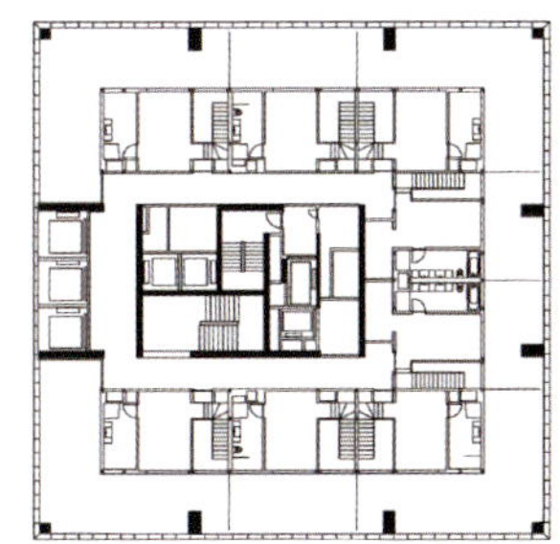

9th-10th and 19th-20th duplex floor plan

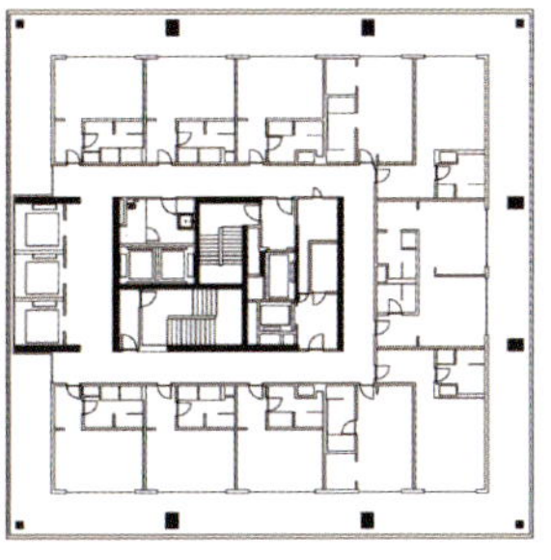

21th-28th floor plan

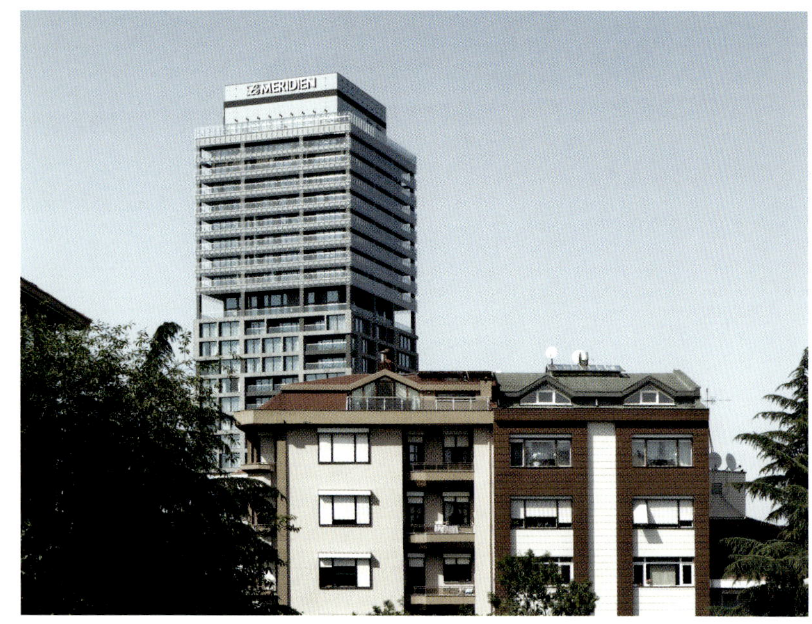

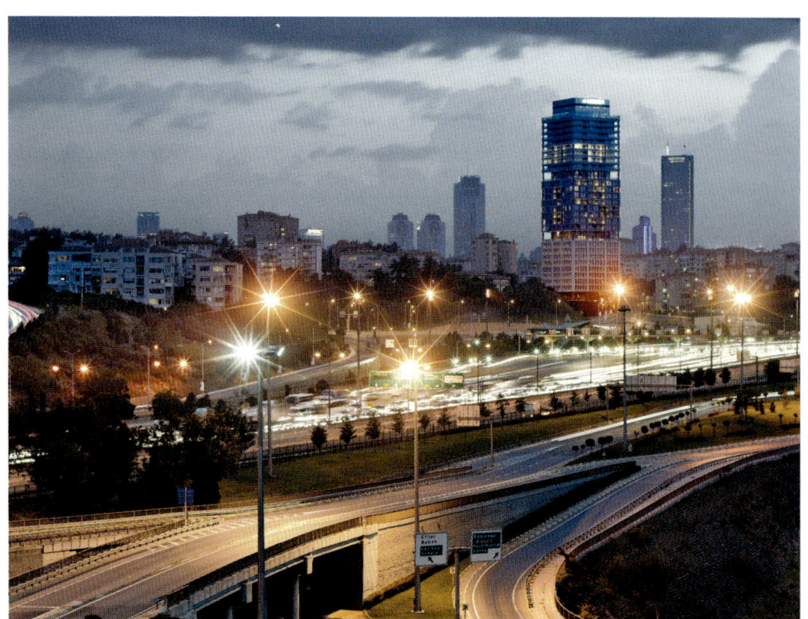

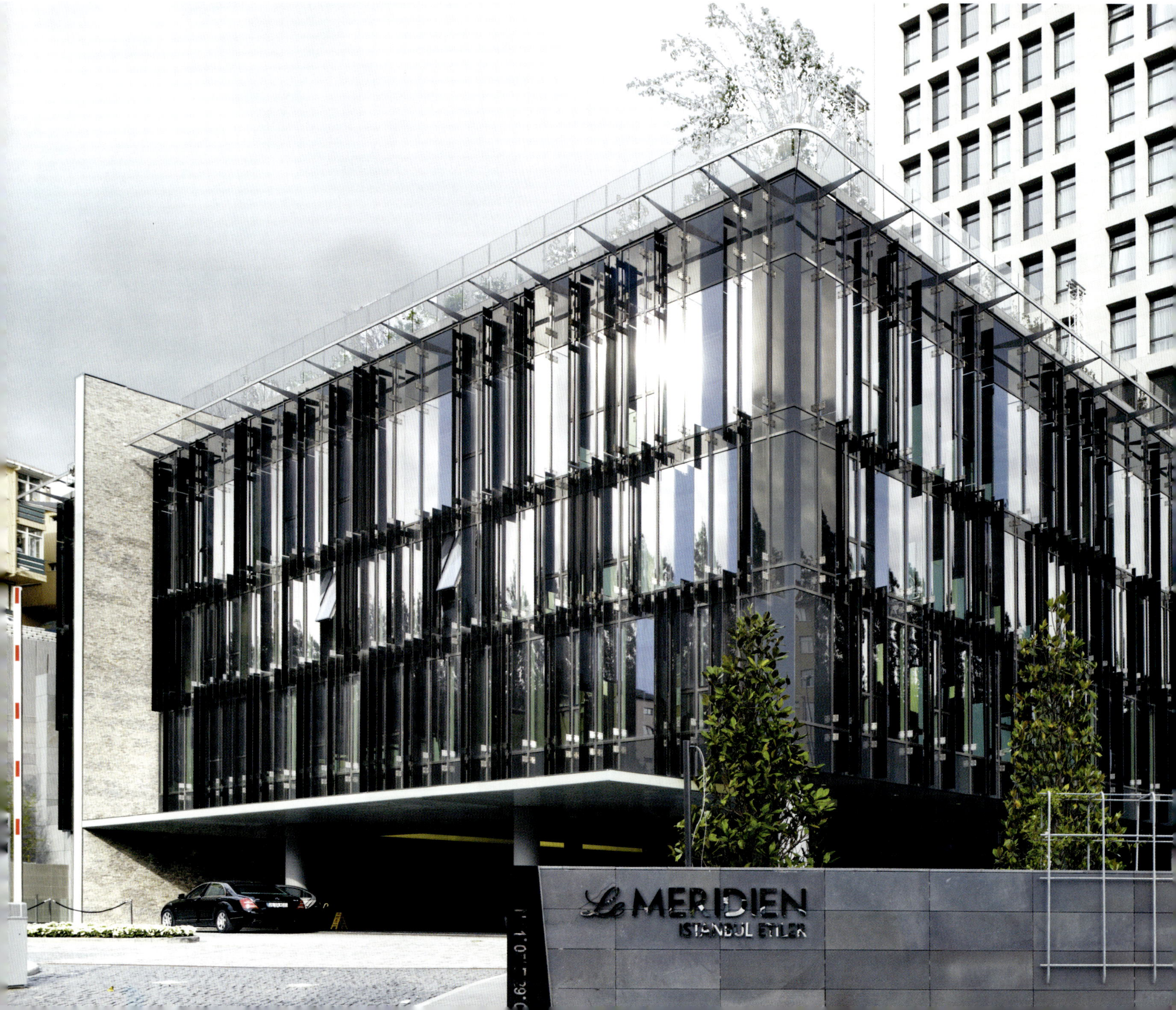
Le MERIDIEN
ISTANBUL ETILER

OPPOSITE, TOP LEFT
View from the southeast

OPPOSITE, TOP RIGHT
Views of the highway at nighttime

BELOW
View of the entrance and base

RIGHT, TOP AND BOTTOM
Views of the facade

Zorlu Center

LOCATION / **Istanbul, Turkey**

YEAR / **2007**

STATUS / **under construction, 2013**

TOTAL AREA / **720.000 m²**

At 720,000 square meters (7.75 million square feet), this project is one of the largest undertaken by EAA. Begun in 2007, it was still under construction when this book went to print. The site is located at the junction of the Bosphorus Bridge European connection and the glamorous Büyükdere axis that connects the city center with the Maslak business district. It is one of only a few sites in the region that faces south, offering a view of the old city.

The architects explain that "the ground is reconstructed with a topographical interpretation, a kind of shell that is transformed into an in-between layer for the different functions combined in the complex." A public square marks the so-called Boulevard Level, where the shell takes form. A public sequence rises 28 meters (92 feet) to the Urban Balcony, which provides a spectacular view of the Bosphorus. A private ring completes its rise 4 meters (13 feet) higher and provides access to the residential units of the mixed-use complex.

The Boulevard Level includes several retail units, and a level below includes cinemas, a children's entertainment center, a gourmet market, and other leisure facilities. A concert hall with a capacity of 2,500 persons opens into the public square. Residential units with Bosphorus views are located both under the shell on the first level and in three identical towers set above the shell on pilotis. A fourth tower houses the luxury Bosphorus Hotel.

View from the north

11. 2008

12.05.2010

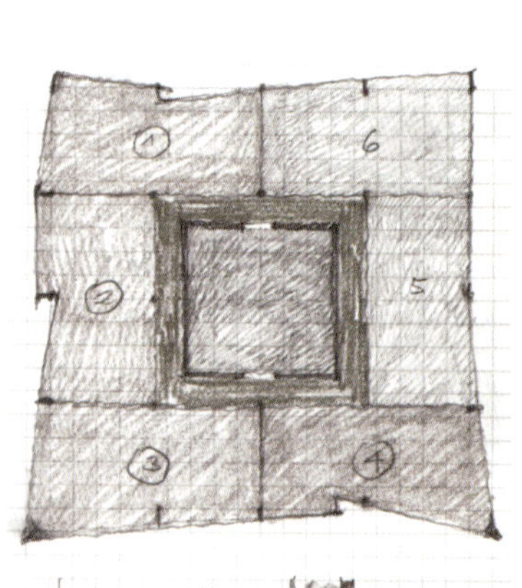

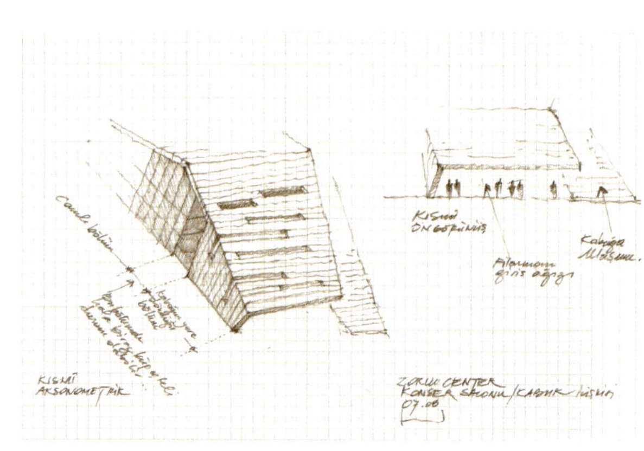

12.05.2010

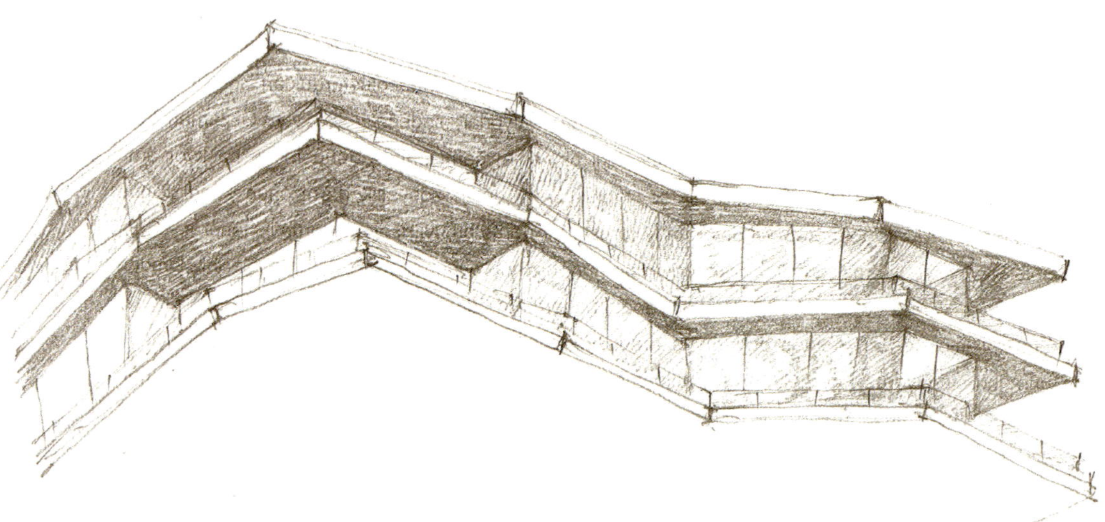

OPPOSITE, TOP LEFT
Conceptual sketch

OPPOSITE, TOP RIGHT
Sketch for the performing arts center entrance

OPPOSITE, MIDDLE LEFT
Residential floor plans

OPPOSITE, MIDDLE
Sketch for the shell edges

OPPOSITE, MIDDLE RIGHT
Sketch for the layout

OPPOSITE, BOTTOM
Sketch for the tower facade

BELOW
Studies for the terrace housing plans

BOTTOM
Floor plans of the podium

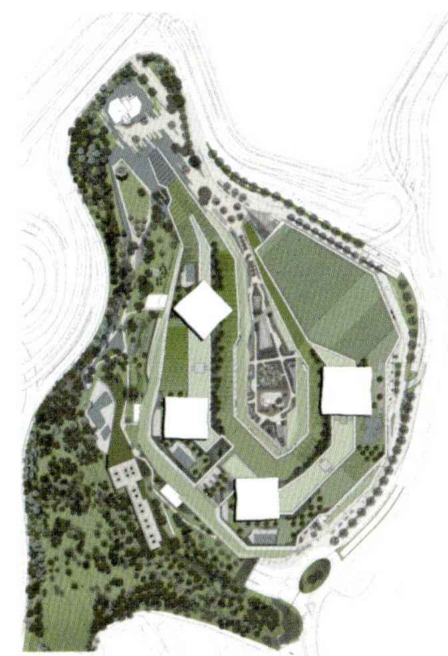

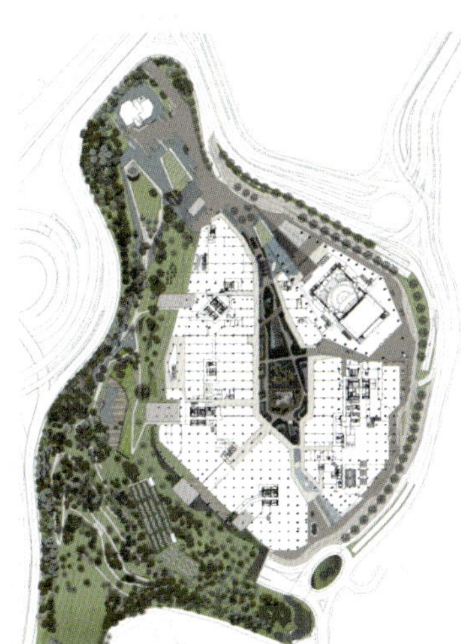

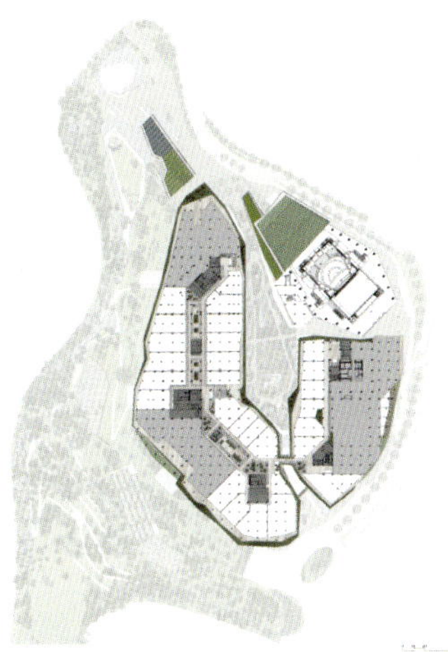

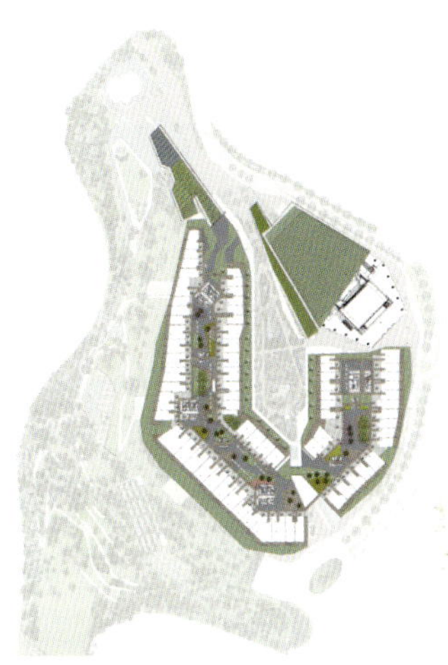

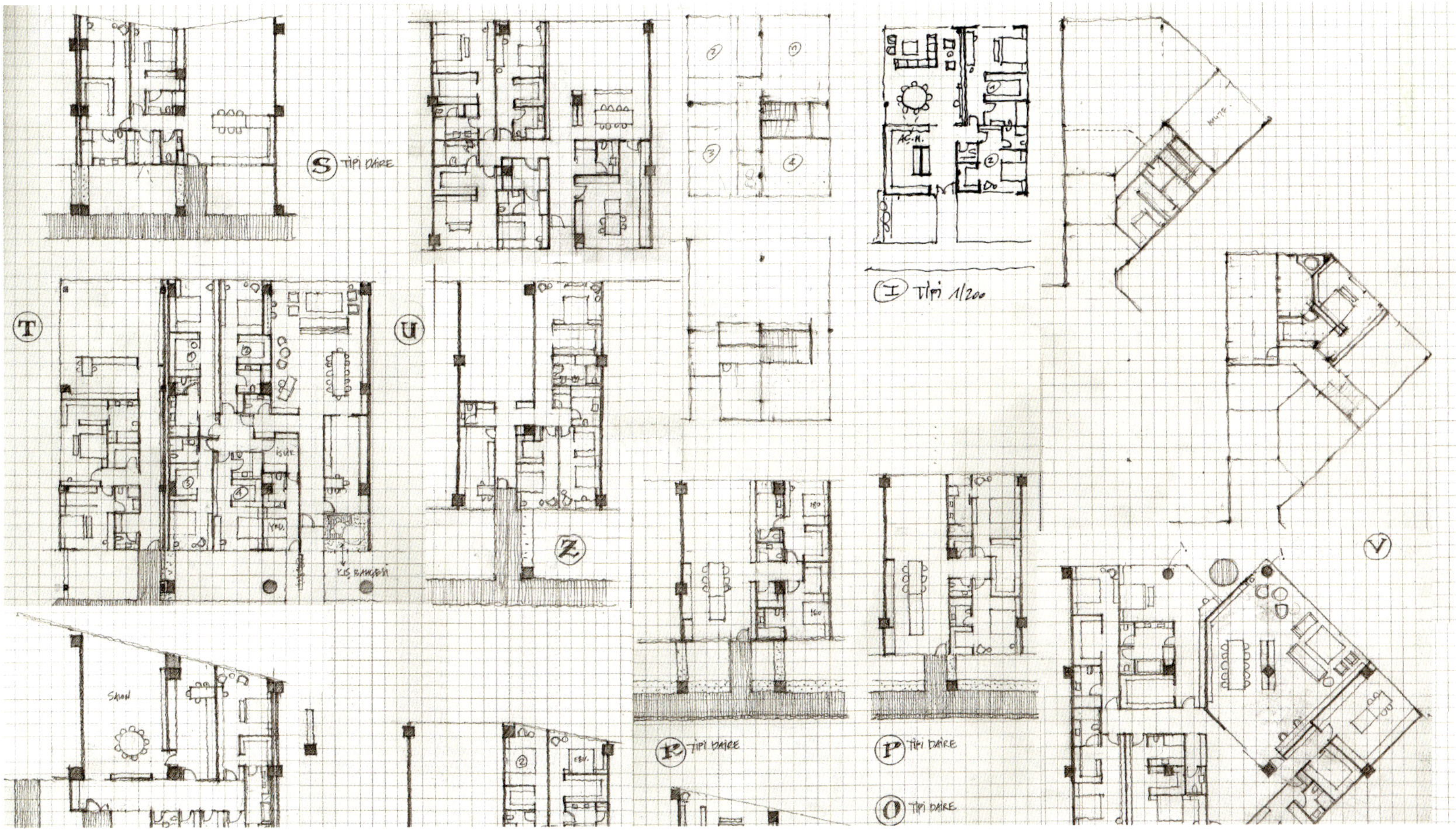

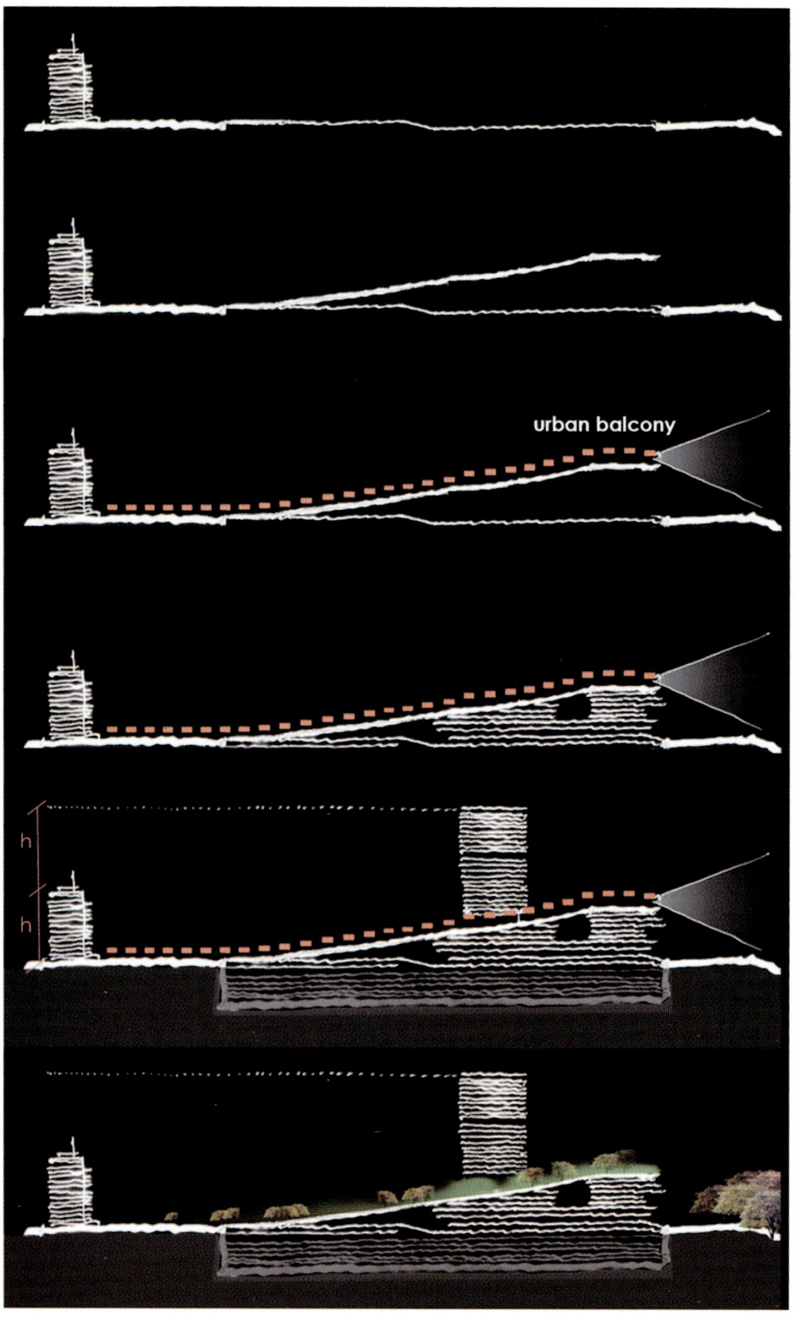

TOP LEFT
Conceptual diagram

TOP RIGHT
Existing land, project render,
construction

ABOVE
Conceptual model

LEFT AND FAR LEFT
Location

TOP
View from the south

ABOVE
View from the terrace houses

ABOVE, RIGHT
View from the concert hall

RIGHT
View from the entrance of the
performing arts center

TOP LEFT
View of the terrace housing

TOP RIGHT
View from the southwest

ABOVE
View from the west

RIGHT AND OPPOSITE
View from the circulation area of
the terrace housing

ABOVE
View from the concert hall

BELOW
View toward the public square

OPPOSITE
View from the public square toward
the terrace housing

Tekfen Kağıthane
Office Park

OPPOSITE
Exterior view from the east

BELOW
View of the site from
the northeast

The Tekfen Tower is a twenty-eight-story structure completed in 2003 and located on the Levent–Maslak axis on Büyükdere Avenue, considered Istanbul's latest backbone of commerce.

The Kağıthane Office Park (2007–12) was designed for the Tekfen Group, which has foreseen the potential in the area. As is usually the case, the architects first carefully studied the site and surrounding area, investigating not only the physical characteristics but also the sociological factors. Solutions involving the fragmentation of the required 53,000 square meters (173,884 square feet) of floor area were privileged to avoid imposing a more monolithic mass on the neighborhood and to allow for more flexibility.

Insofar as the project's appearance was concerned, the architects took into account the relative proportions of voids and building mass and studied the colors and surfaces with respect to inside and outside perception, planned lighting levels, and the use of natural ventilation. "We hope," say the architects, "that this project will be a noteworthy example and even an inspiration for the inevitable transformation that the region is going through."

LEFT
Surface-facade abstraction

RIGHT
Evolution of the volumetric
composition

BELOW
Floor plans

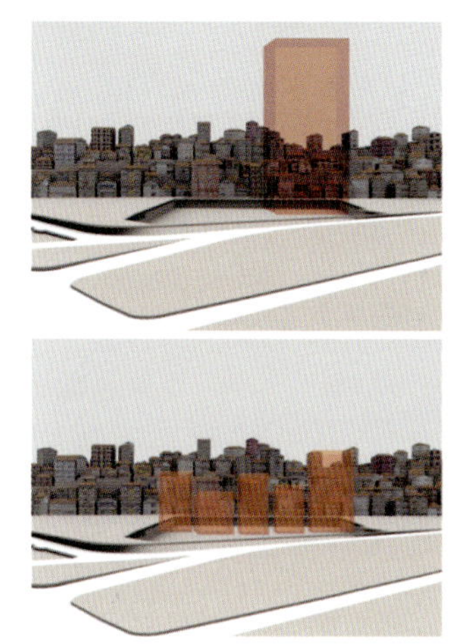

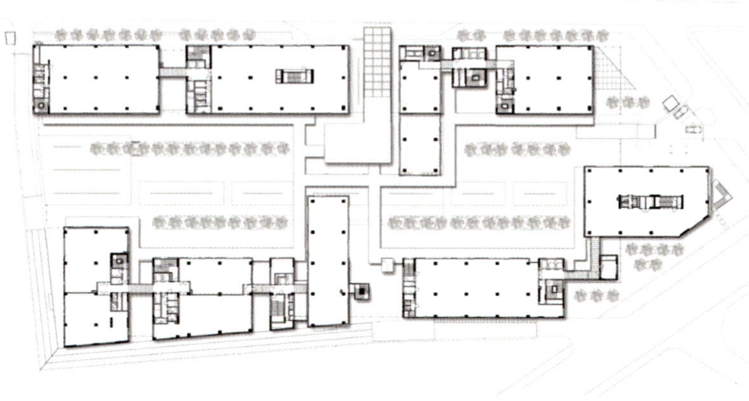

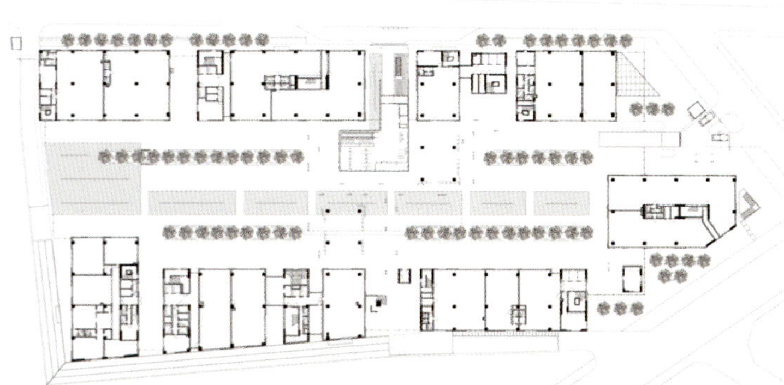

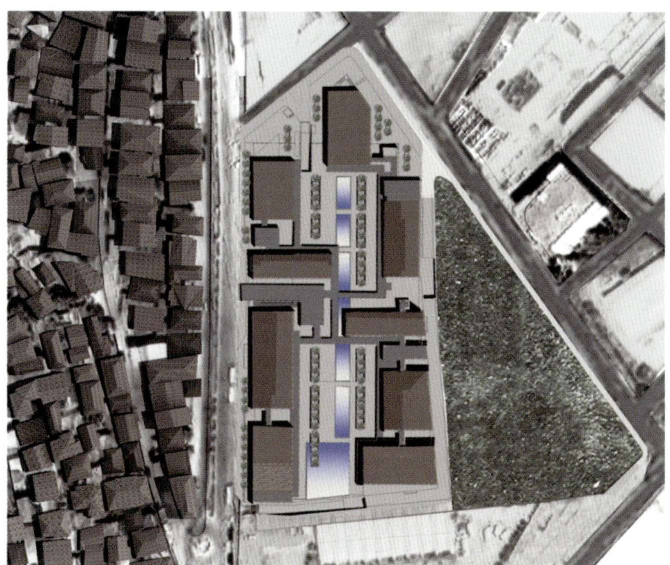

ABOVE
Site plan

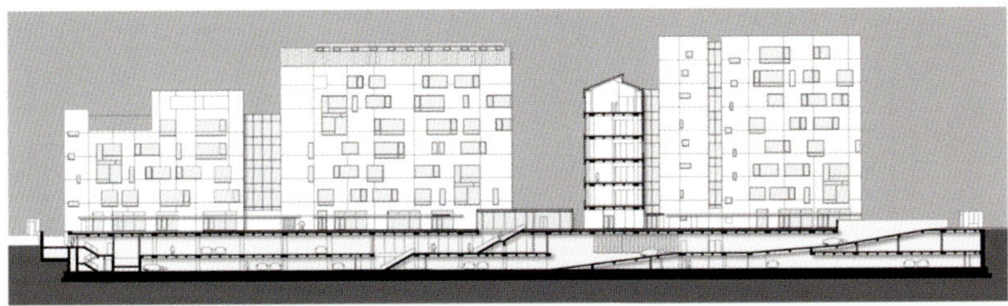

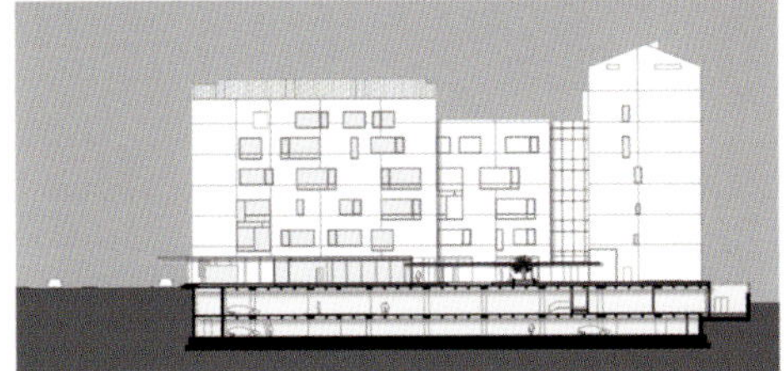

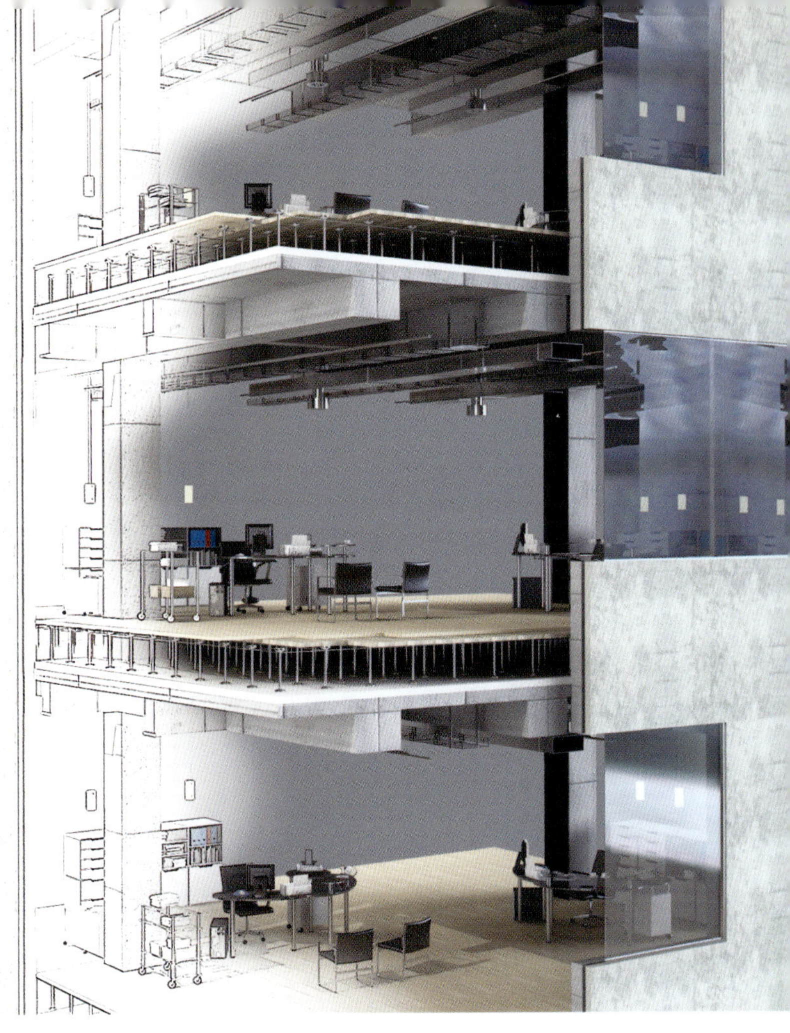

TOP LEFT
Sections

TOP RIGHT
Technical systems

ABOVE
Section perspectives

RIGHT
Facade view from the model

BELOW
Model views

ABOVE
View from the inner courtyard

LEFT
Café at the inner courtyard

RIGHT
View from the courtyard

BELOW
View from the east

BOTTOM, LEFT AND RIGHT
View from the courtyard

OPPOSITE
View from the courtyard toward
the entrance

ABOVE
Views of the dining hall

RIGHT
View from the meeting
rooms corridor

Maslak NO. 1 Office Tower

View of the facade from the southeast

LOCATION / **Istanbul, Turkey**

YEAR / **2008**

STATUS / **under construction, 2014**

TOTAL AREA / **30.000 m²**

Design work for this 30,000-square-meter (322,917 square foot) office building located on the Mecidiyeköy–Maslak axis of Istanbul and its construction were scheduled to be completed in 2014.

The client naturally wanted a prestigious building, but this might be said to be the case of surrounding structures, which were developed with no certain rule, plan, or order. The architects added the concept of vertical gardens to what otherwise remains a rational office block with an 8.25-by-8.25-meter (27 foot) grid, enveloped within a freely formed glazing system. This envelope acts as a secondary facade to the south and west and is detached from the building up to 17 meters (56 feet), allowing for vertical gardens that are 20 meters (65.6 feet) high. The space between the two facades is considered a buffer zone for the acoustic and climatic senses.

The curvilinear plan of the facade formed with 150-by-200-centimeter (59 by 78.9 inch) rectangular modules was designed with respect to the perception of the building from the highway. A silicon glazing system with translucent film layer of varying opacity was employed, with the greatest density on the southern facade.

ABOVE
Location

BELOW
Floor plans

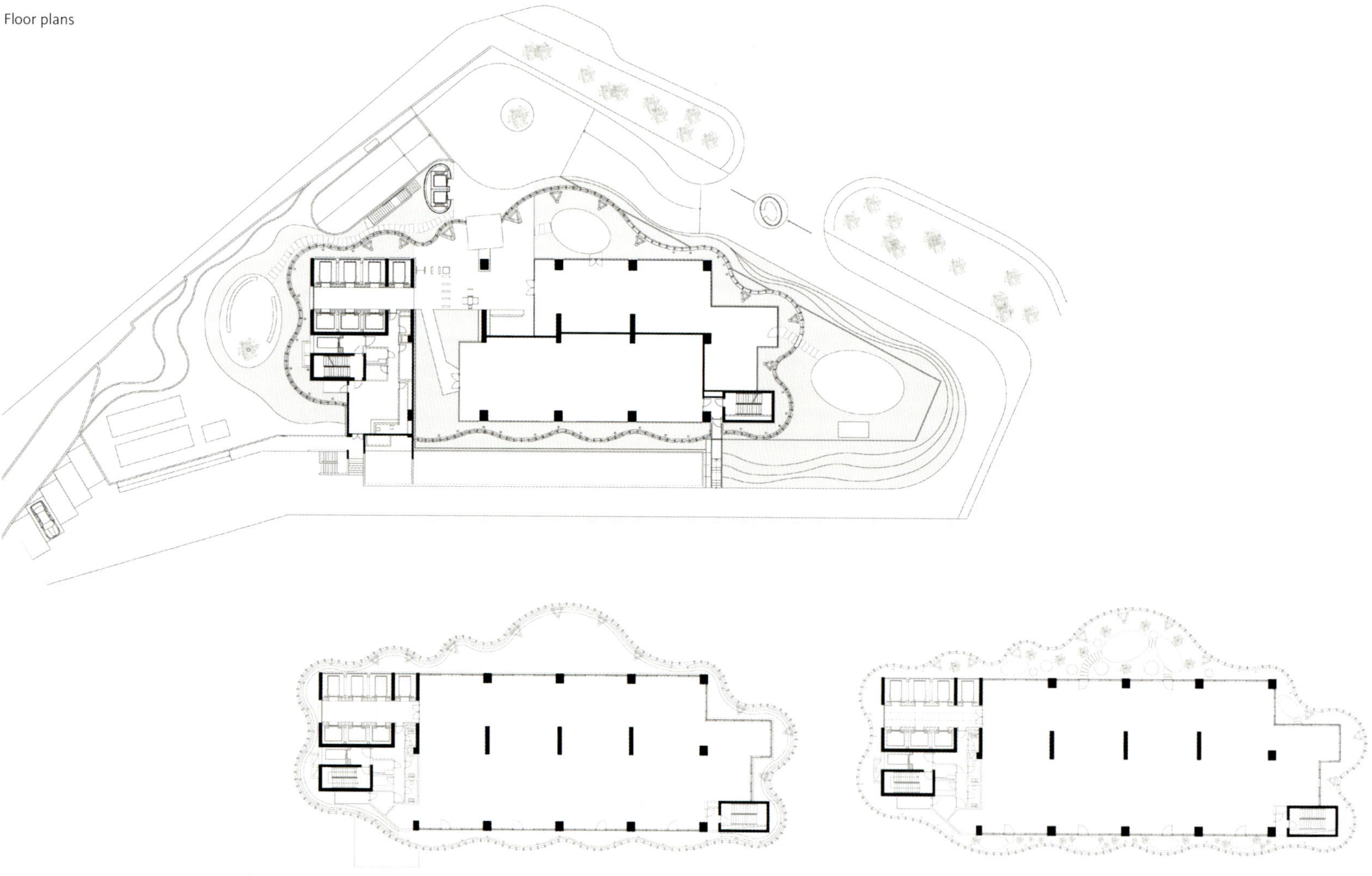

ABOVE
View from the east

RIGHT
View from the southwest

NEXT SPREAD
View upward from street level

ABOVE
Structure of the facade

LEFT
View toward the reception

RIGHT
Vertical garden on the upper levels

Mecidiyeköy Towers

LOCATION / **Istanbul, Turkey**

YEAR / **2008**

STATUS / **under construction, 2016**

TOTAL AREA / **380.000 m²**

The site for this project is in a central, crowded area of Istanbul. The neighboring lots are public on one side and industrial on the other, including a former liqueur and cognac factory designed by Robert Mallet-Stevens in the 1930s. The restoration of the factory was part of the overall project. A continuous green public space was designed between the factory and the former Ali Sami Yen Stadium, another relic of a bygone era in the vicinity.

The 380,000-square-meter (4.1 million square foot) Mecidiyeköy Towers, designed in 2008, adopt the "principle of mass fragmentation" in both the horizontal and vertical planes, inspired by the existing physical context. The architects write, "Creating sky-gardens in different locations and scales, it aims to re-create the essence of the relationship that existing buildings have among each other in the horizontal axis." One of the five high-rise blocks in the complex was intended as office space, another for a hotel, and the remaining three were designed as residential towers. The tactic of fragmentation was also applied to the facades, which face in different directions to best profit from the available views. The architects state that "the fragmentation of the building mass helps the tall building to be perceived as a lighter mass in its urban texture."

BELOW
Facade of the podium offices

BELOW
Aerial view from the northwest

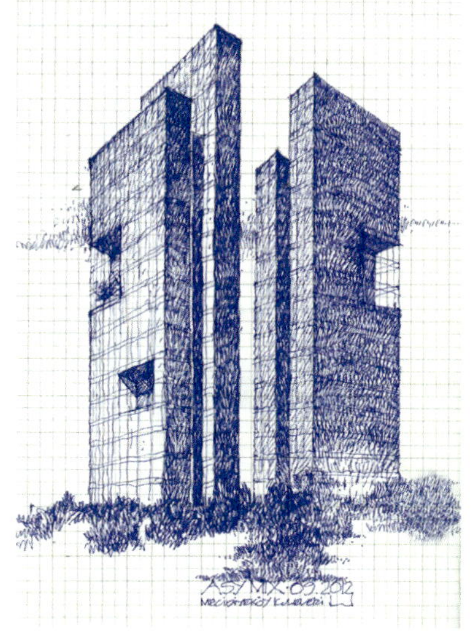

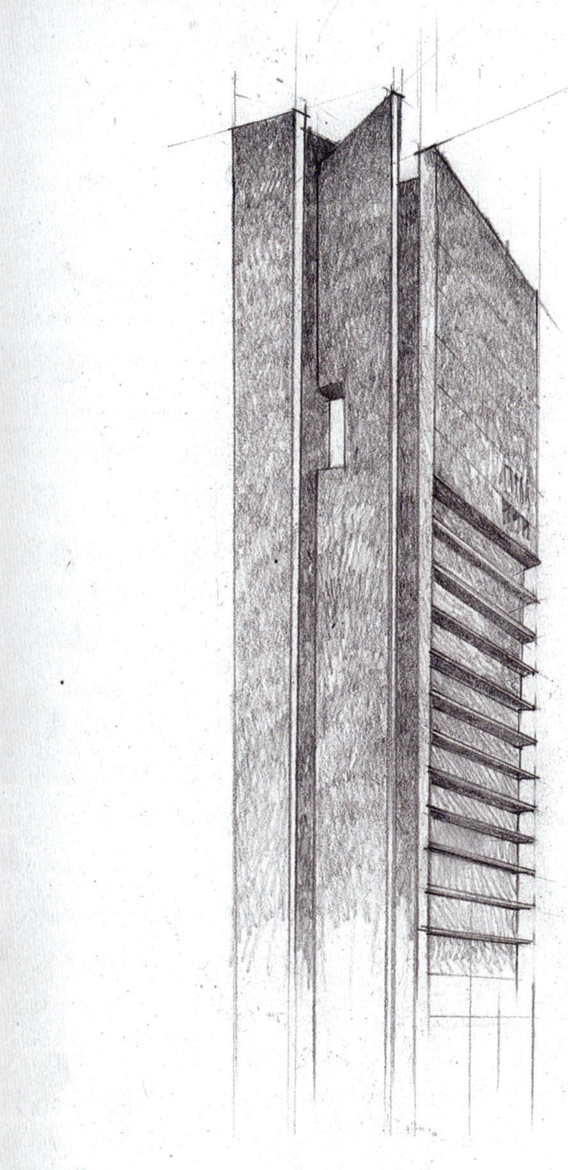

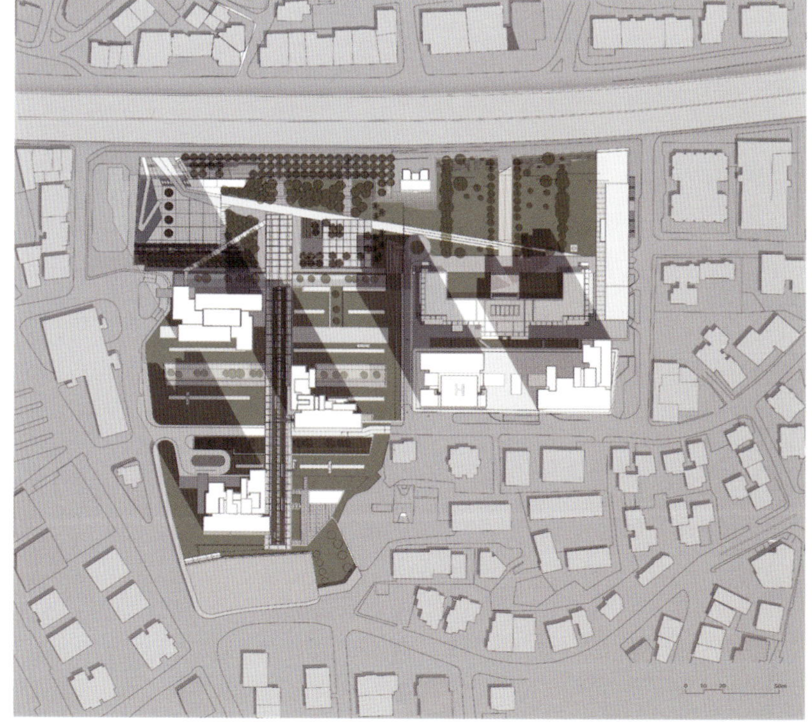

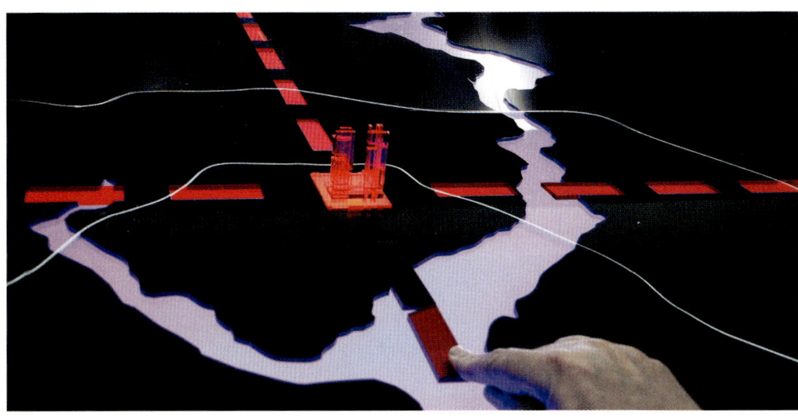

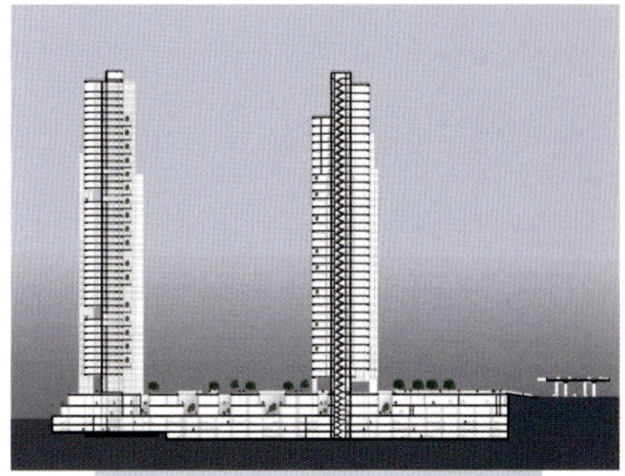

OPPOSITE, TOP LEFT
Photos from the former liqueur and
cognac factory

OPPOSITE, TOP MIDDLE AND RIGHT
Studies for the tower masses

OPPOSITE, MIDDLE
Study for the facade

OPPOSITE, BOTTOM RIGHT
Site plan

OPPOSITE, BOTTOM LEFT
Study for the tower

ABOVE, LEFT
Context model

RIGHT
Sections

ABOVE AND RIGHT
Views from the volumetric model

BELOW, LEFT AND RIGHT
Views from the scale model

LEFT
View from the commercial spaces on
the ground level

BELOW
View from the south

OPPOSITE
View from the south

RIGHT
View from the public area in front
of the towers

BELOW, LEFT AND RIGHT
Views from the office spaces

NEXT SPREAD
View upward from the ground level

Bergama Cultural Center

LOCATION / **Bergama, Turkey**

YEAR / **2011**

STATUS / **under construction, 2013**

TOTAL AREA / **4.000 m²**

ABOVE
View from the interior arcade

RIGHT
View toward the library

This 4,000-square-meter (43,056 square foot) facility, designed beginning in 2011, was due for completion in 2013. Bergama is located in western Turkey, in Izmir Province.

In Greek and Roman times, the city was known as Pergamon, whose altar of Zeus is on display in the Pergamon Museum in Berlin. Historic remnants such as the ruins of an acropolis and a Roman theater can still be seen in the town. The architects note, however, that aside from its ancient culture, modern Bergama had few modern cultural activities.

The new cultural center is located near Cumhuriyet Avenue, where stores and pedestrian walkways are the rule. The architects proposed an arcade with shops as well as cultural spaces such as a library, cinemas, and a theater. Cafés and seating areas serve the cinema and multipurpose room, allowing day-to-day life to integrate itself into the ongoing flow of the city. "With all of these qualities," the architects note, "the Bergama project breaks the image of the 'cultural center' that fails to form a relationship to the citizens, and makes itself a citizen of Pergamon."

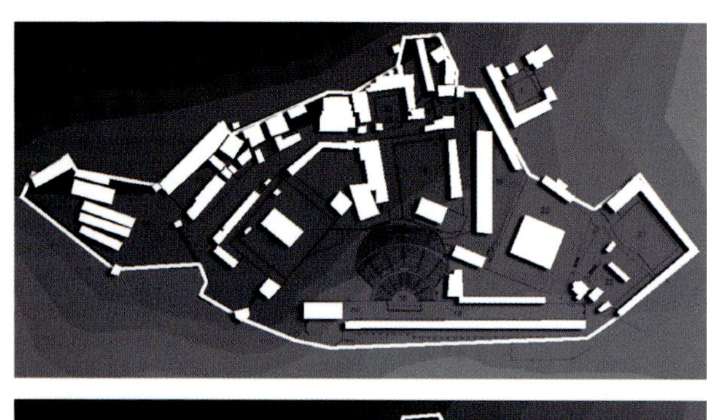

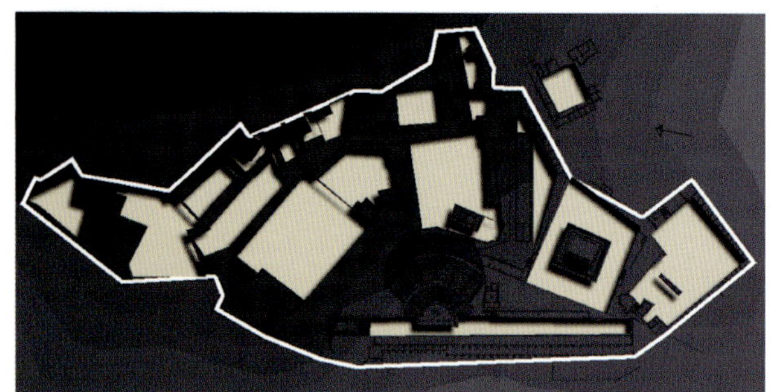

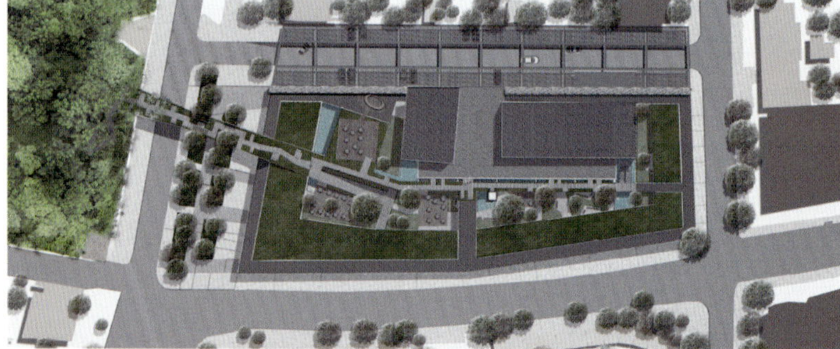

ABOVE
Conceptual framework of
the general layout

RIGHT
Floor plans

BELOW
South and west elevations

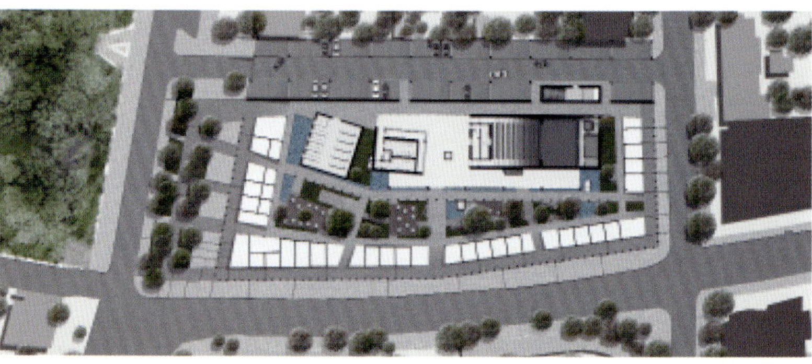
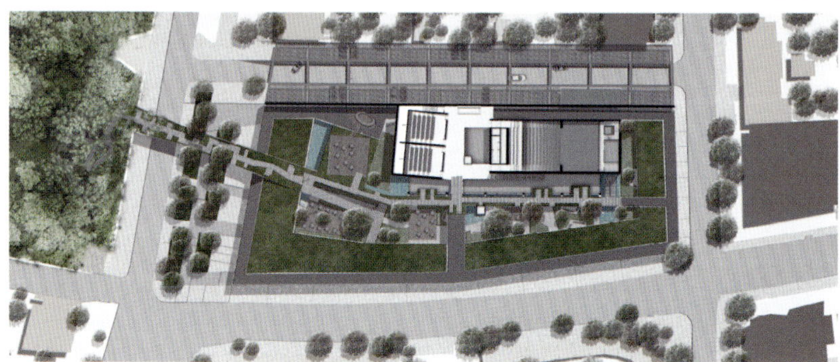

THIS PAGE
Different views from the scale model

ABOVE
View from the southwest

RIGHT AND BELOW
View from the inner courtyard

OPPOSITE, TOP
View through the arcade

OPPOSITE, BOTTOM
Night view from the southwest

Vicem Bodrum Residences

The area around Bodrum is among the most popular holiday destinations in Turkey. The strip of land between the sea and the coastal road to Içmeler remains relatively natural despite the dense construction inside Bodrum itself. The Vicem Residences are located along this strip, which posed the problem of relatively high density in a natural setting.

The architects again have experimented with what they call "mass fragmentation" for the 9,500-square-meter (102,257 square foot) housing complex, completed in 2013. They employed a strategy that takes into account the three-dimensional topography of the site. They explain, "In order for the buildings to integrate with the natural texture and even to dissolve into the rocky site, the buildings are designed as fragmented masses, and the surface articulation of the parts that sit on the ground is kept as a natural as possible. Thick stone walls provide an efficient insulation and keep the inner space cool in summer and hot in winter." Wooden louvers are placed on facades that face the sun. Cross ventilation is used along with shady courtyards to provide a cool breeze in the summer. The landscaping aims to stay within the context of local vegetation, and the "rocky texture" of the site is thus considered as the overall source of inspiration.

LOCATION / **Bodrum, Turkey**

YEAR / **2010**

STATUS / **under construction, 2013**

TOTAL AREA / **9.500 m²**

OPPOSITE
Side facade of a fragmented mass

RIGHT
View from the west

LEFT
Study of the mass fragmentation

BELOW, LEFT
Typical plans of the residences

BELOW
Contextual coherence

BOTTOM CENTER
Sketches for the layout

BOTTOM RIGHT
Site layout and floor plans

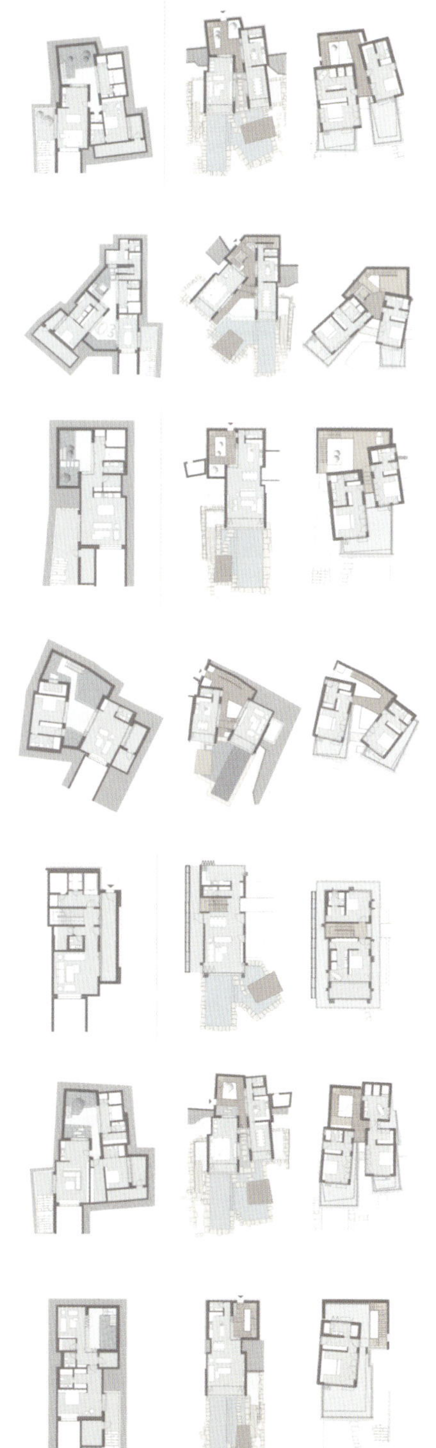

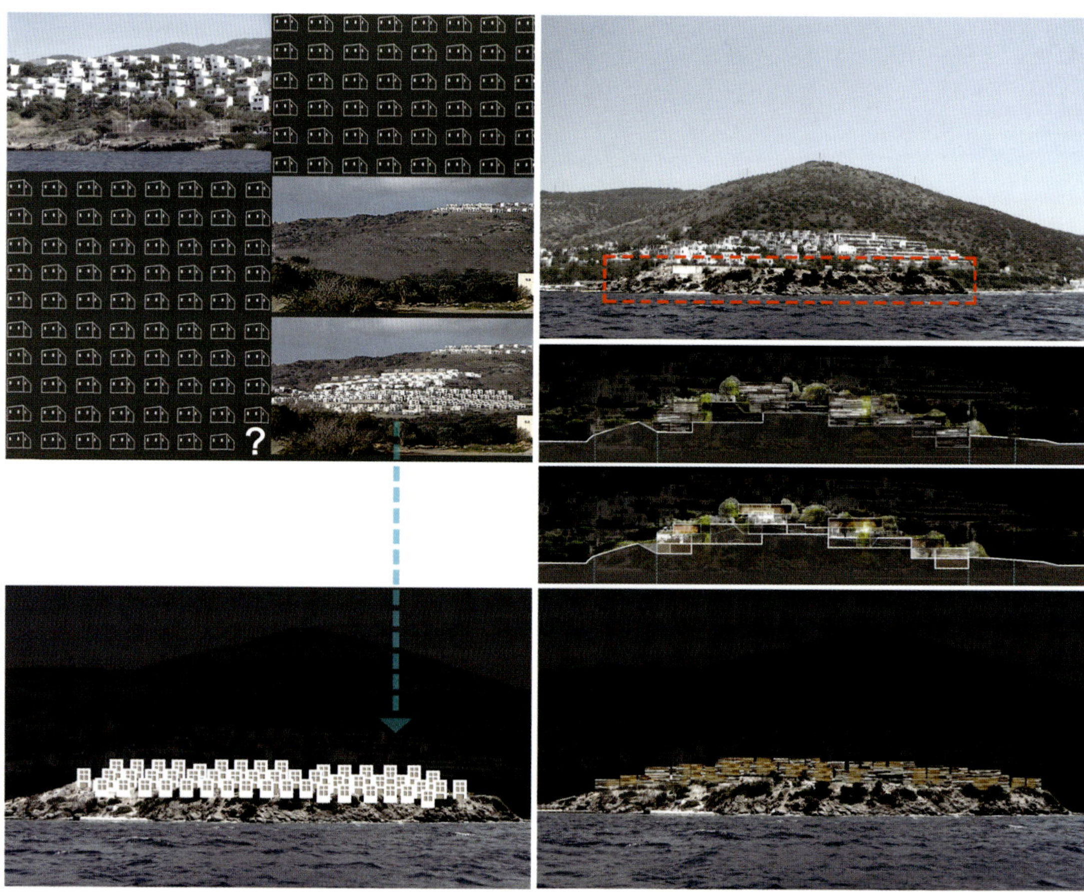

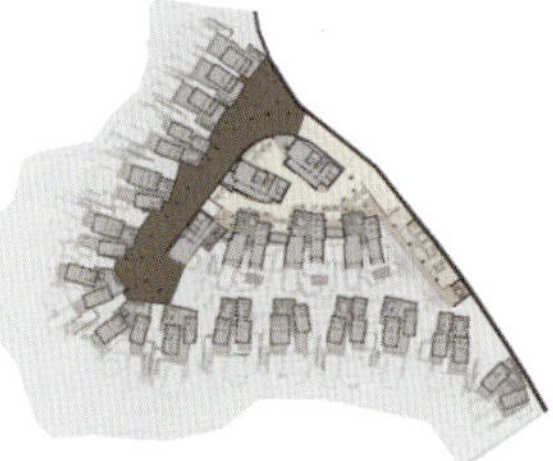

LEFT
View from the Aegean Sea

BELOW, LEFT
View from the east

BOTTOM
Views from the scale model

BELOW
Construction site

OPPOSITE, TOP
Close-up views of
the facades

OPPOSITE, BOTTOM
View of a residence
from the west

OPPOSITE, TOP
View of the living space of a residence

OPPOSITE, BOTTOM, ABOVE,
AND RIGHT
Views of a residence

Antakya Museum Hotel

LOCATION / **Antakya, Turkey**

YEAR / **2010**

STATUS / **under construction, 2013**

TOTAL AREA / **34.000 m²**

Begun in 2010, this project has a floor area of 34,000 square meters (365,973 square feet). The Antakya Museum Hotel is located near the Church of Saint Peter, an important Christian pilgrimage site.

The client wished to build a five-star hotel, but significant archaeological artifacts were found as soon as excavation began. The double nature of the project that emerged, combining a hotel and a museum, was the driving force, as were the ancient ruins. Usually relatively "anonymous," the hotel in this instance had to be designed for its highly specific circumstances. Rather than a compact volume, the individual programmatic elements are spread across the site under a protective canopy. The precise location of the archaeological findings dictated the complex process of placing the support columns for the elevated structure. Further, the hotel was designed to take full advantage of its unique situation overlooking a significant archaeological dig.

The main body of the building is made of prefabricated hotel room units that are stacked on top of one another on a steel frame, with connections established by walkways and bridges. In this respect, the project evokes the temporary structures sometimes associated with archaeological work. Terraces and gardens are located, like the rooms themselves, under the main canopy. The lobby, restaurant, and lounge are on the lower levels, nearer to the archaeological site.

RIGHT
Site plan

BELOW, RIGHT
Section perspective

BOTTOM RIGHT
Floor plans

BELOW
Structural concept

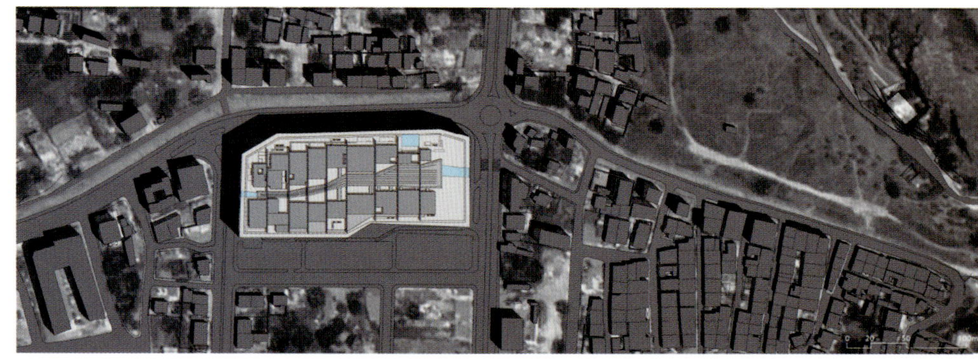

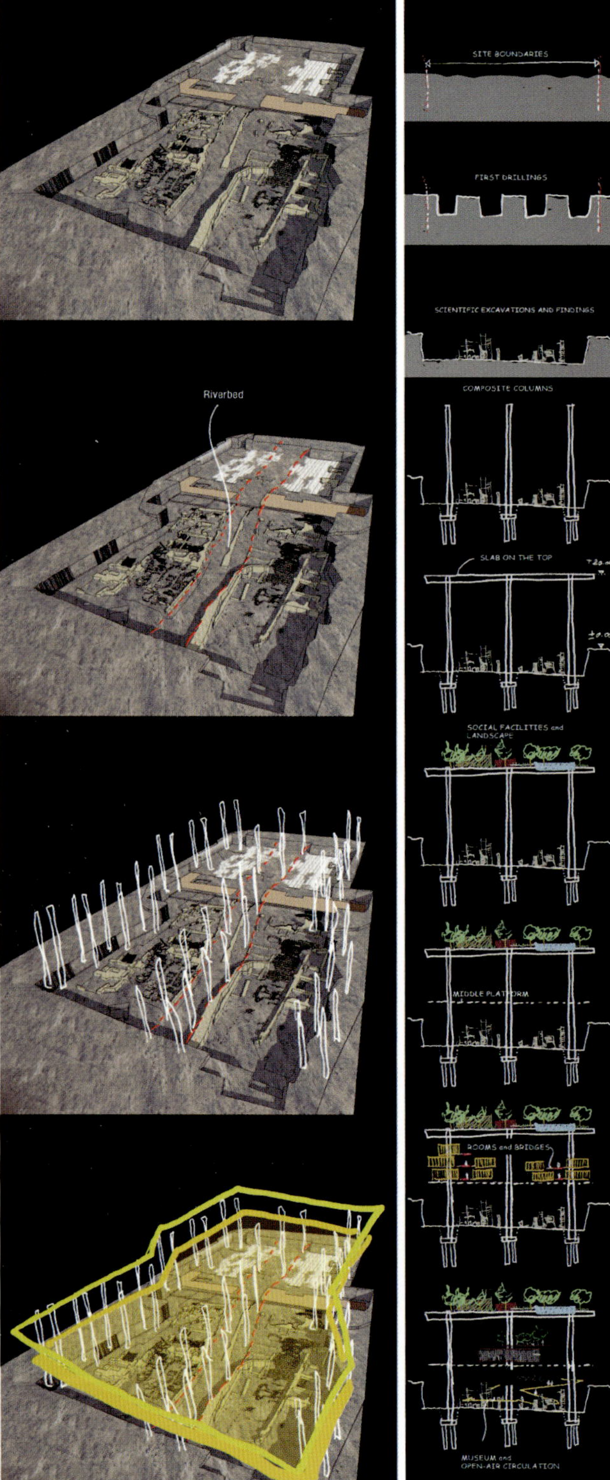

Riverbed
SITE BOUNDARIES
FIRST DRILLINGS
SCIENTIFIC EXCAVATIONS AND FINDINGS
COMPOSITE COLUMNS
SLAB ON THE TOP
SOCIAL FACILITIES and LANDSCAPE
MIDDLE PLATFORM
ROOMS and BRIDGES
MUSEUM and OPEN-AIR CIRCULATION

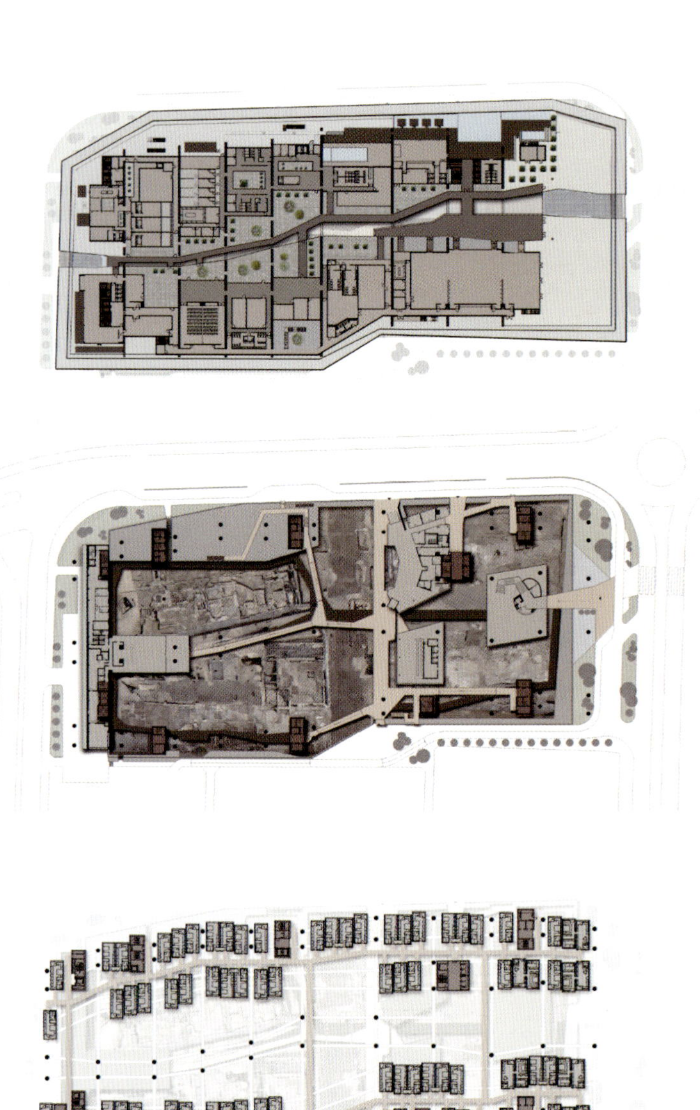

ABOVE, LEFT AND RIGHT
Views from the level of remains

BELOW
Production of the steel columns
in the factory

E1

BELOW
Views from the ground level

ABOVE
View from the southwest

RIGHT
View of the exterior facade from
the southeast

BELOW
View from the terrace above the
main canopy

BELOW
View from the open area on the main canopy

BOTTOM
View from the foyer of the ballroom

BELOW
Bridge leading to a room

MIDDLE
View of the dining hall

BOTTOM
Interior of the ballroom

BELOW
Interior of a room

MIDDLE
Interior of a room

Sancaklar Mosque

View from northwestern side on the lower level

This relatively small (700 square meters, or 7,535 square feet) project is located in Büyükçekmece, a suburban neighborhood on the outskirts of Istanbul. With this project the office sought to address the fundamental issues of designing a mosque while distancing itself from current architectural discussions that concern form only, focusing instead on the essence of religious space.

The site is in a prairie landscape that is separated from surrounding suburban gated communities by a busy highway. The high walls encircling the park on the upper courtyard of the mosque form a clear boundary between the chaotic outer world and the serene atmosphere of the public park. A long canopy stretching out from the park is the only architectural element visible from the outside. The building itself blends in with the topography. The interior of the mosque is a simple cavelike space inspired by verses of the Quran. The *qibla* wall, marking the direction of prayer, is designed with slits and fractures that allow daylight to filter into the prayer hall.

The project plays on the contrast between human-made and natural materials and spaces. Thus, stone stairs follow the slope of the landscape, while a thin reinforced concrete slab spanning more than 6 meters (19.7 feet) forms the canopy.

LEFT, ABOVE LEFT AND RIGHT
Conceptual sketches

OPPOSITE, TOP LEFT
Sections

OPPOSITE, TOP RIGHT
Plan

OPPOSITE, MIDDLE RIGHT
View from the area between the mosque
and the social spaces

OPPOSITE, LOWER MIDDLE RIGHT
View of the interior of the mosque

OPPOSITE, BOTTOM
Approach to the site from the upper level

OPPOSITE, MIDDLE LEFT
Interfere with the land

NEXT SPREAD
Interior space under construction

ABOVE
Sketch for the imperfect landscape

RIGHT
Sketch of the light washing the main wall

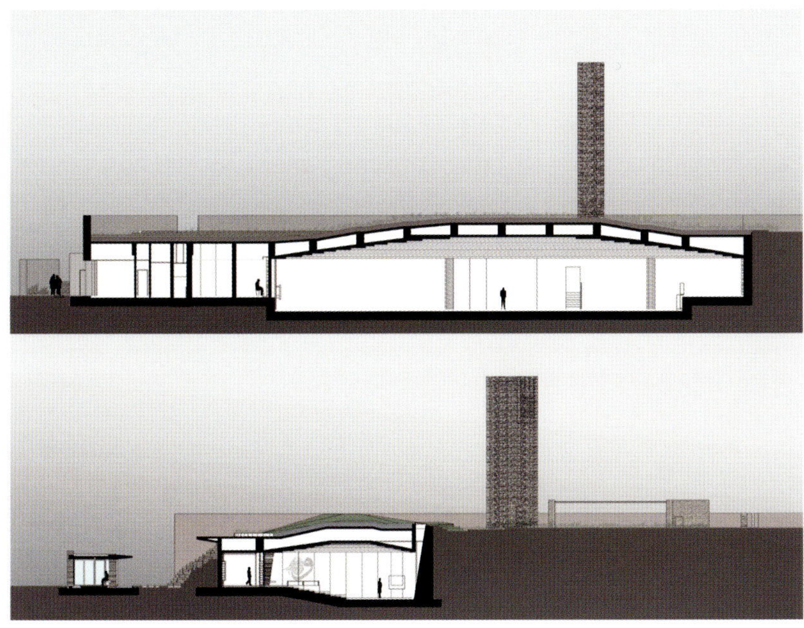

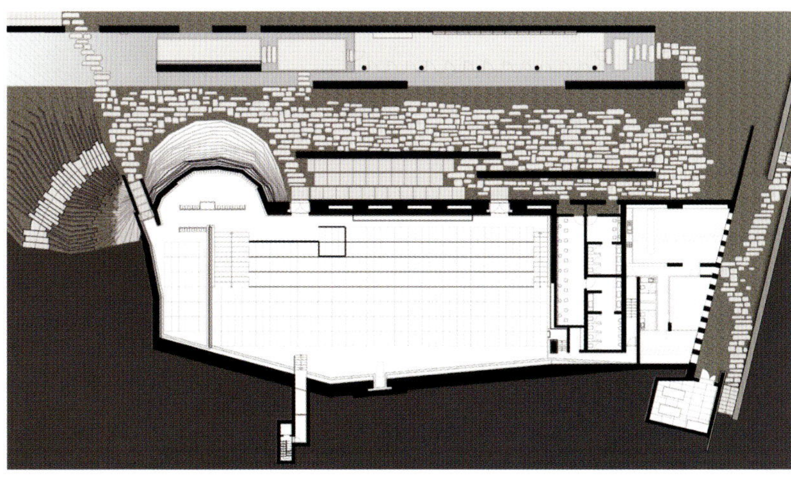

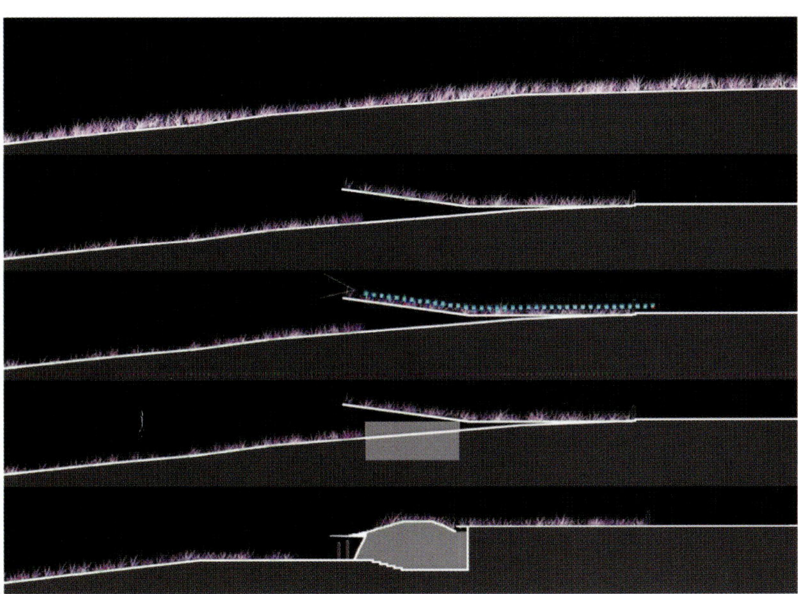

LEFT
Light washing the wall

OPPOSITE, TOP
View of the landscape through
the walls

OPPOSITE, BOTTOM LEFT
View under the main canopy

OPPOSITE, BOTTOM RIGHT
Wall textures

Cendere Valley Urban Design Project

LOCATION / Istanbul, Turkey

YEAR / 2011

STATUS / unbuilt

TOTAL AREA / 332.000 m²

The Kağıthane Cendere Valley, which was an agricultural zone under the Ottoman Empire and later an industrial zone, is today an area of Istanbul that appears to be "forgotten," its high-rise apartment buildings and squatter areas crossed over by a viaduct. It does remain a rather green space, as opposed to most of the rest of the city.

An association of landowners from Cendere valley was formed to organize its transformation in a coherent way. Together with the Istanbul Metropolitan Planning Governate, the association has consulted architectural firms such as EAA. Their goal has been to take the rights of landowners and residents into consideration, to increase areas set aside for public use, and to "protect social, ecological and environmental values." The preservation of low construction density has also been a goal, despite potential investor opposition to this aspect of the plans.

This large (332,000 square meters, or nearly 3.6 million square feet) project involves continuous low-rise blocks with shopping arcades along the main avenues. Semi-open shaded spaces enable multiple uses within the office zone. Instead of zoning in plan, the strategy of separating functions in section was accepted as a way to sustain the mixed use of buildings in the entire area. The green terrace in the office zone divides private areas on the upper levels from public spaces closer to the ground. On the whole, the aim was to preserve Cendere as an ecological corridor for the enjoyment of its citizens.

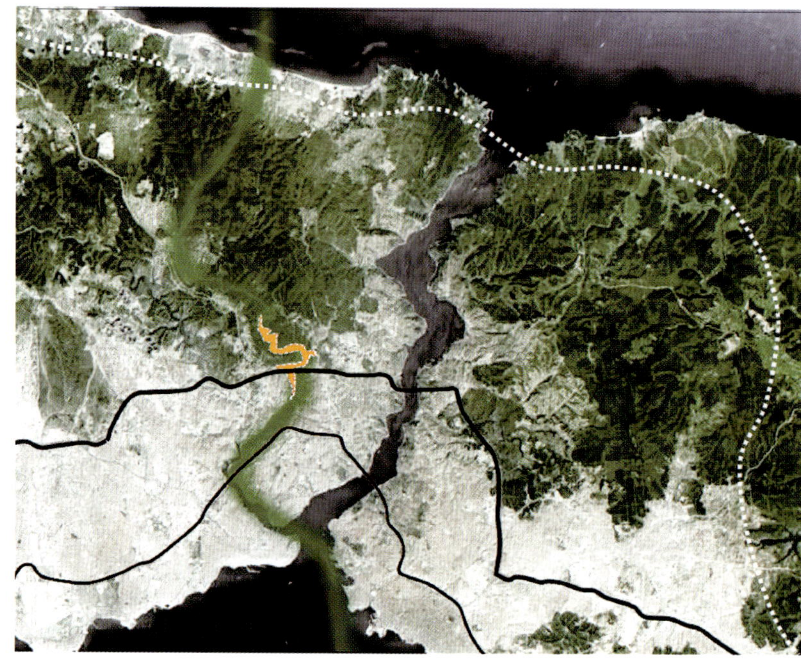

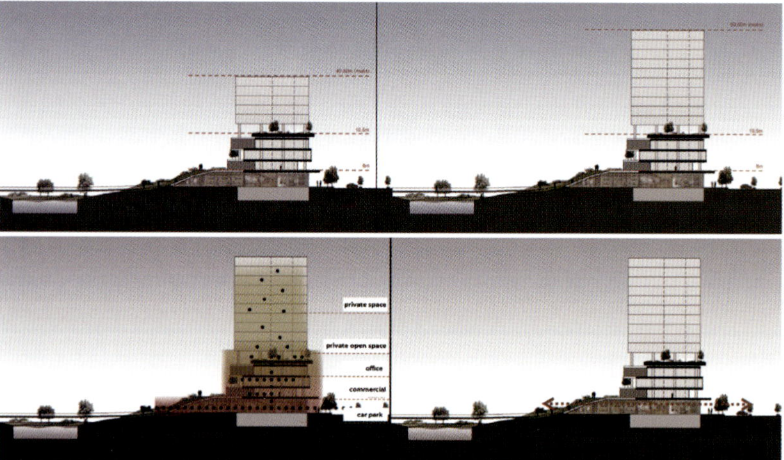

ABOVE
Location

TOP, LEFT
View toward the valley

LEFT
Typical sections showing the
main principles

BELOW, LEFT
Sections through the site

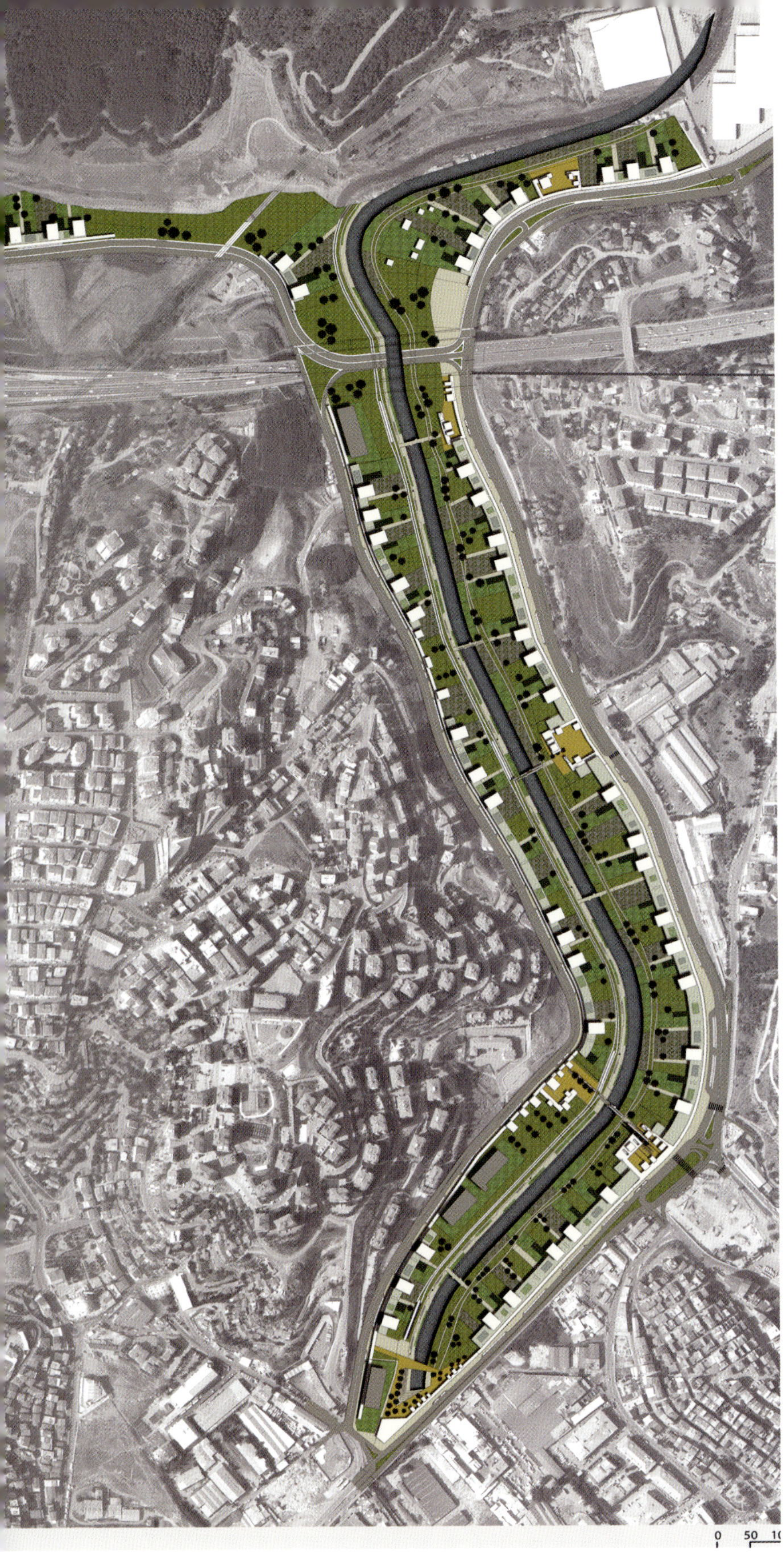
0
50

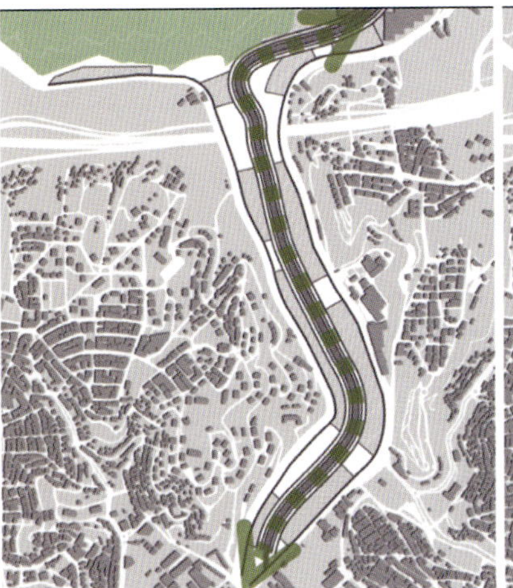

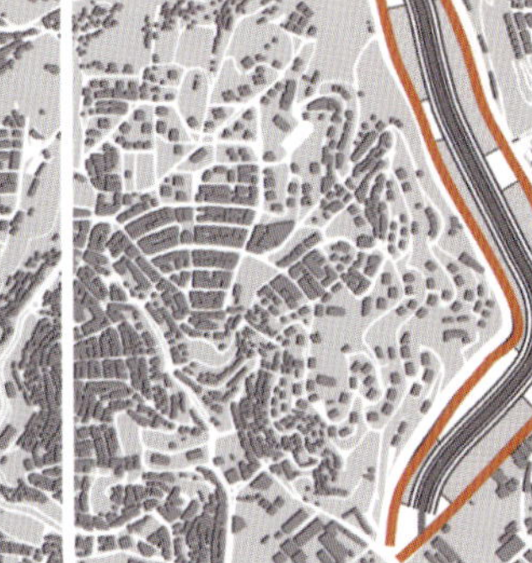

ECOLOGICAL CORRIDOR
CONTINUITY

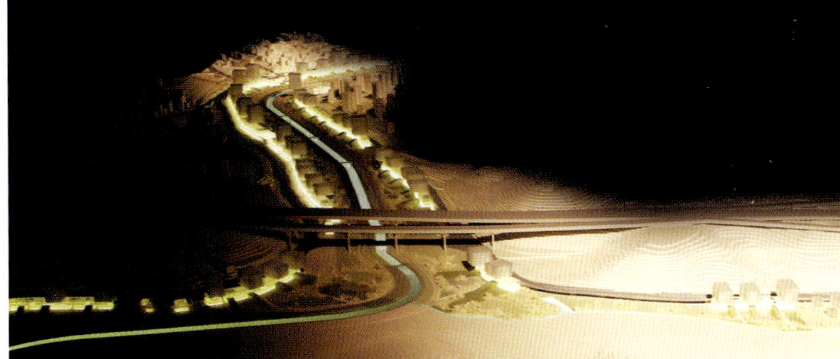

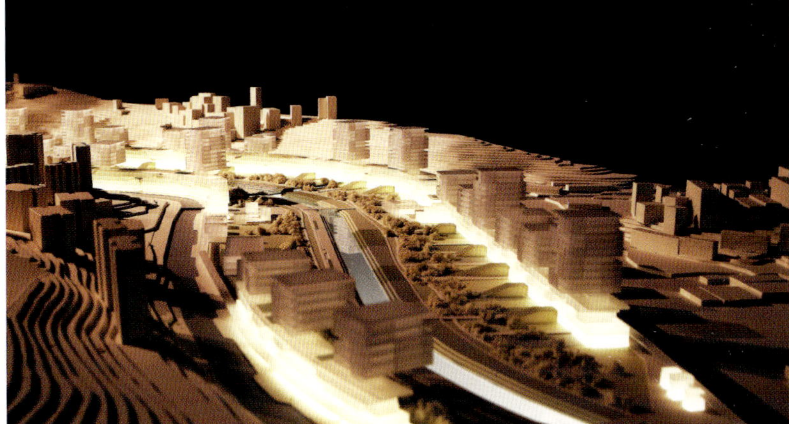

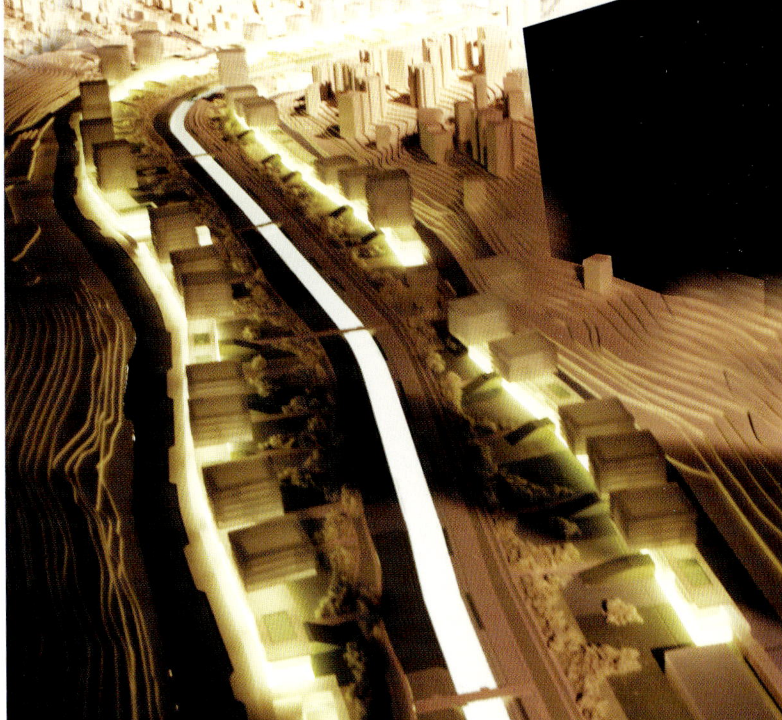

ABOVE
Site plan

ABOVE, RIGHT
Diagrams

RIGHT
Views from the scale model

OPPOSITE, TOP
View from the exterior commercial arcade

OPPOSITE, BOTTOM
View from the green public area

BELOW
View toward a public node

MIDDLE
View from the green public area

BOTTOM
View from the exterior commercial arcade

Çukurova Regional Airport Complex

LOCATION / Adana, Turkey

YEAR / 2011

STATUS / under construction, 2015

TOTAL AREA / 325.000 m²

Adana is an agricultural and commercial center located in southern Turkey. The architects chose to place a priority on the "existing natural texture and the dominant agricultural character of the region."

Efforts were made to minimize energy use in the 325,000-square-meter (3.5 million square foot) terminal, which is intended to serve ten million passengers a year. As described by the architects, a "green shell acts as a second roof that fades away and becomes permeable at some places in the passenger terminal and the multistory parking buildings allowing natural air ventilation." Interior gardens bring sunlight into the passenger areas as well.

Careful attention was paid to the technical aspects of the project, such as passenger-baggage flow, ease of management and maintenance, growth potential, and opportunities for flexible use. The reinforced concrete structure makes no use of stucco, paint, or other finishes. The architects sought to make the passenger hall modest in price but "assertive in the volumetric impact of the materials." They explain that the airport complex emerges as a sort of "man-made topography" that is practically invisible because of its green roof, which requires little maintenance.

ABOVE
Approach to the building

LEFT
Aerial view of the airport

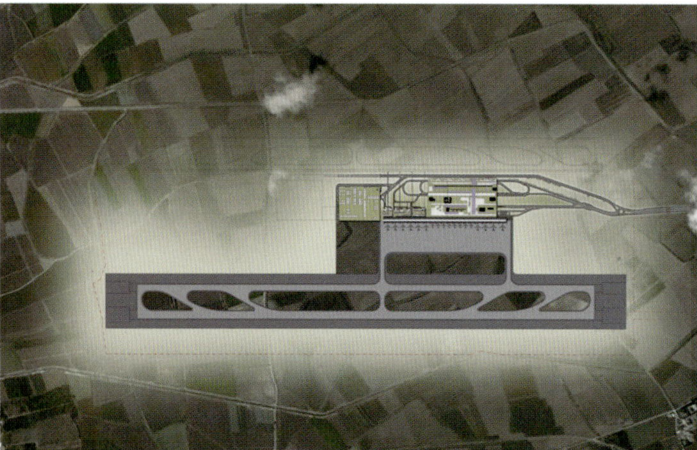

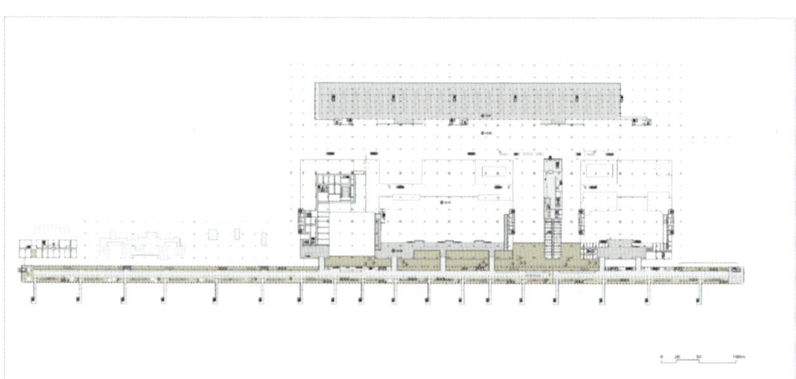

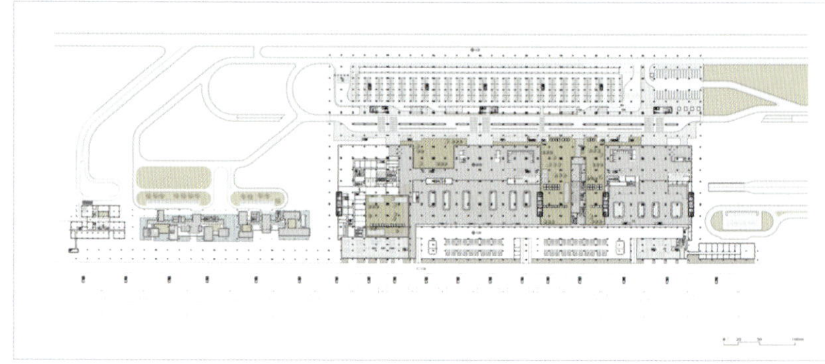

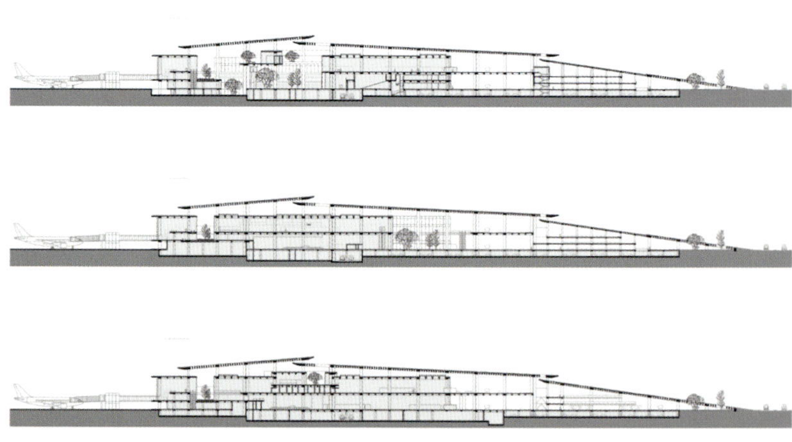

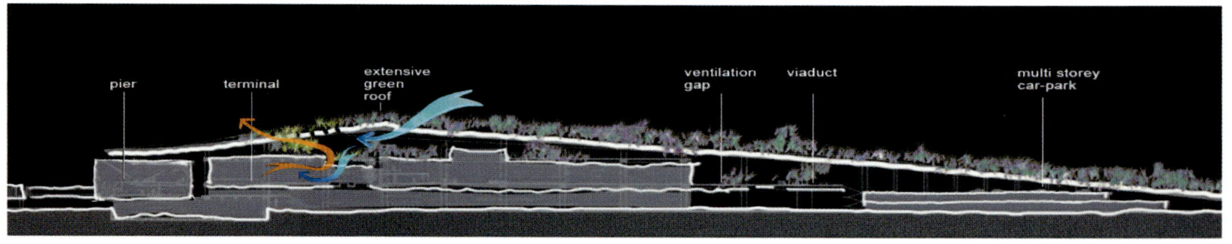

ABOVE
Site plan

ABOVE, RIGHT
Sections

RIGHT
Principal section

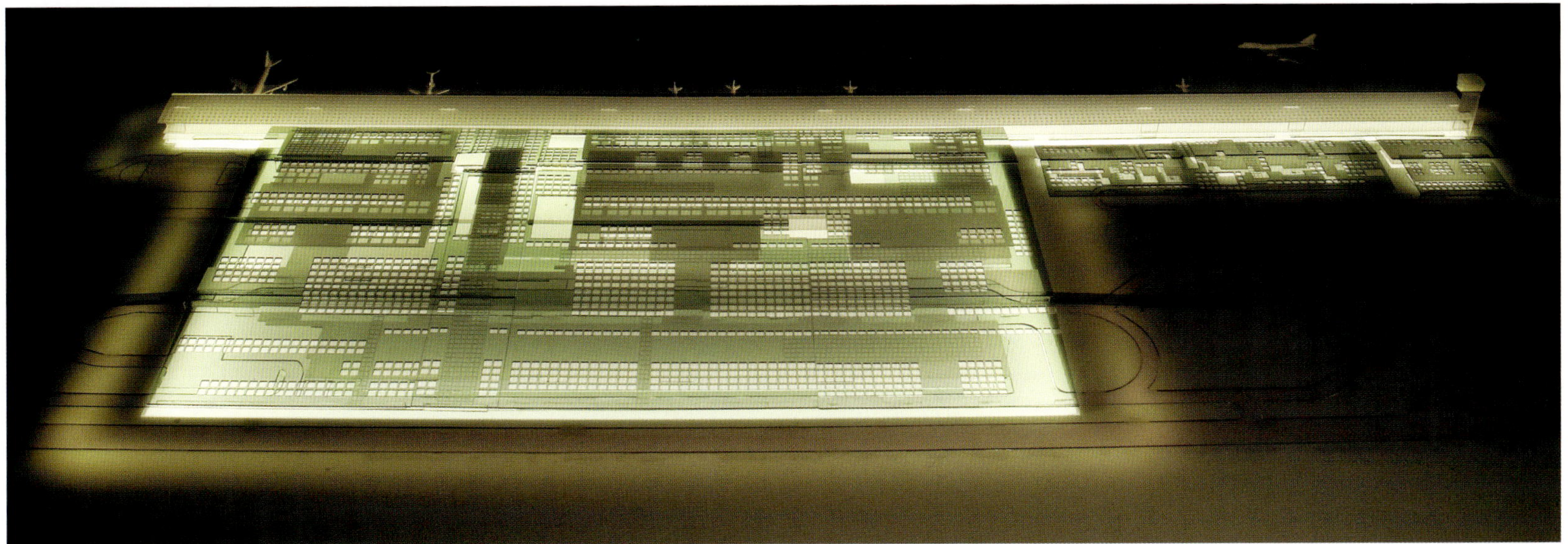

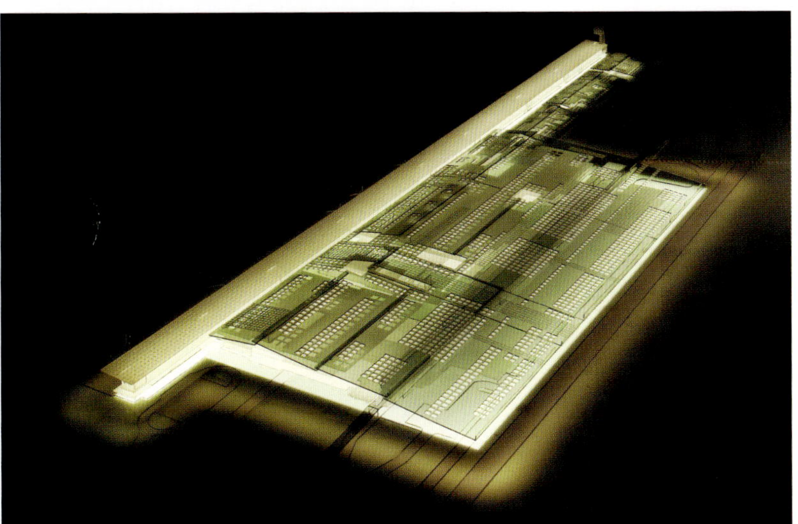

Views of the scale model

BELOW
View of the green shell

BOTTOM
Aerial view of the site

OPPOSITE, TOP
View of the main hall

OPPOSITE, BOTTOM
View from the pier

Prague Turkish Embassy

The architects state that this design, one of their few works outside Turkey, "is driven by the question of how to belong to the site while facing the discourse about being 'Turkish' in a foreign country."

They have sought a "structuralist" or "modernist" interpretation of Turkish regional architecture. A structural grid is employed for the construction, as it is in traditional Turkish houses. The building is divided into four elements to be able to merge into its site, while the structural grid is used as "an abstract image of Turkish architecture."

Designed in 2011, the building has an area of 4,400 square meters (47,361 square feet).

View from the main road

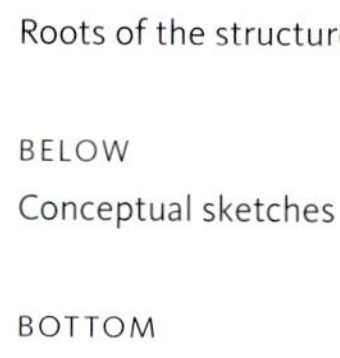

LEFT
Roots of the structure

BELOW
Conceptual sketches

BOTTOM
Section perspectives

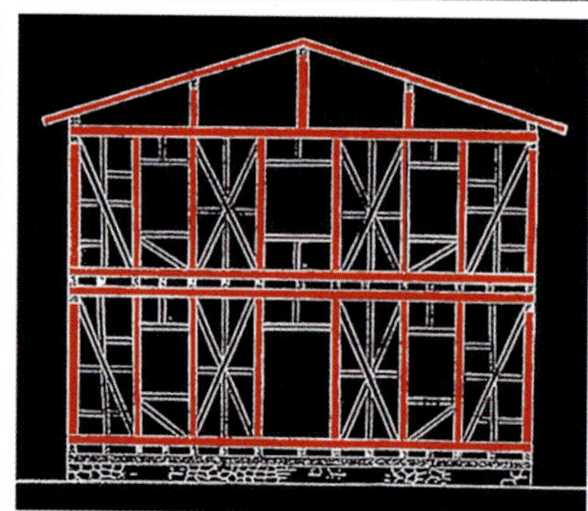

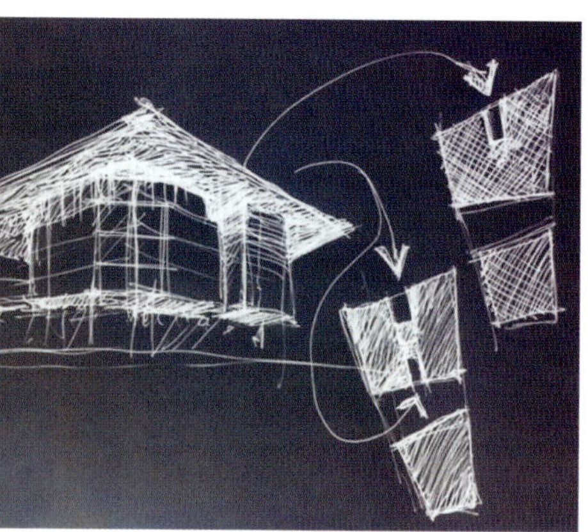

THIS PAGE
Views from the main road

ABOVE
View of the interior circulation spaces

RIGHT
View from the sunken courtyard

Yalıkavak
Marina Entertainment
Island

Marinas on the Aegean and Mediterranean coasts of Turkey have proved to be of significant interest in the development of tourism.

A new owner decided to completely rebuild the marina at Yalıkavak, which is located in a bay on the Bodrum Peninsula. An island in the marina that was previously unused was converted to receive "mega-yachts" as well as to accommodate restaurants, bars, and entertainment facilities. A wall serves to generate gathering spaces, and all surfaces are covered in natural stone.

Now called the Yalıkavak Palmarina, the 10,000-square-meter (215,278 square foot) facility "tries to avoid alienation from its location," according to the architects, "but at the same time keeps in mind that it is a 'newcomer' that aims to be both welcoming and authentic."

BELOW
San Sebastián, Spain

RIGHT
Pavement in Acropolis by
Dimitris Pikionis, Athens

ABOVE
Priene theater

RIGHT
Plan of Miletus

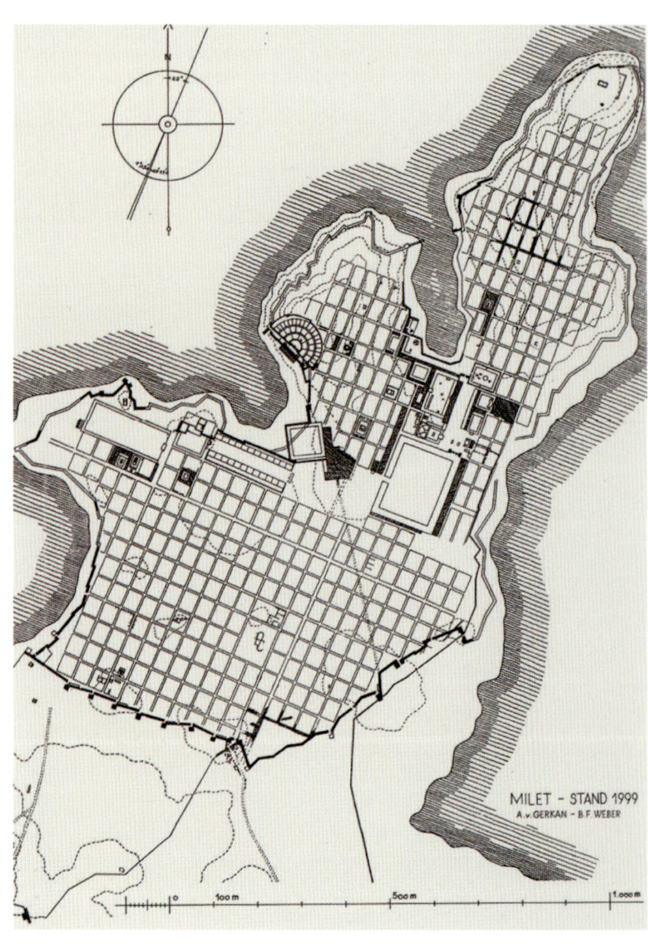
MILET - STAND 1999
A. v. GERKAN - B.F. WEBER
500 m
500 m
1.000 m

RIGHT AND BELOW
Aerial views

BELOW, RIGHT
Site plan

BOTTOM
Longitudinal section,
eastern and western
elevation

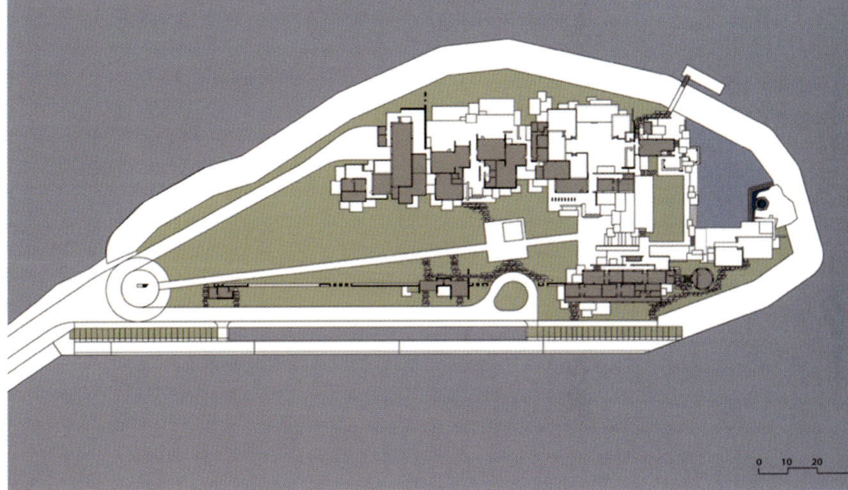

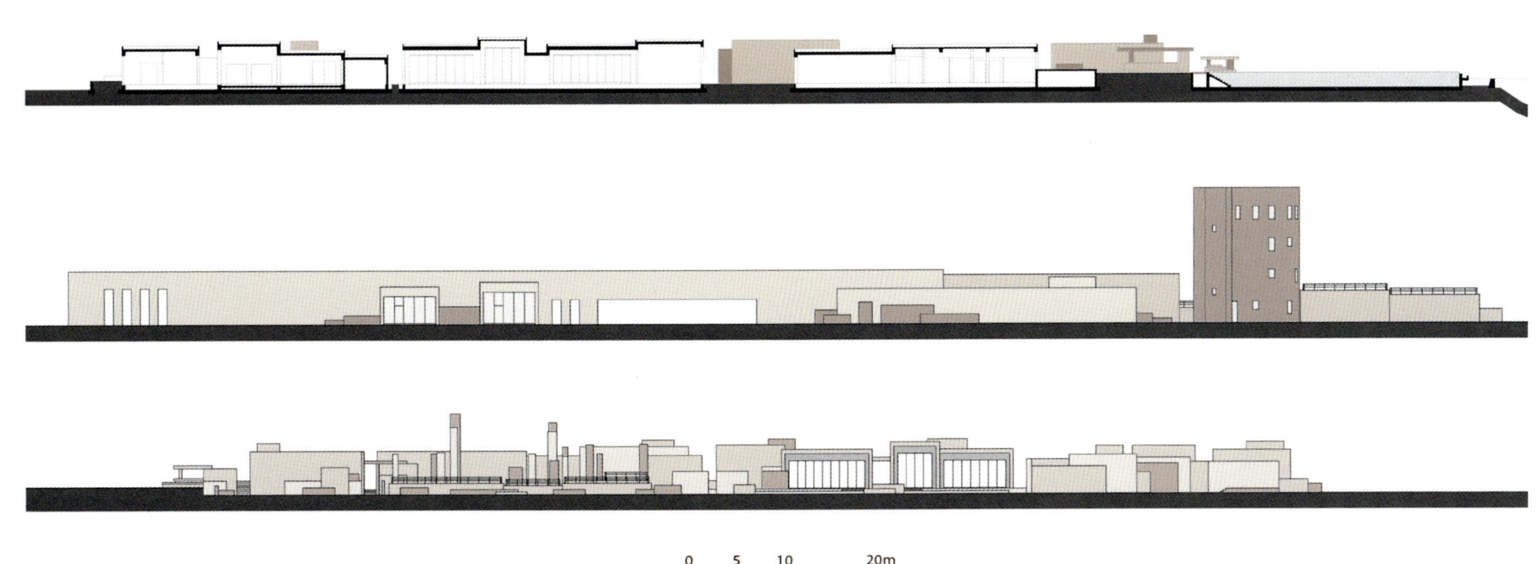

OPPOSITE, TOP
View from the pool area on
the northern edge

OPPOSITE, MIDDLE, BOTTOM, AND LEFT
Articulation and texture of the walls

ABOVE
View from the south

RIGHT
View from the piazza toward the tower

BELOW
View from the piazza

Antrepo 5 Contemporary Arts Museum

This 2011 project involves the transformation of an existing 24,000-square-meter (258,334 square foot) warehouse building into a contemporary art museum. Located in the formerly restricted customs port area of Karaköy, the museum is intended to house fifteen thousand works of art, including the most important examples of Turkish painting from the late Ottoman period to the present.

Originally designed by the well-known architect Sedad Hakki Eldem, the warehouse has a visibly exposed structural grid. EAA retained the reinforced concrete structural elements, but walls and slabs were removed "to obtain a 3-D, naked structural grid which will house the 'containers' of the new museum." The containers are linked by a network of ramps and bridges, and a transparent facade was added outside the structure.

Visitors enter the museum through a spacious hall that houses commercial units, workshop rooms, and public facilities. A Mediamesh on the back wall enlivens the facade that faces a busy road and acts as an interface between the new museum and the city.

LOCATION / **Istanbul, Turkey**

YEAR / **2011**

STATUS / **under construction, 2015**

TOTAL AREA / **24.000 m²**

BELOW
Sketch of entrepôt area,
Sedad Hakkı Eldem

OPPOSITE, TOP
View of the existing area from
the adjacent neighborhood

OPPOSITE, BELOW
View of the existing area
from the sea

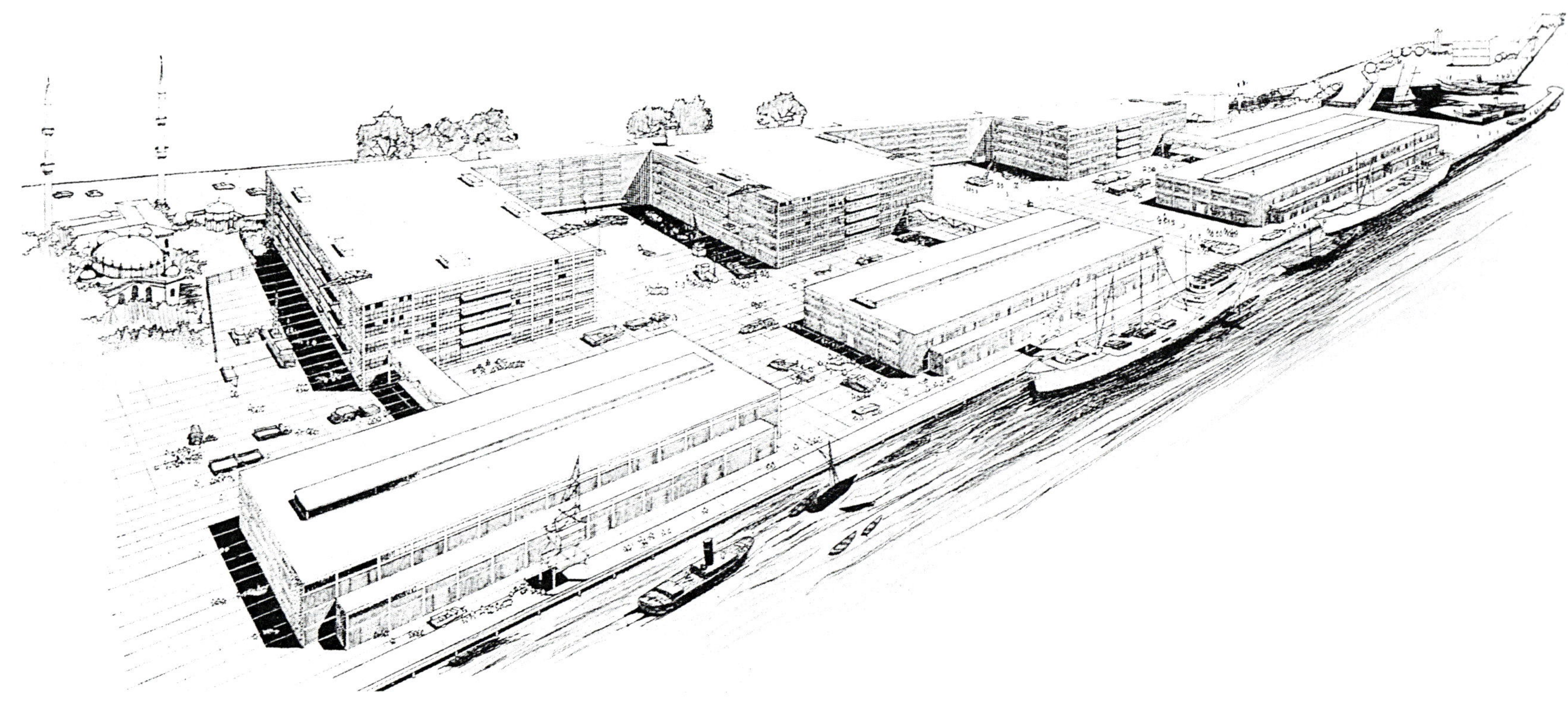

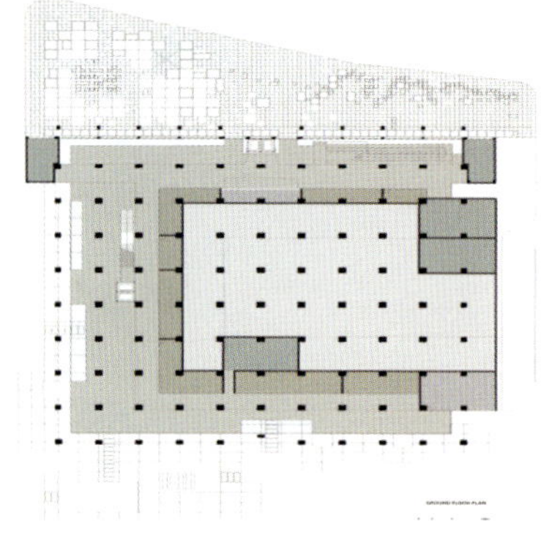
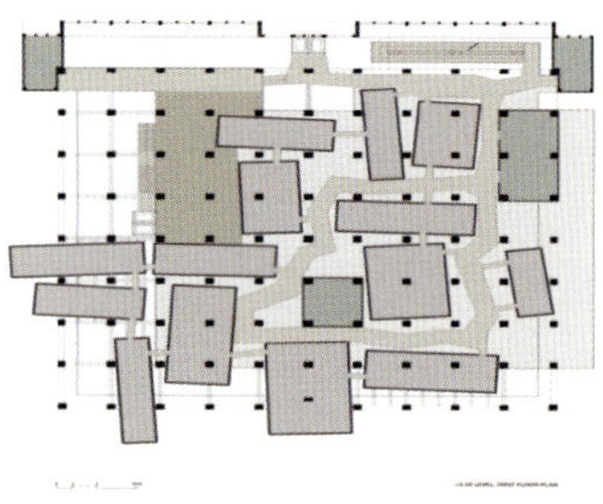
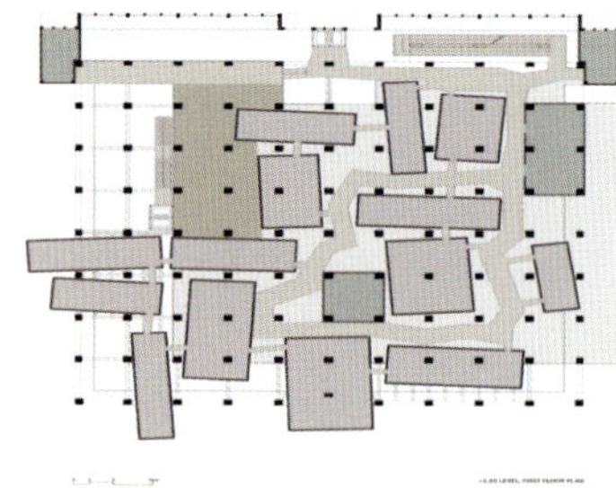
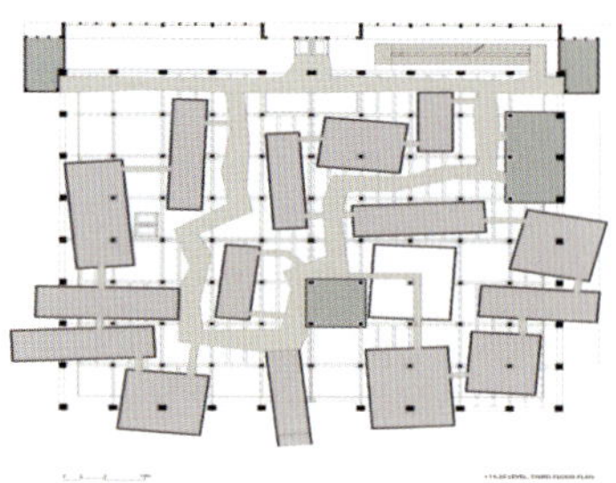
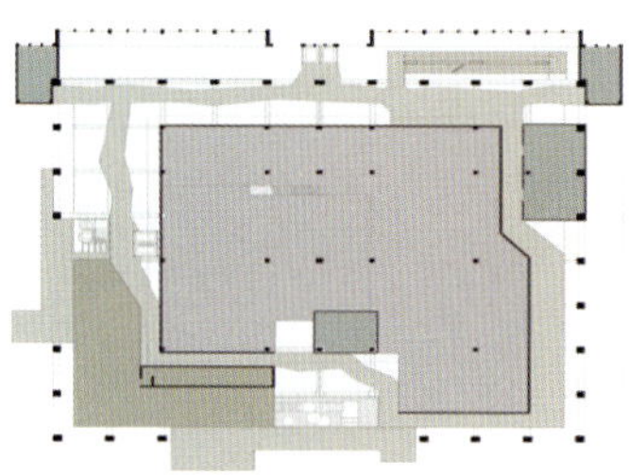
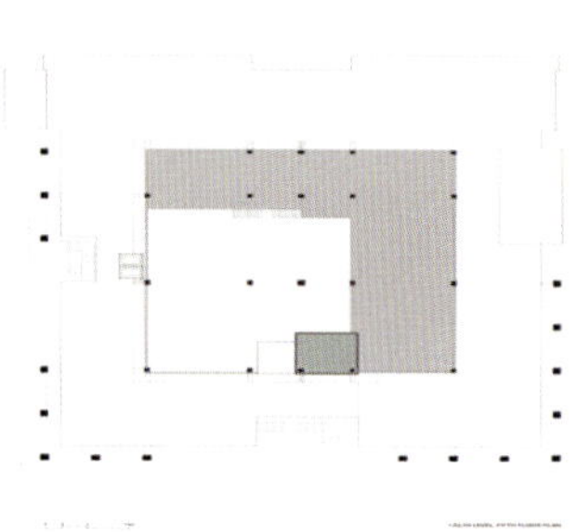

ABOVE AND LEFT
Floor plans

BELOW
Floor layers of the building

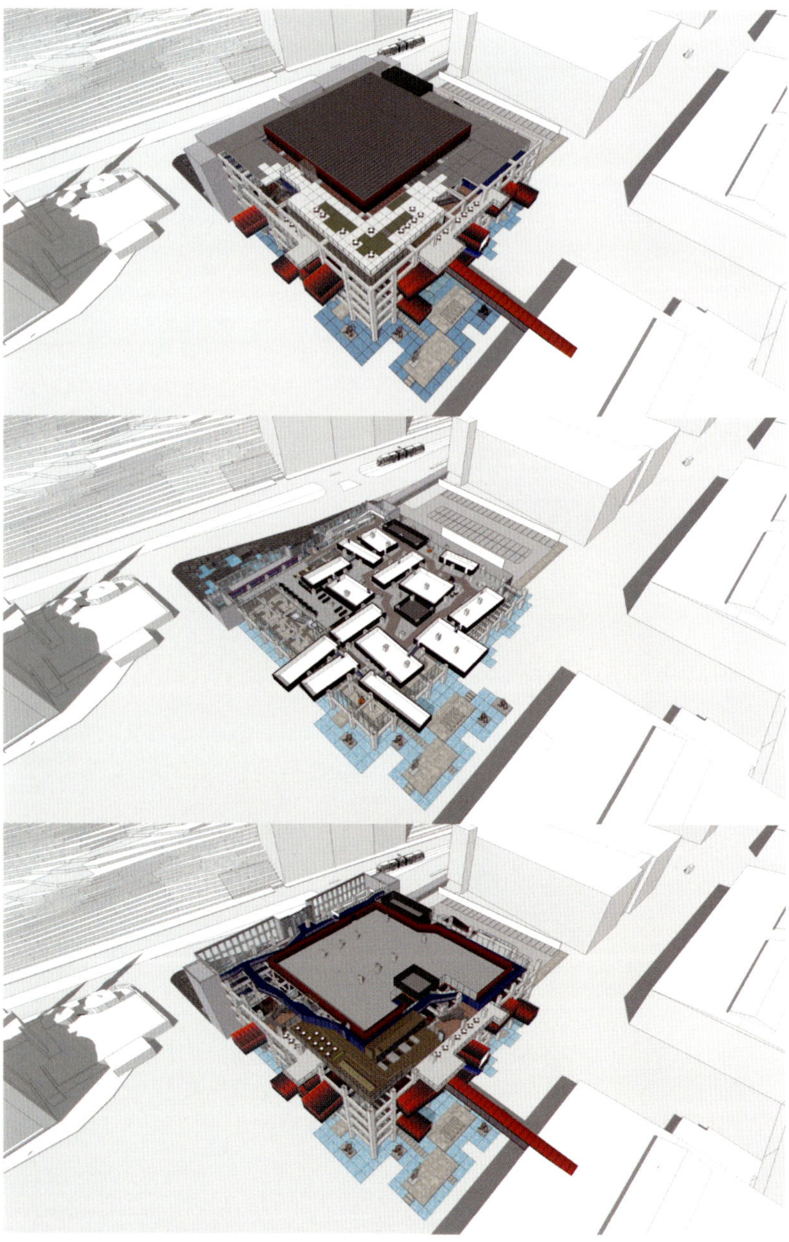
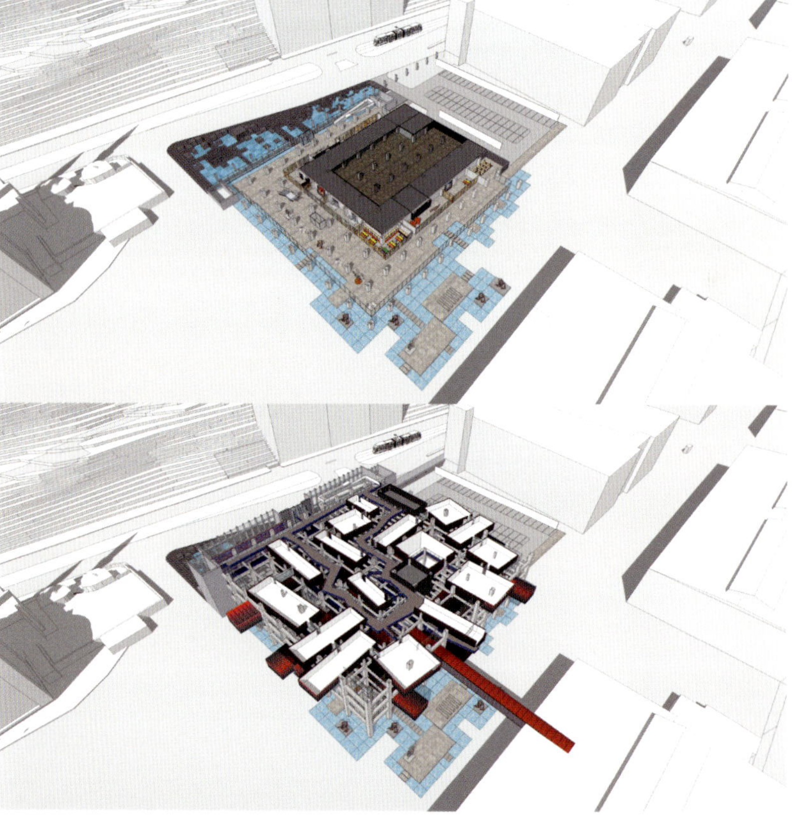

ABOVE
Site plan

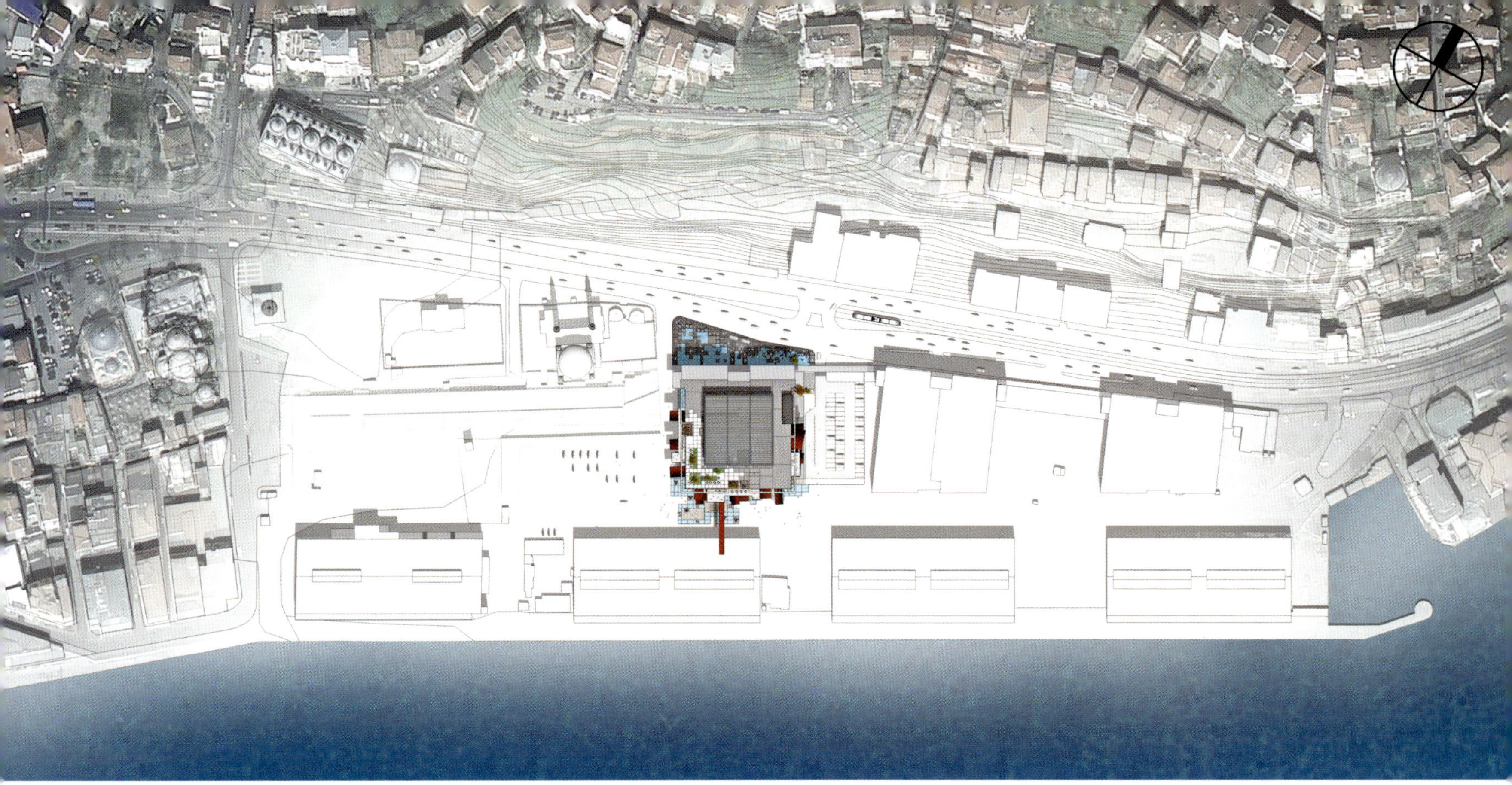

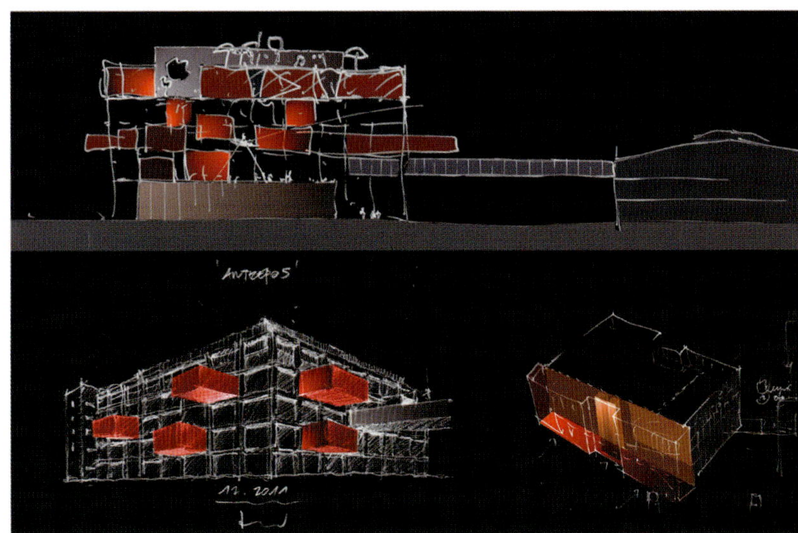

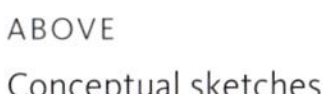

ABOVE
Conceptual sketches

RIGHT
Transformation from a warehouse to a museum

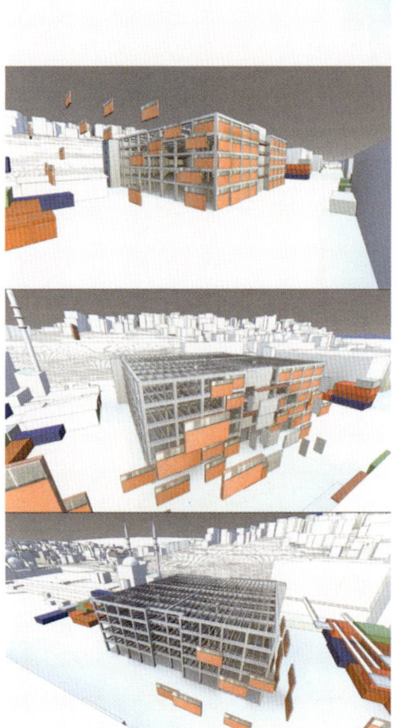

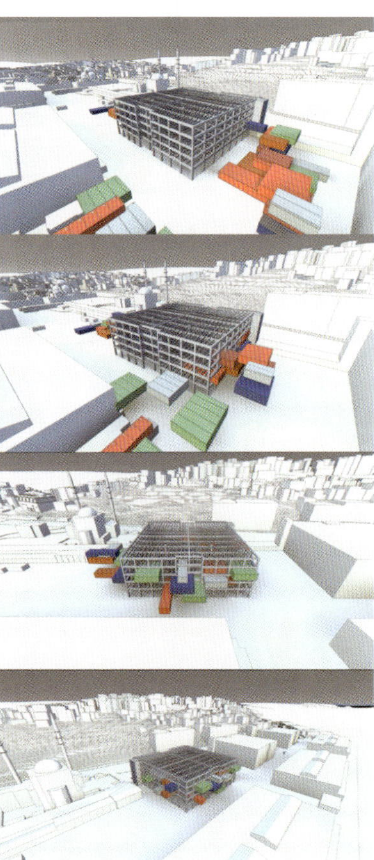

TOP
View from the southwest

ABOVE
View from the terrace

ABOVE, RIGHT
Section perspective

RIGHT
View from the circulation space

OPPOSITE, TOP
Night view of the interface facade
from the road

OPPOSITE, BOTTOM
Night view from the southwest

NEXT SPREAD
View from the sea

AGÜ City Campus

LOCATION / **Kayseri, Turkey**

YEAR / **2012**

STATUS / **under construction, 2014**

TOTAL AREA / **350.000 m²**

This 350,000-square-meter (3,767,368 square foot) project involves the conversion of the former Sümerbank textile factory, built in 1933 by a group of Russian architects led by Ivan Nikolaev. It is located in Kayseri, in Central Anatolia.

The factory, which was shut down in 1999, was long considered an important symbol of industrialization and modernization in republican Turkey. Turned over to Abdullah Gül University (AGU), it is destined to become a new campus that will include both educational and administrative facilities. The goal of the project includes making the new facility into a social and academic center for Kayseri, still considered a "provincial" city.

The architects have given priority to retaining much of the original industrial character of the complex. An existing small warehouse structure, a more recent addition to the factory, will see its roof removed, replaced with a canopy and the addition of upper-level spaces. New buildings will house a food court, and the old "orangery," which will serve as an urban farm for the growing of local herbs, was conceived as the interface between the city and the university.

OPPOSITE
Reuse of the factory

BELOW
Reuse of the warehouse

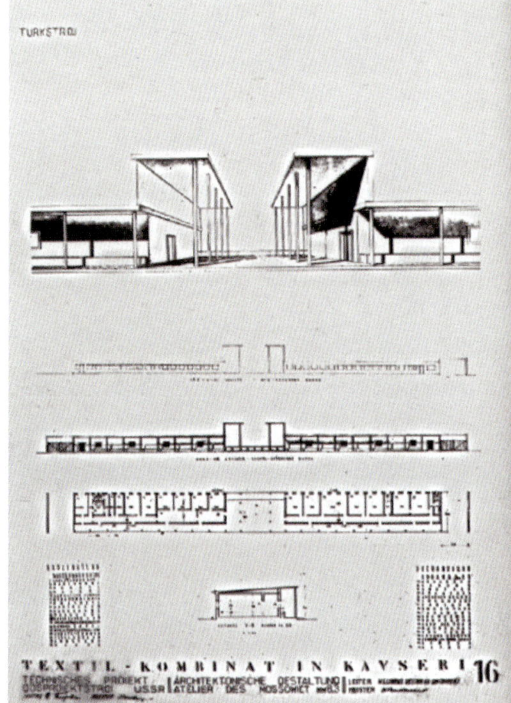
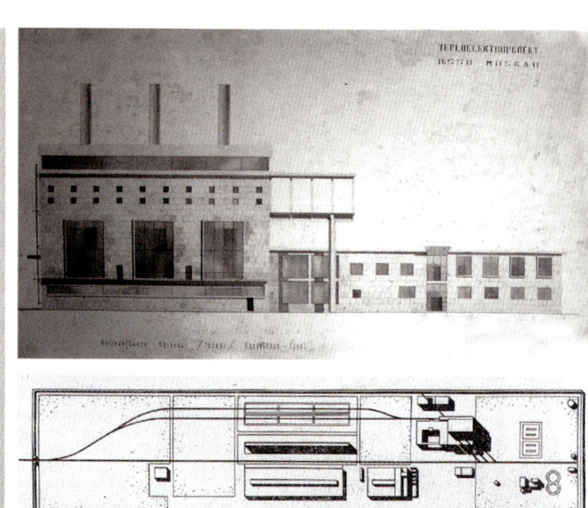
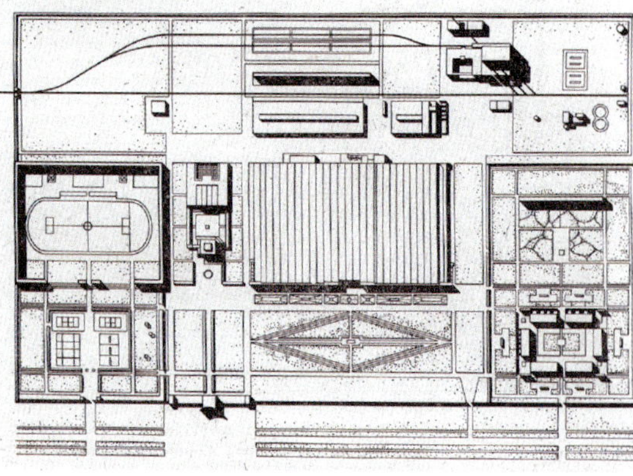

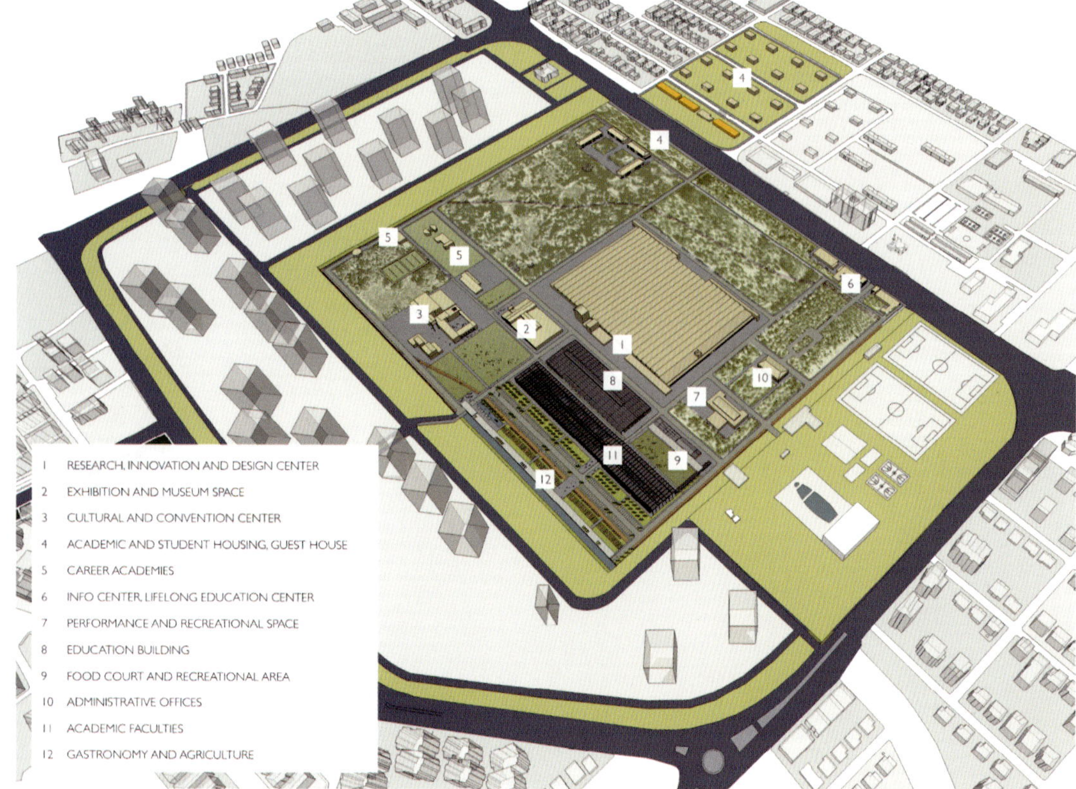

LEFT
Site layout

BELOW
Silhouettes and sections
through the site

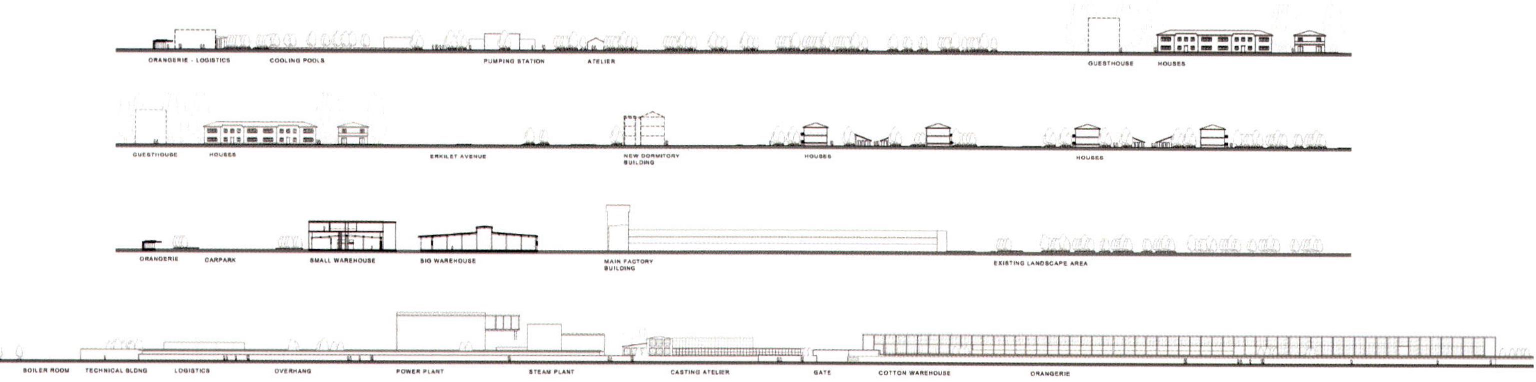

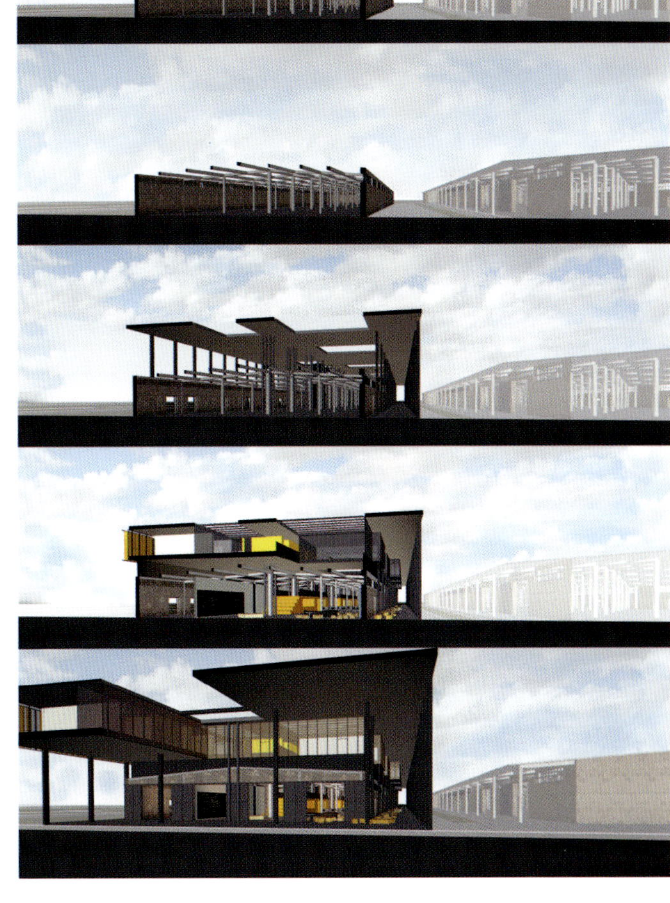

ABOVE
Structural development

BELOW
Warehouse reuse floor plans

RIGHT
Conceptual development

BOTTOM
Aerial view of the general layout

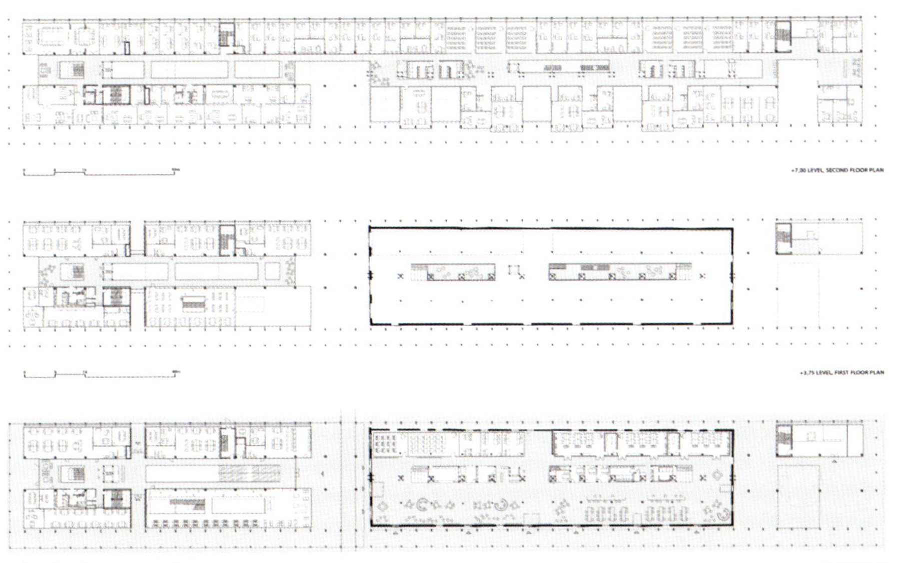
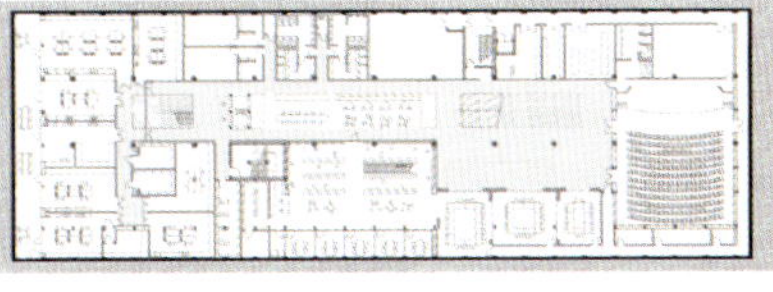

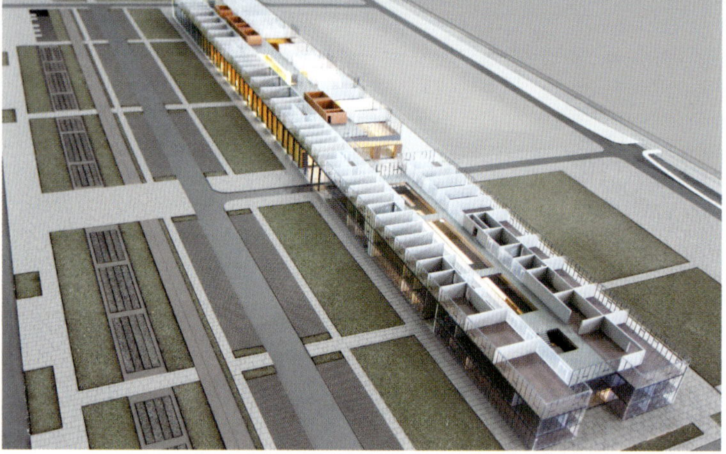

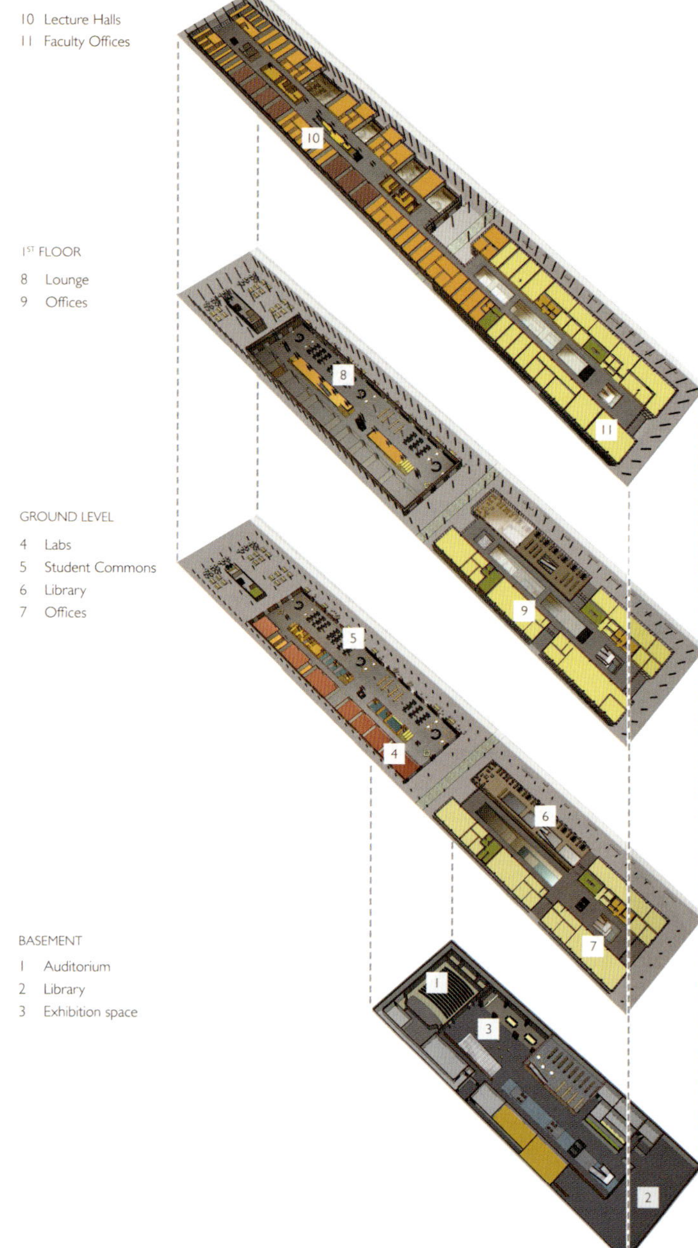

TOP
Aerial view of warehouse reuse

ABOVE
View of the scale model

RIGHT
Warehouse reuse floor plans

BELOW
Existing factory

BELOW, RIGHT
Existing factory exterior

LEFT
Facade of the existing building

BELOW
Existing warehouse

BOTTOM
Power plant reuse

ABOVE
View toward the entrance gate

BOTTOM
View from the social spaces

BELOW
View from the orangery

RIGHT
View from the entrance

BELOW
View from the social spaces
and café

RIGHT
View toward the reused warehouse and
additional building

BELOW, RIGHT
Passage between the reused warehouse
and additional building

OPPOSITE, TOP
Interior of the reused warehouse

BOTTOM AND OPPOSITE, BOTTOM
Views from the interior of the library
inside the additional building

Varyap Yalıkavak Villas

LOCATION / **Yalıkavak, Bodrum, Turkey**

YEAR / **2012**

STATUS / **ongoing**

TOTAL AREA / **4880 m²**

View of a residence and platforms

The site of the Varyap Yalıkavak villas is a rocky hillside with a unique landscape that includes olive trees and endemic plants and offers a panoramic view of Yalıkavak Bay.

To integrate the architecture into this landscape and inhabit the slope, the buildings are considered as series of horizontal platforms that extend into the site and house the mass of the internal spaces. The platforms are placed on different levels, forming roofs, canopies, terraces, balconies, pools, and sundecks. A sunken garden at the rear forms an intimate courtyard and helps generate cross ventilation. A reversed slope in front of the complex creates a cascading waterfall for the underground living areas. Vehicle circulation and parking lots are also placed underground.

Textured concrete is pigmented with an earthen color, and operable glazing on the front facade is intended to blur the boundary between interior and exterior. The architects state that their intention is for the complex "not to totally merge and disappear into the landscape but to assume the presence of an artifact on the ground." The Varyap Yalıkavak Villas, they conclude, "express a desire to belong to this place."

Landscape of the context

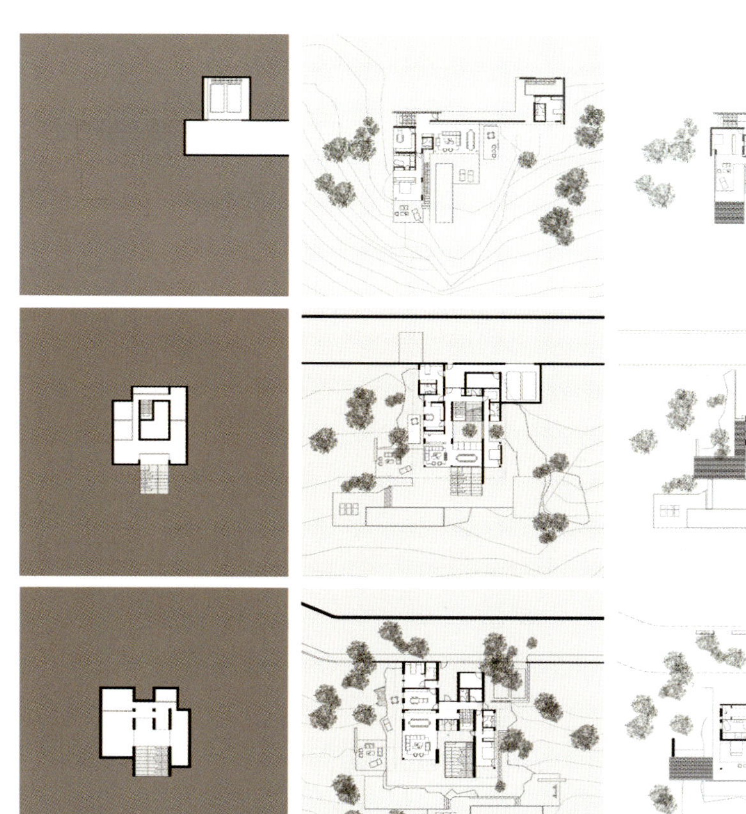

ABOVE
Typical floor plans

LEFT
Textures and materials

RIGHT
Site plan

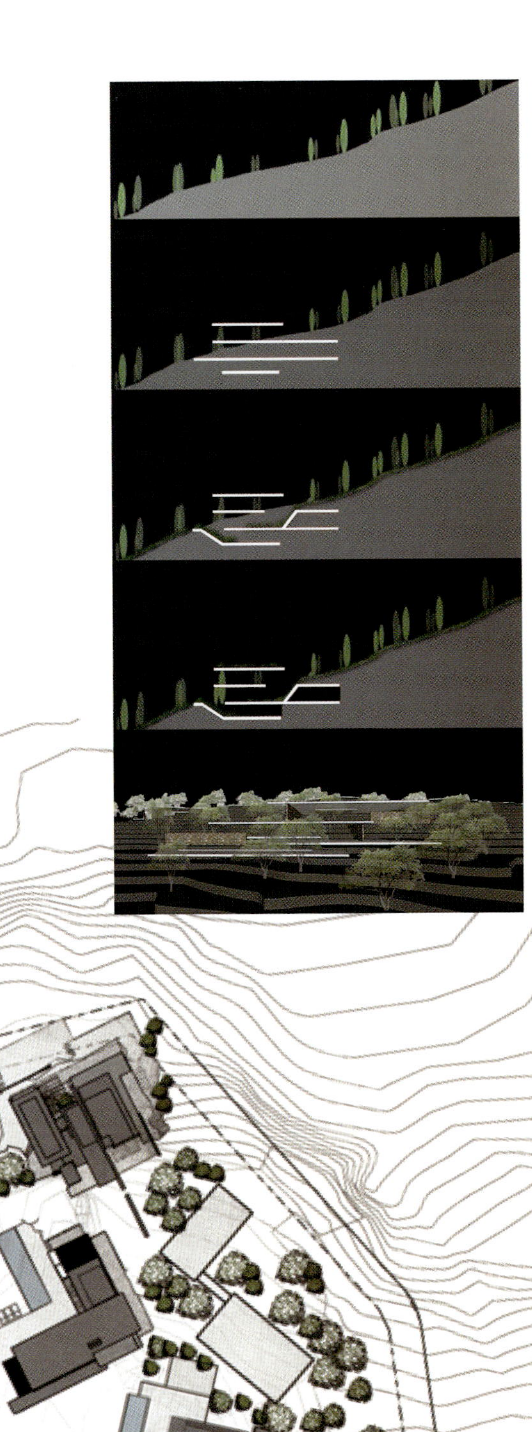

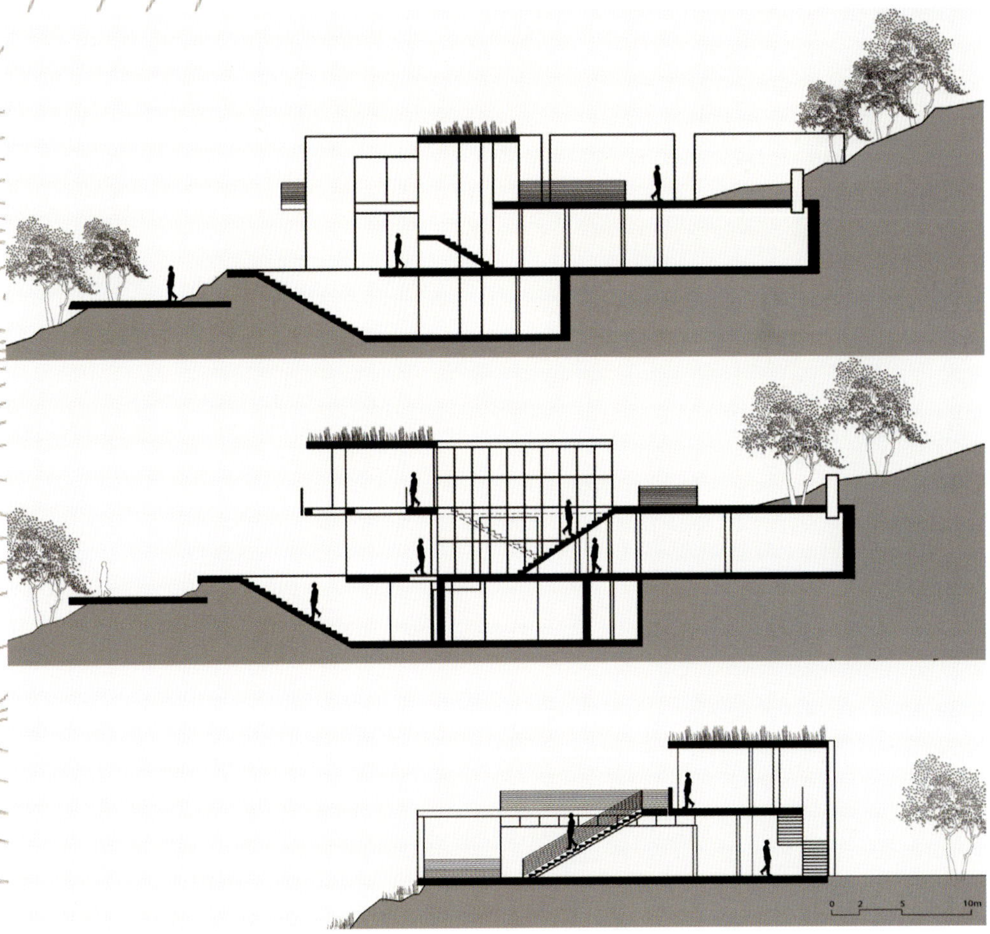

TOP
Principals of relationship with the context

ABOVE
Typical sections

277

ABOVE
View from the back

ABOVE, RIGHT
View from the back garden

RIGHT
View toward the sea

BELOW
Residence with platforms

ABOVE AND LEFT
View from the lower levels

BELOW
View from the side

OPPOSITE
View of a residence from
the lower level

BELOW
Blurring the boundary between
interior and exterior

TOP, LEFT AND RIGHT
Views from the residence and platforms

ABOVE, MIDDLE AND BOTTOM
Views from the interior

METU Research Center

LOCATION / **Ankara, Turkey**

YEAR / **2012**

STATUS / **ongoing**

TOTAL AREA / **10.000 m²**

The Middle East Technical University (METU) is one of the oldest and most prestigious universities in Turkey. Research is one of the most important activities of the institution.

This project was conceived with the plan to unite twenty-three existing research facilities sponsored by the university into a single complex, increasing interaction among those who work within the buildings. An atrium at the center of the space serves as a meeting area. In addition to laboratories, the 10,000-square-meter (107,639 square foot) project includes classrooms, meeting rooms, and conference spaces.

The new research center was conceived to be part of a larger complex that includes the university campus and Techno Park. An alley, which includes "follies" intended to be used as teahouses or cafés, passes over the ring road that separates the Techno Park from the campus and connects both structures with the new METU Research Center.

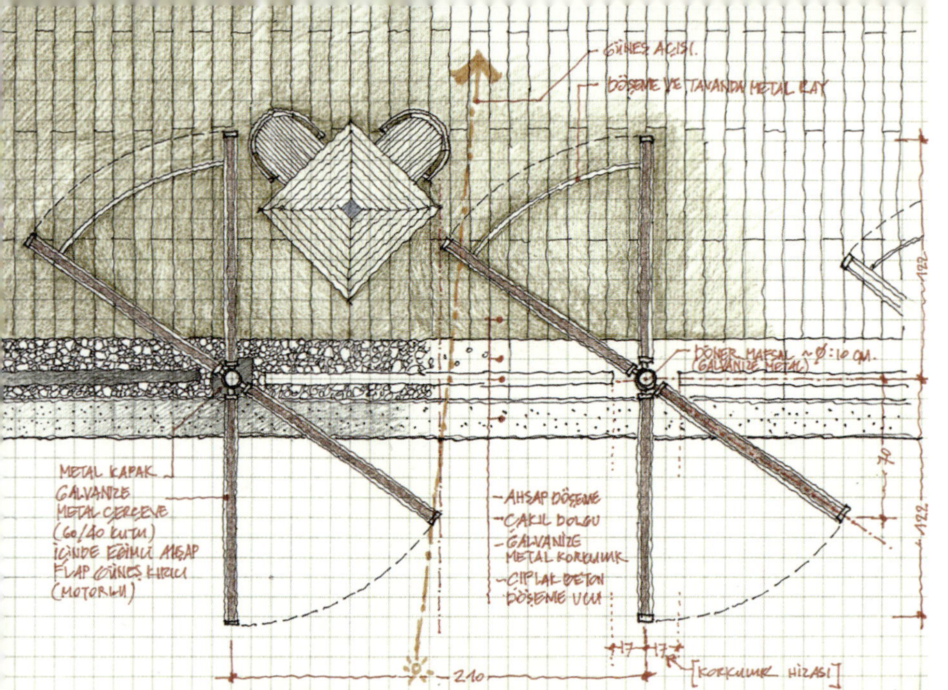

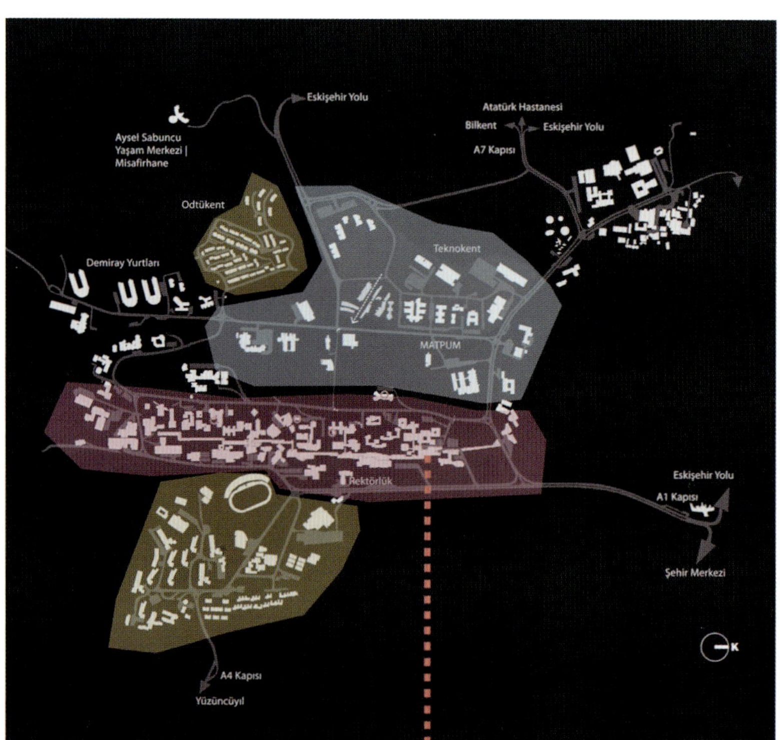

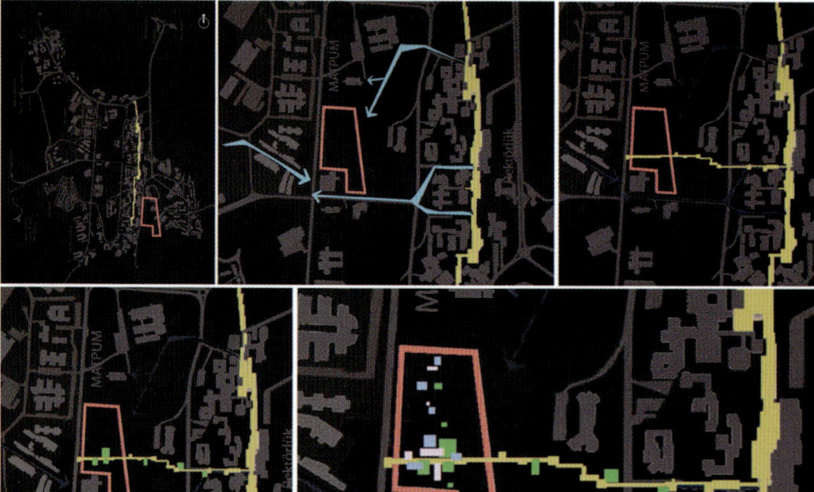

TOP, LEFT AND RIGHT
Study for shutters

ABOVE AND RIGHT
Conceptual framework of
the general layout

LEFT
View from the north

BELOW
Section perspective
through the gallery

BOTTOM
Floor plans

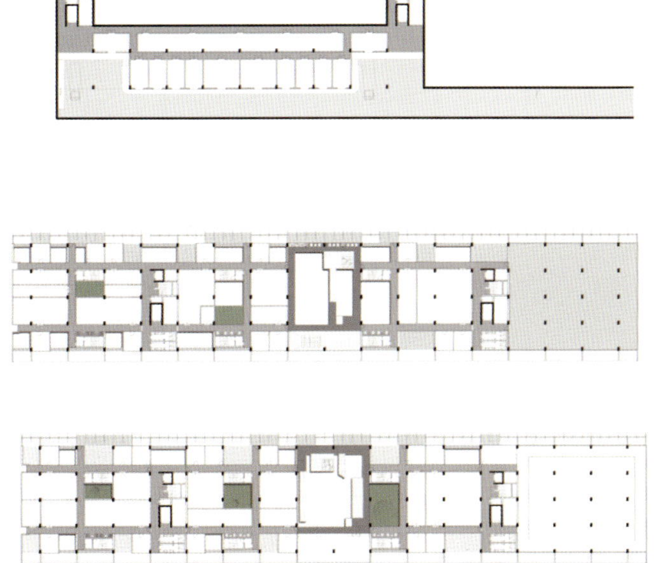

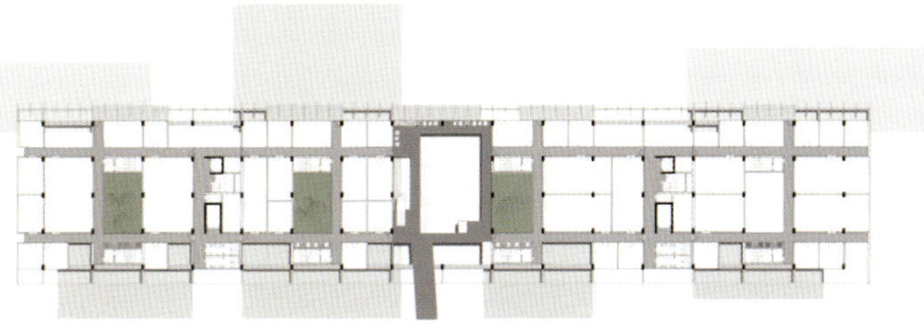

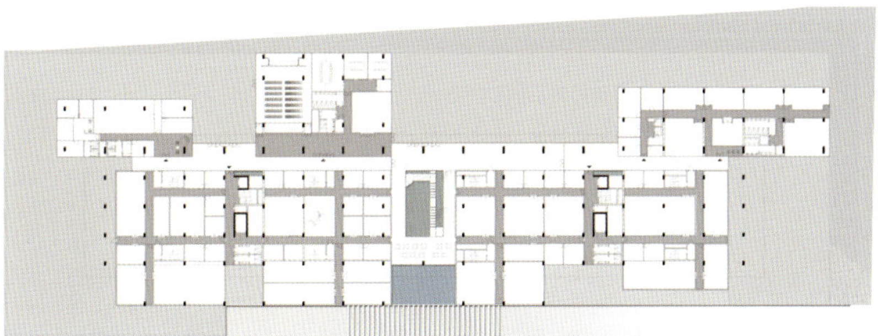

LEFT
Aerial view of the site

BELOW
Approach to the building

BOTTOM
View from the main road

ABOVE AND LEFT
Views toward the gallery

CLIENTS

Abdullah Gül University
Akkök Inc.
ASF Hotels
ATM – Aksa Turkuaz Manas Joint Venture
Ayaydın Miroglio Group
Bergama Municipality of Izmir
Bilgi University
Çarmıklı Inc.
Çarmıklı – Saruhan Partnership
Ermet Construction Inc.
Eyüp Municipality of Istanbul
Folkart Yapı
General Directorate of State Airports
    Authority
Heaş – Airport Management and
    Aviation Industries Inc.
Istanbul Metropolitan Planning
    Department
Istanbul Mimar Sinan Fine Arts University
Kayı Group
Kervansaray Hotels
Koçoğlu Inc.
Makyol Group
Metal Yapı Konut
Middle East Technical University
Palmali Group
Prague Embassy of Turkish Republic
Sancaklar Foundation
Saral Construction
Tekfen Real Estate Development Group
Torunlar Kapıcıoğlu Joint Venture
Varyap Group
Viatrans Meydanbey Joint Venture
Vicem Yacht – Konukoğlu Joint Venture
    Joint Venture
Yapı Kredi Koray Reit – Garanti Reit
Yüksel Construction Inc.
Zorlu Construction Investment Inc.

COLLABORATORS

Architectural Offices

DB (Dalaman International
    Airport Terminal)
İhsan Bilgin, Nevzat Sayın
    (Evidea Housing Project)
NSMH (Santral Istanbul
    Contemporary Arts Museum)
Tabanlıoğlu (Zorlu Center)

**MEP, Landscape,
    Lighting Design**

AE Architecture
AED
Alfa Çelik
Akım
Altıneller
As
Atilla Eser
Aydın Pelin – Can Binzet
Aykar
Babuş
Balkar
Beta Teknik
Birim
Birikim
Bodrum Electra
Buro Happold
Cem&Şan
Çağ Yapı
Çalışan Geoteknik
Çelik Yapı
Deniz Proje
Desibel
Detay
Dinamik Proje
Ds Architecture
Ekiz Proje
Emay
Emt
Enar
English Gardens
Enkom
Enmar
Entegre
Ersa
Esan
Esen
Erke Tasarım
Ersel, Moskay
Fdc
Fonksiyon
Galtek

Geocon
Gmd
Gmd-Genel Mekanik Dizayn
Gn
Göktem
Hb Teknik
Hidromekanik
İmc Proje
Ims
İtez
Kemal Erdoğan
Kitay
Köroğlu
Lal Gardens
Levent Aksaray
Lidea Lighting
Mak-El
Marka
Medusa
MKM
Msd
Necdet Torunbalcı
Nodus
Nükleer
Ofis Architecture
Okutan
On Tasarım
Optimum Lighting
Osm
Pmp
Pronet
Pro-Plan Ltd
Proses
Protek
Ram
Rainer Schmidt
    Landschaftsarchitekten
Reel
Sasel
Seba
Selkom Proje
Sensormatıc
Sentez
Setta
Sigal
Sıla
SLD – Studio Lighting Design
Stm
Tanrıöver
Tezkon
Toptaş
Trafo Architects
Tuncel
Viramer
Yapı Teknik
Yeşil Vadi
Zetaş
ZKLD

Other Consultants

Altensis
Altes
AMPC & SSD
Anova
Artı
Axis Facade
Başak Atalay
BDS Facade
Cwg
Colliers
Duyal Karagözoğlu
Etik
Fyp
Gülsün Tanyeli
Haluk Abbasoğlu
Hatice Pamir
Icts
Itina
Jll
Karina
Mehmet Çalışkan
MFC
Mustafa Ilıcalı
Mustafa Özgünler
Park Sistem
Servotel
Sey
Std
Talayman Acoustics
Turkeko
Yönsis

Modeling and Rendering

Atölye 77
Atölye K
Kent Maket
Maketsan